Fortress Kent

Fortress Kent
The Guardian of England

Roy Ingleton

Pen & Sword
MILITARY

First published in Great Britain in 2012 by
PEN & SWORD MILITARY
An imprint of
Pen & Sword Books Ltd
47 Church Street
Barnsley
South Yorkshire
S70 2AS

Copyright © Roy Ingleton 2012

ISBN 978-1-84884-888-7

Typeset by Concept, Huddersfield, West Yorkshire.

Printed and bound in England by
CPI Group (UK) Ltd, Croydon, CRO 4YY.

Pen & Sword Books Ltd incorporates the Imprints of Pen & Sword Aviation, Pen &
Sword Family History, Pen & Sword Maritime, Pen & Sword Military, Pen & Sword
Discovery, Wharncliffe Local History, Wharncliffe True Crime, Wharncliffe
Transport, Pen & Sword Select, Pen & Sword Military Classics, Leo Cooper, The
Praetorian Press, Remember When, Seaforth Publishing and Frontline Publishing.

For a complete list of Pen & Sword titles please contact
PEN & SWORD BOOKS LIMITED
47 Church Street, Barnsley, South Yorkshire, S70 2AS, England
E-mail: enquiries@pen-and-sword.co.uk
Website: www.pen-and-sword.co.uk

Contents

Introduction and Acknowledgements

Since the dawn of civilisation, Britain has been menaced by foreign powers and invading hordes, anxious either to pillage and plunder or to invade and rule over this green and pleasant land.

Situated on the extreme south-eastern corner of England, the county of Kent is the nearest point to continental Europe, and has so been the preferred landing point for most of these incursions. From the time of the Romans and the Angles, Jutes and Saxons to the Second World War, the Men of Kent and Kentish Men have had to erect and maintain defensive structures, from Iron Age forts to 1940 pillboxes, from the Royal Military Canal to the anti-tank ditches carved out of the hills around the Kent coast during the Second World War, culminating in the construction of deep shelters in anticipation of a nuclear attack.

This book is the story of these measures: the threats that led to the erection and construction of various defensive obstacles, their up-keep and garrisoning, and, in some cases, their ultimate destruction. It is laid out in more or less chronological order, with chapters devoted to the main periods of construction, although there is some overlap and the dates may not always fit comfortably within such periods.

Many of the illustrations are the author's own, and as far as the remainder are concerned, where copyright is known or believed to exist, acknowledgement has been made or permission sought. To the best of my knowledge and belief, any others are in the public domain, but I apologize if there has been any unintentional oversight and will undertake to correct this in any future editions.

Roy Ingleton
Maidstone, 2011

Chapter 1

The earliest constructions:
Iron Age (first century BC)

Prior to the last days of the so-called Iron Age, that is to say the last century before Christ, there is little known of any significant fortifications in Kent: indeed, the sparse population of Kent, and the lack of foreign would-be invaders willing to face the perils of the English Channel or the North Sea in any numbers during those early days, probably did little to convince the population of any such need.

Around 500 BC, a number of immigrants arrived from Gaul and Flanders, but their landings were generally unopposed; after all, with a population of under a million scattered over the entire country, there was plenty of room for everyone. These newcomers to Kent (*Cent* in Old English, *Cantia regnum* in Latin) joined the existing settlers in constructing wattle-and-daub huts to live in, engaged in arable and livestock farming and gave little thought to defending themselves from hostile invasions from overseas. They were, perhaps, more concerned about their near neighbours for, although it has long been thought that this period was a peaceful and settled one, recent discoveries have prompted a rethink. In 2011, archaeologists exploring a hill fort at Fin Cop in Derbyshire discovered the remains of a large number of women, children and babies who appear to have been massacred by a rival tribe around 400 BC. Slavery having been an increasingly important export during the Iron Age, the menfolk were probably carted off to serve as slaves or warriors by the victorious tribe before the less valuable women and children were stripped of their meagre belongings and stabbed or strangled before being tossed unceremoniously into the fort's defensive ditch, where a 13-foot limestone wall was toppled onto the pitiful cadavers.

Although no similar evidence of such violence has been found in Kent, it is probable that such forts as were constructed here during the latter part of the Iron Age were used more as a refuge against other local tribes than from foreign invaders. However, by 100 BC things had changed considerably and the seemingly irresistible expansion of the Roman Empire was forcing many of the existing peoples of Europe – the Franks, Visigoths, Lombards and other 'barbaric' tribes – to seek land outside the influence of Rome, and no doubt many cast covetous eyes on that green and pleasant land just across a narrow strait of sea. The Celtic people of Kent were not unaware of this. They had for some years been trading with merchants from as far away as the Middle East and gained their news of the outside world from this source.

Among the first to arrive in Kent in any numbers were the Belgae who crossed over to East Kent from the Low Countries during the early part of the first century BC. Their gradual but inexorable migration westwards prompted the existing population to set up a number of hilltop camps, the remains of just a few of which still exist. As the name implies, these defences were usually built on a hilltop that provided a good view and represented a significant obstacle to invaders. The site was generally levelled with one or more rows of ditches dug into the hillside to further impede assailants, the excavated earth being piled up to form an earthen rampart, often reinforced by a timber palisade or stone wall. Although often seen as simple, un-sophisticated defensive structures, many Iron Age earthworks incorporated ingeniously arranged diversions in which the attacker could be trapped and eliminated. This represented a military sophistication not seen again in this country until around the fourteenth century.

On the southeast coast, the great white cliffs that Shakespeare described as the '... high, upreared and abutting fronts [that] the perilous ocean parts asunder' (*Henry V*) extend for 13 miles, and the only gap in these towering obstacles occurs at **Dover**, where the shallow River Dour debouches into the sea. This, coupled with its close proximity to France, has placed Dover at risk and needing to be defended since the earliest days in the county's history. In 1992, a Bronze Age boat dating from 1300 BC was discovered beneath Townwall Street, clearly demonstrating that Dover has been a significant maritime centre for more than three millennia.

On the cliff top on the eastern side of the river, where the present castle stands, there was once a great Iron Age hilltop fort, built to provide refuge for the people working and living in the tiny settlement huddled below in the river valley. When Julius Caesar arrived off Dover in 55 BC, it was possibly the sight of these great earthworks that prompted him to seek an unopposed landfall further up the coast. Successive rebuilds of this great fort have meant that very little identifiable remains are now in existence of this structure, which is not mentioned in the records from Roman times.

Some 2 miles west of Canterbury, however, the remains of **Bigbury** hill fort are still visible. Bigbury was probably the first native settlement to be stormed by Julius Caesar when he made his second probing assault in 54 BC. Hurriedly thrown up shortly before, the camp was 1,000 feet from east to west and 700 feet north to south, covering around 25 acres. Deep ditches with just one fortified entrance surrounded the whole camp. The site was described by Caesar in *The Gallic Wars* as 'a position with extremely good man-made defences for some war between themselves … many trees had been cut down and used to block all entrances to it.' The Seventh Roman Legion piled earth up against the defensive banks to form ramps, which they then clambered up and made short work of overcoming the defenders. It seems the fort was then abandoned.

Much more substantial was the hill fort carved out of the hillside at **Oldbury**, near Sevenoaks. Around the third century BC, Wealden people crossed from France into Sussex and some, following the ancient tracks northwards through the dense forest, had arrived at Oldbury by the beginning of the first century BC. There had been some form of earthworks here since very early times. The site's commanding position and the natural defences offered by its steep slopes made it an ideal defensive position, with earlier occupants having enlarged the natural caves formed in the granite-like rock.

Under the Wealden people, the fort soon covered a space of some 123 acres, stretching about 1,000 yards north to south and 600 yards east to west. It enclosed a small pond, fed by springs, providing ample water for the occupants. The fortifications, to which there were five entrances, consisted of a single deep ditch and bank on three sides, the eastern side being on top of a sheer cliff and thus sufficiently unassailable.

Around AD 20, alarmed by the steady approach of the Belgae from the east, the Wealden settlers set about making further improvements to this already hugely significant fort by creating an outer ditch around 9 feet deep and an inner bank, on top of which a wooden palisade was erected – the intention being to use the fort as a refuge should the Belgae arrive – which they did. Despite the impressive fortifications, the Belgae invested the fort and soon overran it, killing or expelling the defenders.

It was now the turn of the Belgae to make use of the hill fort and first they further strengthened the earthworks on the more vulnerable north side. News of the impending approach of the Roman legions prompted them to raise a rampart more than twice the height of the original one and to realign the northern entrance, erecting a heavy wooden gate to secure that entrance. Piles of stones were placed at strategic points to be thrown at attackers or used in slings for the same purpose.

The Romans, advancing along the ancient paths to the north, were informed by their scouts of the existence of a hostile fort close to their lines of communication and felt impelled to take some action to neutralize it. A detachment was therefore sent to take the necessary action.

As the Romans approached, the women and children from the surrounding countryside fled to the fort for safety, while the menfolk took up their primitive weapons and manned the ramparts. On their arrival at Oldbury, the Romans were met with a daunting barrage of stones and other weapons, but these were well-trained and experienced troops. Under the protection of their shields, they piled faggots against the northern gate and set it alight. With the gate thus destroyed there was little to prevent the ingress of the Romans and the battle was soon over.

There is no evidence that the Romans ever used the fort defensively, nor indeed the later Jutes and Saxons. Much of the fort was destroyed in the nineteenth century when the stone was quarried to meet the growing demand for road stone, and today the area is covered with trees and undergrowth. Nevertheless, it is still just possible to make out the lines of the ramparts and the remains of the caves that once sheltered various beleaguered peoples from bloodthirsty attackers.

There are vestiges of other Iron Age forts in Kent, at Nettlestead and Westerham for example, but none are as large or impressive as Oldbury. It appears that the use of these hill forts ceased by the first century AD, being abandoned by the British and ignored by the Romans as unsuitable for their purposes.

Chapter 2

Roman defences (55 BC–AD 410)

Julius Caesar's exploratory probes in 55 and 54 BC showed the Romans that Kent was not to be overcome without a fight. It is probable that the hill fort at Bigbury was taken during the second visit, but the Romans were unable to remain for long and soon withdrew to continental Europe, no doubt intending to return the following campaigning season. But this was not to be, due to problems in Gaul, and it was nearly a hundred years before a further landing was made, this time in greater strength and with the intention of remaining in England.

This is not to say that there was no contact, albeit indirect, between England and Rome. Britain was exporting precious metals, agricultural produce, cattle and hides, hunting dogs and slaves to Roman-controlled Gaul, and importing luxury goods such as fine pottery, wine, oil, jewellery and silver- and glass-ware. The Men of Kent were far from the blue-painted, naked warriors so often depicted, but they were prepared to defend their land, even against the might of Rome.

In AD 43, Emperor Claudius, mistrusting the British leaders who were revealing themselves to be increasingly anti-Rome, despatched Aulus Plautius with some 40,000 men to finally and decisively conquer Britain and bring it formally under Roman rule. After a number of delays, the invading force set out from Boulogne in three divisions, the greater part of which landed at Richborough where they set up their base camp. The earthen banks they threw up to protect their beachhead can still be discerned within the walls of the later fort.

It is worth mentioning here that the Kentish coastline in those days was noticeably different to that which exists today. The River Wantsum that separated the Isle of Thanet from mainland Kent was a wide channel, up to three miles wide in places. This is why Richborough, today some three miles inland, was then an island in the Wantsum, perfectly accessible by sea. A

The ditches of the earth fort within the stone walls of the 'Saxon Shore Fort' at Richborough.

similar situation existed at Lympne, near Hythe: the Roman port (*Portus Lemanis*), built there in the early days of their occupation, now lies a considerable distance from the sea. The Romney Marsh had yet to be formed by the retreat of the sea and the islands of Ebony, Oxney and Midley were true islands.

Although the Celts had expected the invasion, the delays in its implementation had resulted in the Celts disbanding their forces, and the landing was effectively unopposed by the independent groups and tribes of Belgic Kent. Such individual forces as were hastily reformed made their way to East Kent to oppose the invaders but they suffered from the lack of a coherent strategy and were swiftly routed by the highly efficient Roman legions. The only effective resistance took place on the Medway, somewhere near Rochester, where the battle exceptionally lasted two whole days, but this too was doomed to failure, and with the Britons fleeing westwards, Kent was firmly under Roman rule.

With Kent pacified, the Roman occupation force spent the next four centuries consolidating their gains, building impressive townships such as Canterbury (*Durovernum*), Rochester (*Durobrivae*) and Dover (*Dubris*), usually enclosed within substantial stone walls and interconnected by straight, hard-surfaced roads, 12 feet or more in width, many of which remain to this day. Substantial villas were built for the more important Romans and the remains of some of these may be seen at Folkestone, Lullingstone and Darenth.

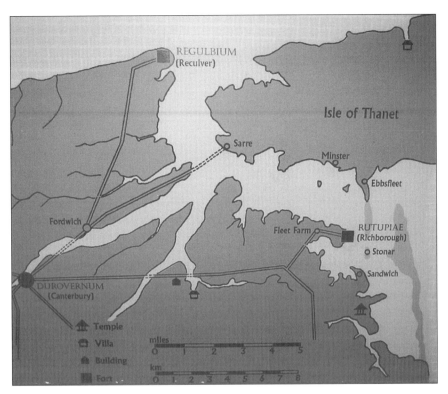

North-east Kent at the time of the Roman invasion, AD 43.

The walls and towers erected by the Romans, whether to encircle a town or a military fort, did not normally incorporate any buildings and were entirely free-standing. The towers provided a field of fire across the length of the wall, but, perhaps more importantly, provided a solid base for the great siege engines that were mounted on top of them. A peculiarity of the Roman forts was that they were designed as military bases from which armies could conduct sorties rather than purely defensive structures; the Romans were attackers, not defenders, relying on the sheer manpower within the fort to deal with any threat to it.

By the third century AD, raids by well-equipped and well-trained Saxon assailants led to the southern and eastern coasts of England being referred to as the Saxon Shore. In response to this, a total of eleven coastal forts were erected, four of which – Reculver (*Regulbium*), Richborough (*Rutupiae*), Dover (*Dubris*) and Lympne (*Lemanis*) – were in Kent, while the remains of the one at Portchester (Hampshire) are particularly well-preserved and impressive. Exceptionally, these square forts departed from the usual design in that they were constructed to withstand a siege, leading to a suggestion

The remains of the Roman fort at Reculver.

that, given the prevailing political situation, they were designed as much to resist attacks by other Roman legions as by the Saxons. The walls were some 12 feet thick and 30 feet high, with towers on each corner and at intervals along the walls.

The walls of the Richborough fort provide some good examples of Roman building techniques. Holes can be seen at regular intervals where horizontal scaffolding poles had been placed. The builders would construct the wall as high as they could comfortably work from the ground and then place poles across the width of the wall. These poles would then have been built upon (thus securing them) and planks lain along the poles where they protruded from the wall to form walkways. In this way, work could proceed on either side of the wall. Once the wall was finished, the poles were pulled out and the holes plugged. It is evident that the walls were built in sections by different gangs, as one can clearly see where two sections meet up.

It has been postulated that **Canterbury** was already one of the great *oppida*, or proto-urban Iron Age centres prior to the Roman invasion. What is certain is that, as early as AD 43, a Roman fort had been erected to the north of the site of the later Canterbury Castle. This fort was abandoned in AD 70, and it was not until the end of the third century that the town became *Durovernum Cantiacorum* – 'the walled town of the tribe of the Cantiaci by an alder marsh' – when an embankment, faced by a stone wall with a defensive ditch around the whole, was erected to protect the town. There were seven entrances to the town, the outline of the Queningate being still visible embedded in the wall near the entrance to the cathedral precincts while three others, Londongate, Worthgate and Ridingate, have been identified by excavations. Worthgate, giving access to the town from Wincheap, was later used by the Normans as the entrance to their castle, while Ridingate controlled the old road from Dover. Northgate was sited where the road from the town led to the port of *Regulbium* (Reculver) and was demolished in 1820, but the adjoining Roman town wall remains in a very good state of preservation. No traces have been found of the Roman Burgate although its site is well known.

In Roman times **Dover** (*Dubris*) was an important trading post, and the well-preserved *pharos*, or lighthouse, close to where the Normans built their great castle, is a testament to the Roman occupation. This had been complemented

The Pharos *or Roman lighthouse at Dover.*

by a second lighthouse and a sizeable settlement on the Western Heights in the latter half of the first century AD.

As the harbour at Dover was improved and enlarged, the Roman fleet – the *Classis Britannica* – moved there, and the importance of Richborough declined. The fleet headquarters was a large structure, covering 2 acres in the present-day York Street area and enclosed several large buildings, metalled roads, sewers and drains, and fresh water supplies. It fell into disuse when the fleet moved away in the early part of the third century, but later, towards the end of the century, a great new military fort was built, partially over the remains of the fleet headquarters and including the present Market Square and Biggin Street. Earth was piled up against the inside of the walls, burying the beautifully decorated Painted House that was rediscovered in the late twentieth century.

Being the site of the first landings, **Richborough** was probably the first fort to be built, and with that built at Reculver, both ends of the Wantsum, separating the mainland from the Isle of Thanet, were secured. Originally a simple settlement of wooden buildings on a small island at the mouth of the Wantsum Channel, Richborough owed its importance to its role as a port and supply depot. Its defence was largely restricted to a series of ditches with earthen ramparts.

The importance of Roman Richborough cannot be overestimated: it represents, with Hadrian's Wall, the most important Roman building in England.

Around AD 85, most of the buildings were destroyed and a great triumphal arch was erected there. Frequent raids by Saxon pirates meant that the Romans could not continue to rest on their laurels, and in the middle of the third century, a sizeable wooden fort was erected. This was converted around AD 275 into a strong, stone-built fortress, surrounded by a double ditch to delay intruders long enough for them to come under fire from the fort. The great triumphal arch was demolished and the stone used to build the walls of the new fort.

The stone fort remained in use for the whole of the remainder of the Roman occupation and was the headquarters of the Count of the Saxon Shore (*Comes Litoris Saxonicum per brittanicum*), who commanded the forts from Brancaster in Norfolk to Portchester in Hampshire. The famous Watling Street starts at the west gate at Richborough and continues, through Canterbury, to London and beyond.

The Roman governor of Britain and Gaul, Marcus Carausius, increasingly detached himself from Rome between 287 and 293 and in due course declared himself Emperor of Britain, much to the displeasure of the joint Roman emperors, Diocletian and Maximillian. Having overcome Carausius' control over Gaul, Maximillian landed with an army in Hampshire and approached Richborough from the land. Being specifically constructed to repel seaborne invasions, Richborough was unable to repel this terrestrial approach and soon fell to Maximillian's legionaries, and Rome once more took control.

In AD 367 Britain was subjected to large-scale, concerted attacks by various barbarians (Picts, Scoti, Franks and Saxons) who rampaged through the countryside, raping and pillaging and causing many Roman and Romano-British residents of the country to flee their towns and villas. The troops mutinied and chaos reigned until Emperor Valentinian sent his general (later emperor), Theodosius, to restore order. Landing at Richborough with a strong army, he succeeded in driving the barbarians from the land and set about strengthening the existing defences.

The port, fort and settlement remained in use well after the departure of the Romans and were claimed by Geoffrey of Monmouth to have been where the fabled King Arthur landed around AD 470. More tangible, it was at Richborough that St Augustine landed in 597 and stopped to pray at the little church within the fort before continuing on his mission to spread The Word throughout Britain. But the gradual silting up of the Wantsum eventually led to Richborough being abandoned.

Even today, the remains of Richborough Fort are impressive and much of the outer walls remain, reaching up in parts to 25 feet. They are constructed of flint with occasional courses of tiles.

The walls of the 3rd century AD 'Saxon Shore Fort' at Richborough.

The **Reculver** fort dates from around AD 210, as confirmed by a dedication stone uncovered in 1960. Originally a square fort with walls 600 feet long, surrounded by two ditches, and covering some 30,000 square yards, the sea has claimed more than half of it over the years. Probably half a mile or more from the sea when it was built, the height of the walls and the flatness of the surrounding countryside gave the sentries an excellent view far out to sea, but by Hasted's time (c.1800) the great walls, 10 or more feet thick, had begun to tumble into the encroaching sea. It was evidently abandoned for a time in the third century but was reoccupied in the fourth century when the First Cohort of Baetasians that originally came from Brabant in Belgium garrisoned it. Some reconstruction was attempted around this time but the fort was finally abandoned shortly afterwards.

Once the Romans had gone, missionaries, following in the footsteps of St Augustine, occupied Reculver. In AD 669, they used stone from the Roman walls to create a church in the middle of the site. Only the imposing twin towers of this Saxon edifice now remain, and even these have been under threat over the centuries. Fortunately, in more modern times, Trinity House has saved the towers (which had provided a landmark for mariners for hundreds of years) by strengthening them and erecting groynes to keep the sea at bay.

The Saxon Shore Fort at Lympne, later called **Stutfall** (from the Saxon 'Stout Wall'), was built around AD 280, but very quickly suffered from erosion by the sea. The south wall has completely disappeared and much of the remaining walls have been moved out of position by repeated landslides.

The remains of the Roman fort at Stutfall (Lympne).

It appears to have been abandoned within a hundred years from its construction. Although the Saxons built churches and other buildings within
the Roman walls at Dover, Richborough and Reculver, Stutfall's position
on such unstable land was undoubtedly the reason why the Saxons did not
make similar use of this crumbling edifice.

The loss of Stutfall was tempered somewhat by the construction of a new
Roman fort at **Saltwood**, near Hythe, on the remains of which the existing
thirteenth-century castle and an earlier Jutish fort were built. No trace of the
Roman fort remains.

Once the Romans withdrew from England, around AD 410, the bewildered
and disorganized Britons were apparently unable or unwilling to make use
of their forts to defend themselves against the Saxons. In due course, the
Saxons proved similarly reluctant to use them, with the result that they
rapidly fell into disuse, the masonry being taken to construct dwellings or to
build walls around their fields.

Chapter 3

Jutish and Saxon Kent (410–1066)

It is sometimes difficult for us today to appreciate just how long the Roman Empire incorporated Britain in general and Kent in particular. With close to four hundred years of occupation, the Kent that Aulus Plautius found when he arrived at Richborough in AD 43 would have been considerably different from that which they left on their departure around 410. It was a similar period of time to that which separates twenty-first century Britain from the Civil War between the Royalists and the Roundheads. The Romans had settled in the county and intermarried with the indigenous population; they had built towns and villas, the early wooden forts had been replaced by sturdy stone walls and fortifications, and the prehistoric track ways, which led from one Roman settlement or town to another, had been widened and surfaced.

But the invasion of the Roman Empire by Vandals, Visigoths, Huns and other barbarian hordes from the east in the fourth century meant that Rome was sorely pressed and had to recall the legions stationed in distant parts of the Empire, such as Britain, to assist in the defence of those parts that were seriously at risk.

Despite popular myth, Britain under Roman rule was a civilized, prosperous and regulated society, but relied heavily on the Romans for its defence and the maintenance of order. With the departure of the legions and the whole Roman administrative structure, it was to be plunged into a period of death and disorder, of pillage and plunder, of rape and ransack, lasting some two centuries. The Angles, Jutes, Saxons and Franks from mainland Europe, and the Scoti from Ireland, received news of the military abandonment of the country with glee and wasted little time in crossing the seas to take advantage of what was a virtually undefended country. Meanwhile, the undefeated Picts from the north swept southwards over Hadrian's Wall into England, some even marauding as far as Kent. Petitions to Rome for a return of the Roman troops were rejected and Britain was left to fend for itself – something it had not been required to do for four hundred years.

The period, lasting about three centuries (AD 500 to 800), which followed the departure of the Romans and the collapse of the Western Roman Empire, is often referred to as the Dark Ages. This is for perhaps three reasons:

- Early historians tended to regard this period as being ignorant and backward, during which a great deal of previously amassed knowledge and learning was lost, as well as being regressive in that people tended to return to simpler lives in smaller communities and many of the larger towns disappeared;
- Few written sources are available from which historians can confidently describe what happened and what life was really like;
- The constant threat to life and livelihoods posed by the continual raids by brutal foreigners, together with attacks from those Britons who were seeking to make a name for themselves and seize power and whatever property they could.

In fact, more recent archaeological discoveries tend to indicate that the period was not quite as bleak and ignorant as earlier historians painted it.

During the early part of this period England was split into an indeterminate number of 'kingdoms', the first of which was Kent, established as a Saxon kingdom in AD 449 under Hengist. Around 425 a great 'king' named Vortigern controlled Kent (and probably a large area beyond) and was greatly occupied in defending his kingdom from the Picts and other invaders. The Romano-Britons were not a particularly war-like race and had become soft with their easy living under Roman rule so Vortigern had to look elsewhere for recruits for his defensive army. Tradition has it that, in AD 449, Vortigern called upon a powerful group of Jutish mercenaries from Jutland and Frisia, under their leaders, Hengist and his brother Horsa, to help rid him of these troublesome neighbours. According to the *Anglo-Saxon Chronicle* (which was written three or four centuries after these events took place and is not necessarily entirely reliable) Hengist replied, 'Take my advice and you will never fear conquest from any man or any people, for my people are strong. I will invite my son and his cousin to fight against the Irish [the Scoti] for they are fine warriors.'

This stratagem proved very successful, and Kent enjoyed a short period of comparative peace. The Jutes, who had arrived in Thanet – which was then still very much an island – were allowed to settle there, but impressed by their new home sent messages back to their people back home, telling them (according to the *Anglo-Saxon Chronicle*) 'of the worthlessness of the Britons and of the excellence of the land.'

With added numbers continually arriving from their homelands, these Jutish immigrants soon began to spread westwards, across the Wantsum into mainland Kent. The fact that these new arrivals were now well established on Kentish soil (Thanet) rendered the old seaward-facing Roman forts of the Saxon Shore obsolete, for, as the 6th century monk Gildas complained, the enemy had already been welcomed and had been '... invited in among them (like wolves into the sheep fold) ... Those very people whom, when absent, they dreaded more than death itself, were invited to reside, as one might say, under the self same roof.'

The Britons resisted this encroachment robustly and there were a number of pitched battles between the two sides. One, at Aylesford in AD 455, resulted in the death of Horsa, as well as the leader of the Britons, Vortigern's son Catigern. The outcome of this particular battle is unclear, but Hengist subsequently claimed the throne of Kent for himself and his son Æsc. The Britons were up against fierce and experienced fighters and at a fourth battle, held in AD 457 at Crayford, they were defeated and largely driven from the county, some eventually as far as Wales.

Kent, which was probably about the same size then as it is today, was now firmly under Jutish control. The *Anglo-Saxon Chronicle* claims that Æsc ruled Kent from 488 to 512, and it is reputed that he immediately built himself a wooden fort at **Saltwood**, where the present castle now stands. The Saltwood fort appears on a charter signed by King Egbert in 833, and with but a few gaps, all the succeeding owners have been recorded.

By the time Æsc's great-grandson, Æthelbert, became king and ruled Kent from 560 to 616, he was not just the king of a small corner of England but was also the Bretwalda or overlord of all the provinces south of the Humber. It was during his reign, in AD 597, that Augustine arrived with forty monks to bring Christianity to England.

By this time the Jutish and Frankish influence had diminished through migration and intermarriage, and the people of England were lumped together, at least by later historians, as Anglo-Saxons or simply as Saxons. The Angles had dominated the north and midlands (Northumbria, Mercia and East Anglia) and the Saxons the east and south (Wessex, Essex and Sussex), but Kent, the seventh kingdom in the English heptarchy, remained a largely independent kingdom whose rulers traced their lineage back to Hengist. It was perhaps because of its position as the gateway to England, and thus the first to be established by the Germanic invaders, that Kent was so relatively powerful in the early Anglo-Saxon period, especially under the rule of Æthelbert, the first Christian king. It was after his death that the power of Kent began to decline.

In 686, Caedwalla of Wessex subjugated Kent, after which the kingdom fell into a state of disorder. There was a brief period during which Mercia exerted considerable influence, but, when Wihtred became king at the end of that century, peaceful relations with Kent's neighbours were restored. However, with the death of Wihtred in 725, followed rapidly by that of his three sons, Kent became fragmented and its history increasingly obscure.

It was probably the internal wrangling and squabbling within the 'kingdom' that encouraged Offa, the great king of Mercia, to make a takeover bid. In 764 he gained supremacy over Kent, and he and his successors ruled over the county, with certain interruptions, for the next sixty years, although there were still minor 'kings' of the county – often more than one at the same time, who were subservient to the king of Mercia.

The victory of King Ecgberht of Wessex over the declining Mercia in 825 at the Battle of Ellandun brought Kent under the control of the victor. Wessex, which now included Kent, had become a powerful and expanding kingdom, covering the greater part of southern England. It was an almost entirely rural and woodland realm, the only significant urban area being Hamwith, near present-day Southampton. (London was also an important town but did not come under Wessex control until the late 9th century.) The population of Wessex at this time would not have been much more than half a million souls, scattered around the kingdom in hundreds of villages, hamlets, farms and tiny settlements.

Up until the ninth century, Britain appears to have been wholly pre-occupied with internal power struggles and domestic squabbles, and very little was done to prevent incursions from other tribes or invasions by people from Europe. Few, if any, forts were built around the Kentish coastline in emulation of the Roman Saxon Shore fortifications and the latter were them-selves destroyed by successive waves of Germanic settlers – the materials of which were often used to build churches. However, raids by pagan Vikings from around AD 800 made the Anglo-Saxons very conscious of their vulnerability, especially when Rorik, a Danish chieftain from Frisia, stormed Canterbury and London with 350 ships and spent the winter of AD 850 on the Isles of Thanet and Sheppey. It was not until Alfred the Great took the throne of a united southern England (871–899) that serious steps were taken to repel the increasing raids by these Danish warriors who were now beginning to settle in various parts of the country, especially the kingdoms of Northumbria and East Anglia.

Given the geographical extent of the kingdom of Wessex and its tiny population, it would have been impossible to build and garrison a significant number of coastal forts (it has been estimated that Alfred's army never exceeded 4,000–5,000 thousand men, and these would only have been mustered as the need arose). The site of a Saxon fort has been identified in the present town of Dover, but much of the populace resided in the fortified town constructed on the cliff top (where the Norman castle now stands), which incorporated an earlier Iron Age hill fort and where the church of St Mary in Castro still preserves many of its Saxon origins.

However, instead of protecting the shoreline as the Romans had done, Alfred generally concentrated on fortifying the existing centres of population and creating a complex of new ones, known as *burhs*, together with a few simple forts. The purpose of these was quite clearly described as 'to shelter all the folk.'

Bayford Castle was one that had its origins around this time, as Alfred erected a fort here in the ninth century to counter the Danish incursions. With **Tonge** and **Castle Rough**, it formed a trio of such defences near Sittingbourne, guarding the Swale and Milton Creek from seaborne invasions and raids. It continued to be used for the rest of the Saxon period and into the Norman era. At some point around the time of the Norman Conquest, the wooden structure was replaced by a more substantial stone building, but by the end of the fifteenth century it had ceased to be viable and was reduced to the role of a farmhouse. The stone castle no longer exists and only the much-damaged earthworks remain, a later large house known as Bayford Court occupying the site, probably built using materials from the old castle and incongruously surrounded by a modern industrial complex.

The thirty-three *burhs* that Alfred built across the whole of Wessex varied considerably in size and importance. According to the contemporary *Burghal Hidage*, the most important were Wallingford (Oxfordshire) and the capital, Winchester. Only one of these fortifications was in Kent, a very minor fort at a place referred to as Eorpeburnan and generally believed to have been near where the present-day tiny village of Newenden now stands, close to the border with Sussex. This belief is supported by the discovery of ninth-century remains there in 1971.

A typical Alfredian *burh* would have been a small- to medium-sized town, the very smallest *burhs* being simple forts to provide refuge for the few nearby residents. Some made use of a Roman fort, as at Exeter, or used the reconstituted remains of one, as at Winchester. Most, however, including the great centre at Wallingford, were entirely new Saxon constructions, typically involving turf-covered earth ramparts with timber revetments and in some cases a palisade, occasionally strengthened by some stonework. The size of the sole Kentish *burh* suggests that it was only intended to provide refuge for around 320 families, which gives an idea of the sparsely scattered population in the county at that time.

The aim of the system was to ensure that no settlement in Wessex was more than 20 miles from a refuge of some kind, and it is therefore notable that, apart from the fort near Newenden (which is virtually in Sussex anyway), there were no Kentish *burhs* listed in the *Burghal Hidage*. This is presumably because, by the late ninth century, a separate system of garrisoned fortresses existed in the county, and the two main centres in Kent, Canterbury and Rochester had already been strengthened (rather than being built from scratch), as had the cliff-top fortified town of Dover.

Canterbury (*Cantwara-burh* or 'the fortified town of the men of Kent') had been the royal centre of the kingdom of Kent, and in the ninth century, was a crowded refuge for the locals against attacks by the Vikings. In AD 850, when Rorik stormed Canterbury, documents indicate that the walls of Canterbury were of considerable height, as some of the attackers were apparently destroyed by being thrown from the top of them.

The fortified town of **Rochester** was besieged by Danes in AD 885, but it was strong enough to withstand the assault until Alfred was able to relieve the occupants and drive off the Danes.

In AD 892, a force of between 5,000 and 10,000 Danes sailed from Boulogne in 250 ships up the now long-lost Lymen estuary (roughly following the course of the present east-west section of the Royal Military Canal), bringing their women and children and horses with them, obviously intending to stay. A small old Saxon fort near St Rumwold's church in **Bonnington** was overwhelmed and destroyed and all the occupants killed. Moving on, the Danish invaders built their own giant fort at Appledore, where they were soon joined by earlier Danish immigrants who had settled in East Anglia and elsewhere under a peace agreement made with King Alfred. Using this fort as their base, they made repeated sorties into the surrounding countryside, razing to the ground a large Anglo-Saxon settlement near Ashford.

Alfred massed his troops at the Eorpeburnan (**Newenden**) fort, and from there retaliated, driving the Danes further and further inland, harrying them until they eventually gave up and returned to France (from whence, a century or so later, their successors made a more successful landing at Hastings under William, Duke of Normandy).

It seems probable that it was this determined and concerted action, plus the provision of the *burhs*, that saved Wessex from being completely overrun, as all the other English kingdoms were by 871. The disgruntled Danes were obliged to concentrate their attentions on the north and east of the country, confining their activities to those parts which had been agreed between Alfred and the Danish leader, Guthrum. It is noticeable that Kent never came under Danish influence, much less Danish occupation or control, which explains the complete lack of Danish place names in the county.

In AD 909, following Alfred's death, his son, Eadward the Elder, felt strong enough to launch an offensive against the Danes, who retaliated fiercely, but they were defeated by the English in a great battle fought near present-day Wolverhampton. Both the joint kings of Northumbria were killed, leading to the unification of virtually the whole of England under one king, Eadward's son, Æthelstan.

As the reader will have gathered, the whole of the Anglo-Saxon period was marked by continual battles between the existing population and immigrants from northern Europe, and between the various sects, clans, tribes and nationalities who had already settled here. Such fortifications as were erected were usually *ad hoc* and thrown up to meet an anticipated immediate or impending assault, whether from overseas or from within the domestic boundaries. Such constructions were of a transient nature and were soon either destroyed by the assailants or left to rot once the immediate danger had passed. Nature soon took over and obliterated the sites, aided by succeeding populations. Only the *burhs* of Alfred's time were, on the whole, solidly constructed, and most of these have been absorbed by the modern town or city. In the same way, although not part of the Burghal system, little of the Anglo-Saxon fortifications of Canterbury or Rochester may be discerned, in many cases the Saxon buildings having been rebuilt and converted by the Normans for their own purposes.

Chapter 4

Norman and Plantagenet Kent
(1066–1300)

The uncertain line of succession to the throne of England, following the death of the childless Edward the Confessor, led to a number of claims from men with a more or less legitimate claim. These included the brother of Edward's wife, Harold, Earl of Wessex, who was probably the most powerful man in England. Another pretender was William, the illegitimate son of Robert (the Magnificent), Duke of Normandy, but he was only related to Edward by the female line and was not directly descended from Edward's predecessors. Under the complex Anglo-Saxon rules of succession, which were partly hereditary and partly elective, it was Harold who was crowned King of England on the day following Edward's death.

The slighted William was not about to give up easily and as is firmly implanted in the minds of all Englishmen, invaded England in September 1066. With some 700 hundred ships and 7,000 men, he landed unopposed at Pevensey before moving to a more secure beachhead at Hastings. Harold, who had already been hard-pressed repelling an invasion in East Anglia by King Harald Hardrada of Norway, had to hastily make his way south. His battle-weary men marched the 200 miles to Hastings in five days, in order to join battle with William, where Harold was killed and the English army defeated. William thus took the throne of England by force of arms and began a new royal line.

It was not a popular move and William had to subdue a resentful Anglo-Saxon population. In a matter of a days, William had had simple forts built at Hastings and Pevensey, and just five days after the Battle of Hastings he began his journey towards London. This was not a simple matter: the direct route northwards to his goal was blocked by the almost impenetrable and tactically perilous Wealden forest. Also, William needed to secure his maritime lines of communication (some of his supply ships had mistakenly landed at Romney where they had been soundly repulsed by the townsfolk), so he set off eastwards along the coast into Kent.

Once he reached Romney, the population was severely punished for having had the temerity to tackle the Norman seamen earlier. Dover was the next place of any strategic importance and the town surrendered on demand, although this did not prevent the town from being put to the torch. One of William's first forts was built here before the retinue proceeded to Canterbury, following the old Roman road, where he met with representatives from all the significant places and negotiated their submission.

Legend has it that the people of Kent, led by Archbishop Stigand of Canterbury, surrounded William and his army near Swanscombe, disguised with bushes (in the style of Macduff's army on the way to Dunsinane from Birnam as described in *Macbeth*), which they threw aside as William came near and offered him their loyalty if he would agree to them retaining their traditional rights, such as the law of succession known as *Gavelkind*. Faced with this determined resistance and not wishing to have to fight yet another battle so soon after Hastings, the astonished William agreed, and the people of Kent have henceforth taken as their device the word 'Invicta' (unconquered). This story is well known to be an attractive fiction and the truth is probably that, on his way to Canterbury, William received a deputation of the Kentish nobles, who pledged their loyalty to him in return for the recognition of their ancient rights and customs. Indeed, William of Poitiers, the Conqueror's chaplain, wrote that 'the men of Kent of their own accord, met [William] not far from Dover, swore allegiance and gave hostages.' Another writer speaks of the people of Kent flocking to make submission 'like flies settling on a wound.'

This solution would have been attractive to both sides. The Kentish nobles were alarmed at William's pitiless suppression of any opposition, as shown at Romney and Dover, and were conscious that both Canterbury and Rochester lay in the Conqueror's path. For William, his army was not a huge one and he had lost a good number of men at Hastings; he had to garrison the forts he was erecting along his route and he had no desire to wage another pitched battle if it could be avoided. In any case, he could always review his promises once he had secured the throne and the country.

To safeguard his newly gained possessions, William appointed his half-brother, Odo, Bishop of Bayeux, as the earl of Kent and conferred on him nearly 200 manors. Apart from the king himself, Odo thus became the largest single landowner in the county, most of the remainder being shared out amongst other clerics. The Archbishop of Canterbury possessed the town of Sandwich and twenty-five manors, including Maidstone, Charing, Otford and Wrotham, where 'archbishop's palaces' were built. The Bishop of Rochester's holdings were somewhat smaller, as were those of the various monasteries and abbeys. Only four laymen were tenants-in-chief of Kentish manors: Hugh de Montfort, Richard de Tonbridge, Eustace de Boulogne and Hamo the Sheriff, who were thus rewarded for having fought alongside William or rendered outstanding service to him. Hugh de Montfort held a number of manors in the south-east of the county, centred on his castle at Saltwood.

During the first few years after the Battle of Hastings, William's policy was to govern through the great Anglo-Saxon families and win them over, rather than have to hold the country down by brute force. There is therefore nothing surprising in his allowing the men of Kent to keep their old laws and traditions, especially as these were not, by their nature, likely to embarrass the king. It is perhaps a tribute to the later Anglo-Saxons, and to William's desire to assert the legality of his succession and the continuity of his government that, across the country, the Normans adopted and adapted many of the Saxon ways and customs, including the legal system. When a dispute arose in 1070 between Odo and Archbishop Lanfranc of Canterbury regarding the dubious transfer of land and properties within the diocese, William I called for a trial to be held on Penenden Heath, the ancient Kentish meeting place on the outskirts of Maidstone, before the nobles of Kent, including Richard de Tonbridge, Hugh de Montford and the Bishop of Rochester. Such was the importance of the Anglo-Saxon land-tenure precedents that William also ordered Æthelric, the former Bishop of Selsey, a 'very old man, very learned in the laws of the land', to attend the trial, and he arrived by chariot 'in order to discuss and expound these same [Anglo-Saxon] legal customs.' (Odo lost and was later stripped of his possessions and title, and imprisoned, despite his family links to the king.)

Nevertheless, William's army was tiny compared to the population of England, and he and his followers were determined to demonstrate their power and authority by building a series of forts and castles to subdue and overawe his new subjects. The concept of 'shock and awe' is not an entirely new one! However, this did not occur overnight and William's progress through the country was governed by the establishment of suitable fortifications to his rear, to which he could withdraw should the resistance prove intransigent. It was now that the word 'castle' really entered the English language. Although used in some Anglo-Saxon translations of the Gospels, the word to them meant a village and it was not until the arrival of the Normans that the word took on its more forbidding and war-like aspect. (Other French imports included *fortress, conflict, siege, assault* and *armour* – not to mention *taxes*!)

Some of these castles were built for the purposes of national defence, such as at Dover, Canterbury and Rochester – all built along the main lines of communication. Others, such as those at Chilham, Leeds and West Malling, were built by the Norman barons and knights to protect and oversee the lands (or 'loweys') that the new king had conferred on them. These were not, at first, substantial castles but usually 'motte-and-bailey' fortifications and are more properly described as forts. Like the earlier Roman defences, they were able to serve as military rallying points.

The 'bailey' referred to commonly comprised one or more ditches surrounding a wooden palisade or thick thorn hedge, behind which lay a secure compound (sometimes referred to as the 'ward' but more generally included in the term 'bailey'), in which accommodation and storage huts were built. Within or immediately adjacent to the bailey there rose a hillock or 'motte' constructed using rubble and the spoil from the ditches, and/or taking advantage of an existing natural mound. Excavations have shown that these mounds were not simply hurriedly thrown up but were carefully constructed of alternating strata of varying materials such as chalk, gravel, earth and turf.

On the flattened top of the motte a wooden fort was erected – the final bastion. Entry to the motte and its fort was gained via a single, easily defended entrance, accessible only through the bailey, to which there was similarly a single, defended entrance. Thus, any assailants would first have to overcome the deep ditch or ditches and then find a way over the palisade around the ward, before attempting to launch an assault on the steeply sloping motte and its fort.

These early Norman fortifications were cheap and easy to construct, and were surprisingly effective; William the Conqueror built one at Hastings as soon as he arrived, which can be seen on the Bayeux tapestry. But, once the soil of the mound had consolidated sufficiently, the Normans generally preferred to convert the more important sites into stone constructions to become what we now regard as a 'castle'. The wooden elements of those that were not considered worthy of such a conversion have long since rotted away, but the contours of the substantial ditches can still be seen at various sites throughout Kent.

The numerically weak Normans took advantage of the defeated Saxons to help in the construction of their castles in the form of forced labour, using the old system of *burh-bol* or castle work. Unlike the Saxons, the Normans used similar building techniques to those employed by the Romans, centuries earlier. The walls were massively thick with a core of rubble faced with dressed stonework, using bricks or timbers to bond and strengthen them.

The first priority for reinforcement or replacement by a stone structure was usually the gatehouse, followed by the wall surrounding the top of the motte – rather confusingly usually described as the shell keep. Storage, accommodation and other buildings inside these stone edifices were economically erected using the defensive wall as the back of the building.

Most castles which did not incorporate a motte or a shell keep were provided with a large stone tower that we know as a keep, but was originally described as a donjon (which is still the French word for this type of building). The word 'donjon' became 'dungeon' and was subsequently used to describe a totally different concept.

No two keeps are the same but they do tend to fall into one of two basic categories: a hall keep (where height is less than the width) or a tower keep (where the height is greater than the width). Being built of stone from the start, the keeps tend to have withstood the impact of time, war and weather, and Kent has some fine examples that still exist. Dover Castle has what is undoubtedly the finest hall keep in Europe while Rochester's early tower keep is the tallest in England. Once the stone keep had been built behind its shell keep, the owner could concentrate on the walls of the bailey, and once the wooden palisade had been replaced by a stone wall the whole structure was largely impervious to fire – the greatest threat to any wooden fortress.

The siting of castles was subject to two main factors: strategy and landscape. Strategy demanded that castles had to be built at certain points, such as Dover and Rochester, which blocked the gateway to the continent, but the precise location was subject to the geographical advantages such as the cliffs at Dover and the River Medway at Rochester. Elsewhere the value of the castle was based on the artificial barrier created by the diversion of a river, such as at Leeds. Other castles, like Canterbury, owed their existence to the need to overawe a nearby township.

Such descriptions might give the impression that castles were purely defensive, but this was not the case. It is true that access was made as difficult as possible for unwelcome visitors, but the overriding concept was not passive defence but action and destruction. Shutting oneself in a castle was not an attempt to avoid conflict but a means of making the enemy fight at a disadvantage. The approaches to the castle were planned to provide 'killing fields', and 'hit-and-run' parties leaving the castle through 'sally-ports' could inflict considerable damage on the besieging troops before retreating back inside the castle walls. Those within the castle had shelter, warmth and so long as it lasted, food. Starvation was the greatest threat to the besieged, but, having to live off the land, things were far from easy for the besiegers. Sieges were a great drain on the invaders' human resources, and many a siege was abandoned because the invader could no longer spare the time and men to maintain it for several weeks.

In the early castles, defence was conducted mainly from the battlements on the central keep, and also on the curtain walls and any towers where these

Artist's impression of the original motte-and-bailey fort at Tonbridge.

had replaced the less-imposing bailey palisades. The tops of these stone walls were crenellated – that is to say there were open embrasures in the merlon or protective wall through which the defending troops standing on the rampart could rain missiles on the attackers. As well as arrows and cross-bow bolts, these missiles could include rocks, rubbish, dead cats and dogs, as well as hot water. (The popular idea of boiling oil being used is unlikely given the cost and scarcity of this substance.) One problem with this method of defence was the difficulty in dealing with attackers immediately below without the defenders leaning out through the battlements and thus exposing themselves to enemy fire. This was solved by providing a platform or hoard-ing projecting about 4 feet from the wall or tower with a shield on the outer edge and holes in the floor through which the enemy could be assailed. Where such projections were later built into stone walls or towers, from which they were supported by corbels, they were known as 'machicolations'.

The rampart on the inner side of the wall, otherwise known as an 'allure', had no protection on the inner side so that, should the attackers manage to gain access to it by means of ladders or assault towers, they would be com-pletely exposed to the remaining defenders within.

Internal passages were protected by gratings known as portcullises, which were lowered through slots in the roof and side walls. These were particularly useful in gatehouses, where any attackers who managed to enter the passage would find further progress prevented by the inner portcullis, while the outer one could be lowered, thus trapping them in a killing space, the ceiling containing a number of apertures or *meurtrières* through which the defenders in an upper room could destroy them. These can be clearly seen at Tonbridge Castle.

In more peaceful times, there was a great temptation for the lords to try to make their cold stone castles more comfortable and attractive. Certain modifications and decorations rendered the structure more welcoming to visitors and gave an indication of the lord's wealth. The walls, plastered and painted in bright colours, or hung with tapestries and heraldic banners, relieved the cold stone and presented a fantastic cacophony of colour. Unfortunately, the decorations could not resist the ravages of time, and the present-day appearances give a completely erroneous impression of drab dullness.

At one time, the River Medway at **Allington** was fordable and so the area was populated – if that is not too grand a term to describe a tiny settlement – as long ago as 700 BC, as evidenced by a burial ground discovered there. When the last wave of Belgic or Celtic migrants settled in Kent at the beginning of the first century BC, they called the River Medway the *Elyntun*, which is most probably whence the name Allington was derived. The Romans built a villa here and traces have been found of late Saxon fortifications. After the Norman Conquest the land was bestowed on Odo, the half-brother of William I (like so much of Kent), and a motte-and-bailey castle was built to the south of the present castle.

Following Odo's fall from grace, the first Lord of the Manor to emerge from the mists of time was Ansfrid the Sheriff in 1130. Ansfrid was *ex officio* the governor of Kent, the captain of the local militia and president of the shire court. It was during his tenancy that the original wooden fort was replaced with a more substantial, crenellated stone construction. This was undoubtedly done without royal authority during the notoriously lax reign of King Stephen (1135–54), whose barons did whatever they wished. According to the *Anglo-Saxon Chronicles*,

> Every powerful man built his castles and held them against him [Stephen] and they filled the country with castles. They oppressed the wretched people of the country severely with castle building. When the castles were built, they filled them with devils and wicked men.

Whether Allington was filled with 'devils and wicked men' is not known!

On the death of Stephen the throne passed to Henry II, the son of Matilda, Stephen's great rival, and the grandson of Henry I. Henry II was a much stronger monarch than Stephen, although he came to the throne of a country in chaos, devoid of law and proper administration, and his reign was bedevilled by the continual claims made by his four sons, Henry, Richard (Coeur de Lion), Geoffrey and John (Lackland).

Ansfrid's grandson, William the Younger of Allington, made the fatal error of supporting Prince Henry's claim to the throne against his father, Henry II, in the failed rebellion of 1173/74, as a result of which, since the building had been embattled without royal authority (like so many during Stephen's reign), it was deemed by Henry II to be adulterine and was ordered to be destroyed. The remains of this fortification can be seen to this day.

Some form of dwelling remained, however, since in 1190 the young heiress to the manor was married off to Osbert de Longchamp and the couple apparently lived there. Contemporary documents refer to this being a 'house' so it was presumably a much more modest affair than the demolished castle. There then occurred a case of history repeating itself since Osbert's grandson backed Simon de Montfort in the revolt against Henry III, and when

Allington Castle.

de Montfort was killed at the Battle of Evesham (1265), the family lost Allington.

In 1279, during the reign of Edward I (1272–1307), a new manor house was built on the site by Stephen de Penchester who, three years later, was given permission to crenellate it. Arising out of the moat and surrounding the house, he erected a stout curtain wall incorporating a number of bastions, as well as eight towers and a gatehouse. The very successful Stephen was very close to both Henry III and his son Edward I and was appointed Sheriff of Kent, Constable of Dover Castle and Lord Warden of the Cinque Ports.

Despite the substantial defences erected by Stephen de Penchester, Allington Castle was always more a residence than a fortress and is notable for the early use of bricks in its construction, taking advantage of Penchester's interests in a brickyard in Essex. Around this time the medieval kitchen and the Great Hall were built, extending the manor house southwards.

Following Penchester's death, the castle passed to his daughter who married into the Cobham family, and it remained in their hands until the middle of the fifteenth century when it was acquired by Sir Henry Wyatt, who was responsible for the Tudor additions. Details of these and the new-found role of Allington Castle are to be found in a later chapter.

Binbury Castle, near Detling (TQ812603), also known as Bonbury or Stockings Wood Castle, was one of the earliest motte-and-bailey constructions, originally forming part of Bishop Odo's vast estates until his conviction for fraud around 1072. Today all that remains is the castle mound, greatly reduced from its original height, with the soil removed from the top having been used to partially infill the very overgrown moat. A farmhouse and its outbuildings now occupy the site of the bailey. Unusually for such a minor castle, it appears to have been built of stone, either originally or very shortly thereafter, although the walls were not particularly substantial. It seems to have had a very uneventful history, its only claim to fame being a landslip in the fourteenth century in which Lady Alice de Northwood was buried alive.

Brenchley Castle was another Saxon (or possibly earlier) fortification that was converted by the Normans into a motte-and-bailey and of which very little remains to this day. Almost nothing is known of its history, and its importance by Norman times appears to have been negligible, probably due to being eclipsed by nearby Tonbridge Castle.

As we have seen, **Canterbury** was a highly defended, strategic centre, even before Roman times. Having overwhelmed Bigbury hill fort and driven the defending British from the various other strongholds in the area, the

Romans set about encircling the town, which they called *Durovernum*, with stout defensive walls that the succeeding Saxons for once adopted for their own purposes. Now known as Cantwaraburh, the town had become the monarchical centre of the kingdom of Kent and successfully resisted attacks by the Vikings, the considerable height of the walls playing a major role in this.

However, Canterbury surrendered to William the Conqueror as he made his way towards London, no doubt encouraged by the sacking and burning of Dover, whose castle had proved no great obstacle to the Normans. William wasted little time in adapting the ancient defences to his own purposes. The stone castle that the Normans erected (only the keep of which now remains) was one of the earliest in England, dating from around 1080. It was one of the three original royal Norman castles in the county: Dover, Canterbury and Rochester – all built on the old road from the coast to London.

As an interim measure, a timber motte-and-bailey castle was rapidly erected near the Roman Worthgate, the present mound known as Dane John Mound being what is left of the original motte. The modern name is possibly a corruption of the Norman French *donjon* (keep), in turn derived from the Latin *dominium* or place of lordship. Making use of an existing pre-historic burial mound (which was not an uncommon practice), a

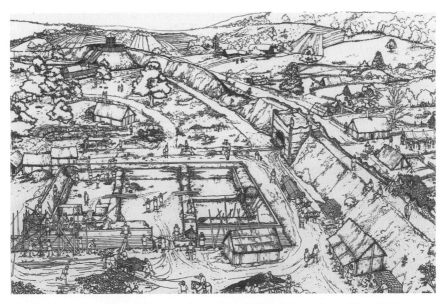

An imaginative reconstruction by Laurie Sartin of the keep of Canterbury Castle being built in the early 12th century. Note the earlier motte-and-bailey fort in the background and the Roman Worthgate. (Illustration courtesy of the Canterbury Archaeological Trust)

temporary castle would have been built, as at Rochester, to serve as an impermanent defence while the more permanent, substantial stone castle was built. Excavations in 1981 revealed what appears to have been the course of the bailey ditch, extending in a semi-circle north-westwards about one hundred metres from the Dane John Mound, the south-eastern approach being shielded by the Roman wall. These discoveries have now been reburied under a housing estate.

The first occupant of the motte-and-bailey castle was Hamo, the son of Vitalis, a Norman knight who appears on the Bayeux tapestry, but Hamo's occupancy was not to last very long, as in 1086 the Domesday Book mentions the construction of a new royal castle nearby. The temporary motte-and-bailey would by then have long been redundant.

When they came to build the more permanent stone castle, the Normans used the existing Roman wall as the south-western outer wall of their stone castle, utilizing the Roman Worthgate as its main entrance. The other three sides of the rectangular courtyard were enclosed within a ditch and stone curtain walls with one further gate opposite the Worthgate (facing up present-day Castle Street). The impressive keep rose in the south-western corner of the courtyard.

Fourteen houses, occupied by tenants of St Augustine's Abbey, were destroyed in the construction process, and it is perhaps an indication of the conciliatory manner adopted by the new rulers that the residents were given the churches of St Andrew and St Mary de Castro in recompense.

The great keep, built at the turn of the eleventh and twelfth centuries, measured around 30 metres by 26 metres and some 24 metres high, the walls of mainly flint and sandstone rubble being 4 metres thick at the base. In accordance with common practice, the only access to the keep was by a (now lost) staircase leading directly to the first floor, to deny easy access to assailants. The ground floor was simply a storage area, lit only by three narrow windows, and there was originally no access from it to the first floor which contained the great hall, a principal chamber, two other rooms and a kitchen. Above this there was a second floor, now demolished, that probably contained private rooms. The keep was solidly set in the south-western corner of the outer bailey in which there was a further great hall and a chapel.

Despite the imposing appearance of Canterbury Castle it was never put to the test by warfare. Various alterations were made over the centuries, particularly in the twelfth and thirteenth centuries when the castle was mainly used a county gaol under the control of the sheriff who sometimes resided there. The emphasis appears to have become one of keeping prisoners in rather than assailants out, and the defensive structures were allowed to decay. The prison cells were in the ground floor basement, reached from

Artist's impression of the Norman castle as originally constructed. (Illustration courtesy of the Canterbury Archaeological Trust)

the first floor entrance by two spiral staircases until around 1221, when a forebuilding with round towers was constructed to cover a new door formed in the south-east wall to give access to the prison from ground level. This forebuilding has long since vanished, but its foundations were discovered in 1939 whilst soil was being excavated to fill sandbags. The actual doorway is still visible, although now blocked.

Most prisoners spent much of their time chained in the castle yard, where they were permitted to beg for food from passers-by. It is possible that other parts of the castle were used for special prisoners, like the mysterious Saracen captive reported to be held incommunicado in Canterbury in 1242. One John Blackman escaped twice from the castle prison, despite being held in fetters, but he was recaptured on both occasions and later hanged. More recently, around forty-two 'godly and innocent martyrs' were held there before being burned at the stake, between 1555 and 1557.

It was remarked in the fourteenth century that a number of houses and gardens had been allowed to be set against the castle and the city walls and ditches, both inside and outside. A commission of enquiry in 1363 noted that the Roman walls were 'for the most part fallen because of age, and the stone thereof carried away, and the ditches under the walls are obstructed.'

This was just the beginning of the deterioration of the great castle, as we shall see later.

The origins of **Chilham** Castle are, like so many Kentish fortifications, lost in the mists of time. Its position on a high hill overlooking the ancient trackway known as the Pilgrims' Way supports a view that the earthworks date from prehistoric times, and there are signs of a Roman encampment and Saxon defences. The Norman keep and inner bailey which now dominate the hill probably replaced a motte-and-bailey castle and were built in 1171 on the orders of Odo, Bishop of Bayeux and Earl of Kent. Uniquely in Kent, the keep is octagonal in shape with two projections: a larger forebuilding and a smaller stair turret. It stands within a small, rectangular courtyard with a well-preserved curtain wall but has been considerably altered over the years – the battlements are missing and a flat roof has been installed.

The castle changed hands repeatedly during the Middle Ages, and one owner, Bartholomew de Badlesmere (who had been born in the castle) was hanged, drawn and quartered in 1322 for his part in an uprising against Edward II. In 1542 Chilham Castle became the property of Sir Thomas Cheyney, the Warden of the Cinque Ports, who pulled most of it down and sent the materials to Shurland on the Isle of Sheppey, where they were used in the construction of Shurland Hall.

In 1616, the castle having become uninhabitable, the then owner, Sir Dudley Digges, who was James I's Master of the Rolls, had an impressive

Chilham Castle.

Jacobean 'castle' erected alongside the Norman remains. This house and the keep were restored by Sir Herbert Baker after the First World War, and the complex passed into the hands of Viscount Massereene and Ferrard who sold it on, and in 2002 it became the property of Tessa and Stuart Wheeler, who, in turn embarked upon a further comprehensive restoration.

Although originally built as a defensive edifice, the Norman castle does not appear to have been involved in any battles or combat for the whole of the last millennium. Like the castles at Leeds and West Malling, Chilham Castle was essentially built as a stronghold by its wealthy landowners and was more a fortified private residence than a castle with strategic significance, such as Dover, Canterbury, Rochester and Tonbridge.

One of the great jewels in the Kentish crown so far as castles are concerned must be that at **Dover**, which has been closely involved in the defence of this country for more than two millennia. Standing proudly above the town and port, the Norman castle is an impressive sight even today, especially after nightfall when the floodlit edifice seems to float over its surroundings.

The importance of the earlier Saxon 'castle' may be perceived by the fact that it was the seat of Godwine, the earl of Kent in the middle of the eleventh century, and that he is reported to have made it a great stronghold in the late Saxon period. The town experienced a foretaste of the Norman invasion as early as 1048 when, according to the *Anglo Saxon Chronicle*, Eustace, Earl of Boulogne, attacked the citadel but was repulsed, suggesting that the fortifications were then of some considerable substance.

Following Godwine's death in 1053, his son Harold (later Harold II) took over and finished the Saxon keep and towers. Some sources refer to him using masons, but it does not seem that any major stone building had been erected by the time of Harold's death at Hastings. Harold further strengthened the fortifications in 1064, but they do not appear to have presented a serious obstacle to William I on his way to London. After the Conquest, William made certain additions to the castle, but the Normans did not consider any further work necessary for another hundred years.

It has been suggested that it was the implacable defence of the castle by its then constable, Bertram Ashburnham, which caused William, while on his tortuous journey to London shortly after the Battle of Hastings, to burn the town, and once the castle was finally taken, to take Ashburnham prisoner and to behead him. However, other accounts opine that the castle put up very little resistance, and even the presence of Ashburnham is questioned, as is the manner of his death.

It would seem that William's undertaking to leave the men of Kent essentially to their own devices, as long as they pledged allegiance to him, was not made until further on in his journey, and it may have been the burning of the stronghold of Dover that encouraged the Kentish nobles to seek an accommodation with the new Norman ruler. And so it was under Norman rule that the town and port next came into prominence.

It was not until around 1180 that Henry II, the first of the Plantagenet kings and an enthusiastic builder, set about replacing the Saxon and early Norman fortifications with a great, stone castle, far larger and far more costly than any castle that had been built hitherto. The work was supervised by Maurice the Engineer and comprised a massive square keep and inner bailey that rose from the central earthwork. At least part of the great curtain wall was built, complete with its towers and a deep ditch, and it is a tribute to the design, construction and strength of this new castle that it has remained virtually intact for over eight hundred years. It was also the earliest known example of a concentric castle in Europe – a form of defence that would be exploited fully in the following century.

Henry's son, the 'absentee king', Richard I, spent more money on it, as did his brother and successor, John, in response to a threatened French invasion; the outer walls were completed and new gate houses provided, as were the D-shaped towers (those built by Henry II were rectangular). The entrance then was through a gate between the Norfolk Towers that is now blocked.

The keep of Dover Castle is one of the largest and finest of its type ever built in Europe, being in the shape of a cube, some 29 metres high and wide. The walls, built from local Kentish ragstone with Caen stone dressing, are

Dover Castle.

over 6 metres thick at their base and incorporate numerous small rooms, latrines and storage places. It is clear that the keep was intended to provide a sumptuous residence for the constable and his retinue, as well as an almost impregnable fortress. Outside, the original curtain wall with its fourteen towers is virtually intact, although the Norman and medieval buildings that huddled against its inner bailey are long gone.

Towards the end of King John's troubled reign, a number of his barons, appalled at his cruelty and savagery and the heavy taxes imposed on them, forced John to sign the Magna Carta, promising reforms and the observance of ancient rights and practices. But John claimed the charter to be null and void, having been signed under duress, and so civil war broke out the following year, with the disaffected barons taking control of much of the south-east, including London. To assist them in ridding the country of its unpopular monarch, the barons invited Prince Louis of France to come and take the English throne.

Louis arrived in May 1216. Ignoring his father's advice that Dover was the key to England, he decided to bypass the port and instead landed in Thanet. He then proceeded to take Rochester and London before moving on to Winchester. He initially had considerable success against King John's forces and soon took control of the whole south-east with the exception of Windsor and Dover; but the latter was to prove a particular sticking point.

King John had appointed as Dover's castellan the great castle designer and builder, Hubert de Burgh, who was renowned and respected for having successfully held Chinon Castle in the Loire Valley against the King of France's entire army for a whole year between 1204 and 1205. He was famed as an outstanding administrator and intellectual, and later, during the minority of Henry III (who came to the throne in 1216 at the tender age of nine), was responsible for the running of the country as the justiciar or chief judicial officer.

By failing to tackle Dover in the early stages of the invasion, Louis had given de Burgh more time to make the castle as impregnable as was possible in those days and to ensure that it was well stocked to withstand a lengthy siege. He had gathered 140 knights and recruited a large army of men-at-arms and professional crossbowmen who, through the enfilading arrow slits in the concentric walls and towers, could hold an entire army at bay for an almost unlimited time.

Without access to the port of Dover, Louis' lines of communication to his allies in France were extremely restricted, and eventually, in June 1216, he set siege to the castle, employing mangonels, siege engines and the latest weapon in siege warfare: the trebuchet. These great catapults caused considerable damage to the outer parts of the castle, but the curtain wall prevented them from being deployed at their most effective range. Louis based half of his army in the town and the remainder set up camp outside the castle's northern wall, anticipating being able to breach the castle's formidable defences through the North Gate, which he had correctly identified as its weakest point.

Meanwhile, the deadly crossbowmen in the castle were imposing terrible losses on the French engineers and their escorts, especially as it was their practice to steep their bolts in excrement before being fired, resulting in many minor wounds becoming infected and life-threatening.

Hubert de Burgh put up a spirited defence and even sent out raiding parties against the French, forcing them to protect the siege engines they had sited to the north. A siege tower was built which was destined to be placed against the great stone walls of the castle, and at the same time, the French dug a number of tunnels and saps under the outer walls. These mining operations caused parts of the outer defences to collapse in September, and the defenders had to withdraw behind the stout main curtain wall. The barbican fell and the besieging forces then concentrated on the North Gate, the weak link in the castle's defences, digging further tunnels in the soft chalk until the gate towers collapsed into the ditch. Fierce hand-to-hand fighting prevented the French from taking the castle, and the defenders set about closing up the gap in their defences with timber beams and tree trunks. Later, steps were taking to hamper enemy mining operations by the digging of countermines, running out from the castle, beyond the castle's defences, to where enemy saps might be anticipated. These countermines could then be used either to cause the enemy's tunnels to collapse or to enable the defenders to break into them and kill the miners.

By September it was evident that the castle was going to resist for a long time yet and the siege was taking up too much of Prince Louis' time and resources. A further irritation was the constant guerrilla attacks on his supply lines by the Robin Hood–like William of Kensham, known as 'Willikin of the Weald'. With the arrival of the autumn rains, some of the French knights simply packed up their rusting armour and headed for home. The sudden death of King John in October relieved the situation somewhat, and in accordance with the 'rules' of siege warfare, Louis invited de Bergh to agree to a period of truce to enable him to consider his options as to where he should devote his allegiance, since the heir to the throne, Henry III, was but a nine-year-old child. Louis' own claims to the English throne could be regarded as having improved with John's death, and so he sent the late king's half-brother, the rebel Earl of Salisbury, to propose that the castle be surrendered to him, in the absence of an adult claimant to the throne.

Hubert de Bergh's response was unequivocal. Supported by an imposing escort of archers his reply was recorded by his close friend, Mathew Paris:

O traitor earl, and if King John our lord and your brother be dead, he has an heir, your nephew, and when all desert him, you who are his uncle ought not to leave him but rather be another father to him. How then degenerate and wicked one, dare you speak thus? Let not Louis hope that I will surrender as long as I draw breath. Never will I yield to French aliens this castle, which is the very key and gate of England. [*Chronica Majora I*]

With the English joining forces to welcome the new king, Henry III, Prince Louis was no longer needed and was politely sent back to France, and the siege of Dover Castle was lifted after a whole year.

Further forays by Louis against England, largely aided by his mother, Blanche de Castile, took place shortly afterwards, culminating in the great sea battle of Sandwich in which Hubert de Bergh, as Warden of the Cinque ports, soundly defeated a much stronger French fleet.

The long siege had highlighted certain weaknesses in the castle's defences, and between 1217 and 1256, under the wise guidance of Hubert de Bergh and the king's regent, William Marshal, Henry III embarked upon a comprehensive (and expensive) overhaul of them. In particular, the original North Gate entrance was blocked off and a new entrance provided further to the west through the magnificent new Constables Gate, which is the one used to this day.

Hubert de Bergh went on to greater things, marrying the King of Scotland's sister in 1221, being made Earl of Kent in 1227 and being mentor to the young king for a decade. Despite understandably making a number of enemies and rivals, he died peacefully at his country estate.

In the fourteenth and fifteenth centuries, although Dover Castle was maintained in a reasonable state of repair, work concentrated on building a town wall that seems to have had a rather short life. Although excavations in 1992 in connection with the making of a dual-carriageway road along Townwall Street revealed substantial buried remains of wall sections up to 6 metres high, by the mid-sixteenth century contemporary writers appeared to have difficulty in locating any signs of the wall above ground.

Throughout its history, Dover Castle has remained an important royal fortress, the role of constable being a highly prestigious one that, since 1226, has been combined with that of the Warden of the Cinque Ports. Notable holders of this office have included Odo, Bishop of Bayeux and Earl of Kent; Henry, Prince of Wales (later Henry V); Henry, Duke of York (later

Henry VIII); the Duke of Wellington; Sir Winston Churchill and Queen Elizabeth, the Queen Mother.

The castle is presently in the hands of English Heritage who have maintained it in an excellent state of repair and have refurbished and refurnished the great chambers and halls to give visitors an idea of how they would have looked in early medieval times. Its role in future conflicts will be examined in subsequent chapters.

The design of **Eynsford** Castle is somewhat unusual in that, unlike most Norman fortifications, it was not originally a motte-and-bailey castle, although it was probably built on an existing, ancient mound. Sited as the castle is, overlooking an important ford across the once-formidable River Darent, it is quite possible that there was an earlier Anglo-Saxon fort here. However, at the time of the Domesday Book, there was very definitely a 'castle' here, the property of Archbishop Lanfranc of Canterbury, and held on his behalf by a knight named Ralph, who took the name of the place as his surname.

Originally a hall, surrounded by a wooden fence, was built on the site, to the west of which a second enclosure was later attached, forming an outer ward. A basic, stone-based watchtower was built on the mound in the centre of this outer enclosure. The wooden wall around this second enclosure was later replaced by a stone wall, and the wooden watch tower was replaced by the existing ruined stone castle. The gap between the mound and the curtain

The remains of Eynsford Castle.

wall was bridged by infilling with earth, which meant that the castle's defenders would be on a considerably higher level than any external attackers. The timber walls of the eastern enclosure and the original hall were destroyed, probably to provide materials for the newer hall and the curtain wall.

Around 1100 Ralph's son, William de Eynsford I (all the subsequent first-born Eynsford sons were somewhat confusingly baptized William), built the existing curtain wall before retiring to Christ Church, Canterbury, to live as a monk. Henceforth Christ Church held the right to appoint the parish priest at Eynsford, an act that was to have serious consequences. William de Eynsford II built the present stone castle on the site of the former timber watchtower and raised the height of the surrounding curtain wall.

William de Eynsford III further extended the castle, and although ostensibly faithful to the Church and his landlord, the archbishop, openly aggravated the ill feeling between Henry II and Thomas Becket. When Becket appointed a new priest to the parish, William III barred the new arrival from entering the church, resulting in his being instantly excommunicated by the archbishop. The overturning of the ecclesiastical decision by the king was but one of the many squabbles between Becket and the king that eventually led to the latter's murder in 1170.

William de Eynsford V originally supported King John against the rebel barons, but by 1215 he was among those who resisted John at Rochester, and once the castle fell, narrowly avoided being hung for his treachery. With the death of William de Eynsford VII in 1261, the estate passed to his sisters and their husbands – William Heringaud and Nicholas de Criol – after which the ownership of the castle became rather complicated. Legal squabbles led to the castle being deserted and gradually falling into disrepair. It was later acquired by the Hart family (now the Hart-Dykes) from nearby Lullingstone Castle who used it in the later-eighteenth century as kennels for their hunting dogs.

Eynsford Castle was a relatively unimportant building and so escaped the sort of continual revamping that was the fate of more significant castles such as Dover and Rochester, and displays many of the domestic arrangements that have been eradicated in other castles.

Before the arrival of the Romans, the Kent coast to the west of Dover was sparsely populated and remote from the more populous areas of the North Downs and the Thames Estuary. Even during the Roman occupation, the main route from Dover ran north-westwards towards Canterbury before joining the Watling Street and continuing through Rochester to London – the route of the present A2 road. The almost impenetrable, and certainly hazardous, Weald Forest restricted access northwards from the coast, apart from the ancient route from the forest's iron industry to what the Romans called *Portus Lemanis* (Lympne port), linked to Canterbury by the Stone Street (B2068). As has been mentioned previously, the safest and most practical route for William the Conqueror to take from Hastings to London was along the coast to Dover and thence via Canterbury and Rochester. It was not until towards the end of the Saxon period that trading communities grew up at **Folkestone**, Hythe and Romney, resulting in the development of their harbours, the latter two becoming members of the Confederation of Cinque Ports in the Middle Ages.

The strategic importance of this low-lying stretch of the Kent coast between the great cliffs at Dover and the Weald was not lost on the Romans, who built one of their 'Forts of the Saxon Shore' at Stutfall, near Lympne. Unlike the Saxons, the Normans continued and extended the concept of coastal defence castles with the great castle at Dover, another at Saltwood and even two in Folkestone, although both have long since disappeared. One probably suffered the same fate as the nunnery (the first in England) built in the seventh century for Saint Eanswythe, which tumbled into the ever-encroaching sea shortly after the Conquest. Evidence of this castle's existence remains solely in the street name, The Bayle, which is to be found on the cliff top adjacent to the medieval parish church of St Mary and St Eanswythe (the latter being the daughter of King Æthelberht of Kent).

'Caesar's Camp' at Folkestone. (Actually the site of an early Norman fort.)

The confusingly named 'Caesar's Camp' on the outskirts of Folkestone does not appear to have ever been used by the Romans, but is in fact an ancient mound that later became the basis of a Norman motte-and-bailey fort. This 'Caesar's Camp' castle was built on one of the two rather high hills adjacent to the Roundhill tunnels on the A20 road, in a commanding position overlooking the town. Like so many other Norman castles, it was built on the site of earlier earthworks that were enlarged and altered by the Normans. No evidence of any stonework has been discovered, leading to the supposition that this castle was never more than a basic motte-and-bailey form. Today, only the considerable earthworks remain, but these clearly demonstrate the arrangement of such defences.

One of the great Kentish castles, with sumptuous gardens like Scotney and Sissinghurst, **Hever** still stands proudly in its moat, in an admirable state of preservation. Unlike the two other castles mentioned, Hever is not owned by the National Trust but by Broadland Properties Limited, but is open to the public in the same way as National Trust properties are.

The oldest part of the existing castle dates from 1270, consisting of the gatehouse and a walled bailey. Although crenellated by William de Hever around 1340 and again by Sir John de Cobham in 1384, the castle was never required to withstand a siege or repel assailants and has always been essentially a fortified dwelling.

Hever Castle: a remarkably well-restored Norman castle. (English Heritage)

The castle's greatest claim to fame is that it was the birthplace in 1507 of Anne Boleyn, the future queen of Henry VIII, who spent her childhood there. Sir Geoffrey Bullen (later Boleyn), a former Lord Mayor of London, purchased the castle in 1462 and converted this fortified manor house into a delightful Tudor residence.

After the execution of Anne in 1536 and the deaths of her disgraced parents, the castle passed to the crown and was occupied by Henry's divorced wife, Anne of Cleves. After 1557 the castle seems to have been largely forgotten and fell into disuse and decay, becoming a simple farm house.

It was rescued in 1903 by William Waldorf, the American millionaire, who later became a naturalized British citizen and was ennobled in 1917 as the Viscount Astor of Hever. He spent a fortune on restoring the castle to its present splendid condition and creating the delightful gardens. Apart from the medieval gatehouse and external walls, the present-day castle has been restored to how it would have looked in Tudor times, with a fine collection of sixteenth-century portraits, furniture and tapestries.

The thirteenth-century gatehouse has been described as one of the finest still existing, with two of its three portcullises still preserved, the outer one being one of the last in England still in working order. The Council Chamber now contains an admirable collection of weapons and armour, together with instruments of execution and torture.

Leeds Castle, always primarily a place of residence rather than a fortress, has been constantly modified over the years so that this magnificent construction, rejoicing in the title of 'the loveliest castle in the world' bestowed on it by Lord Conway, has been altered considerably from its original form.

In AD 857, Ledian, the Chief Minister to King Æthelberht IV of Kent, built the first, wooden castle which straddled two islands in the middle of a large lake formed by the River Len and which were connected to each other by a drawbridge. This was commandeered by the Normans and originally formed part of the extensive estate of William I's half-brother, Odo. When Odo fell out of favour it passed into the Crevecoeur family, and in 1119, during the reign of Henry I, Robert de Crevecoeur replaced the wooden fort with a stone castle, making use of a third, partly natural and partly artificial, island to form a barbican in front of the gatehouse. Subsequent modifications mean that only about half of the original castle remains today, the rest being of later date.

In 1138, during the troubled reign of King Stephen, Leeds Castle was in rebel hands and was besieged and taken by the king. Remaining loosely under the king's control, the castle henceforth changed hands according to the political situation pertaining at the time. Thus it was gifted to the

Leeds Castle: 'The most beautiful castle in England.'

Leyburn (later Leybourne) family during the reign of Henry III, and in 1272 William de Leybourne gave it to the newly crowned Edward I (Edward Longshanks), who adored it. He and his queen, Eleanor of Castile, frequently stayed there and made improvements to the residential quarters and improved the fortifications. King Edward enlarged and machicolated the gateway, strengthened the modest keep or gloriette, and added an outer bailey.

One of the rare occasions on which the defensive qualities of the building were tested occurred in 1321 when Queen Isabella, Edward II's wife, arrived late at night with a large retinue and asked for shelter. When the castellan, Walter Colepeper, refused to admit her without orders from the then owner, Baron Bartholomew of Badlesmere, Edward's commander, Aymer de Valence, laid siege to the castle with an army of 30,000 men. This was possibly a ploy to test Badlesmere's loyalty, and on succeeding in taking the castle after just seven days, Colepeper and twelve others were hanged, Lord Badlesmere was executed and his wife confined to the Tower of London. A number of other, lesser persons were merely imprisoned. As to why this seemingly impregnable castle – surrounded by a great lake and with a strong gatehouse protected by two barbicans – fell after such a short time, it seems probable that it was simply too thinly garrisoned.

By a curious twist of fate, some three hundred years later, Colepeper's descendants were to purchase the castle, be ennobled and remain associated with it for a further three centuries.

In 1394, Jean Froissart, the renowned French historian, stayed at the castle, and even then, commented that the castle was more of a palace than a stronghold. And Leeds continued to live up to the soubriquet of the 'ladies castle', successive owners or occupants including Queens Isabella of France, Anne of Bohemia, Joan of Navarre and Catherine of Valois. The castle was in royal hands for some three hundred years, the last monarchical owner being Henry VIII, who, in turn, made considerable alterations and 'improvements', including the construction of the Maidens' Tower and an upper floor to the gloriette.

Henry VIII passed the castle on to his friend, Sir Thomas St Ledger, and it remained henceforth in private hands, including the Culpeppers of Hollingbourne and the Fairfaxes. The extensive Stuart and Jacobean additions were removed by Fiennes Wykeham-Martin in 1822 and replaced by the mock-Tudor block in the middle bailey. Although criticized for 'desecrating' the castle, Wykeham-Martin did restore much of the original medieval work and added certain sympathetic embellishments.

Although the Fairfaxes had strong connections with America in the eighteenth century (and eventually emigrated to Virginia), the castle remained solidly in British hands until 1926 when the Anglo-American Lady Baillie bought it and immediately embarked upon a monumental restoration project. Much of what one can see today is the result of her care and devotion. During the Second World War, the castle was used as a military headquarters and later as a hospital. When Lady Baillie died in 1974, the castle was, in accordance with her wishes, opened to the public and managed by a charitable trust.

Despite the construction of the M20 motorway and the high-speed rail link nearby, the castle remains a haven of peace and tranquillity and welcomes thousands of visitors each year.

Leybourne Castle follows the usual Norman pattern of being built, first as a wooden motte-and-bailey stronghold on earlier earthworks, and then, in the thirteenth century, replaced by a substantial stone castle. The original castle formed part of the vast Kentish estate of Bishop Odo, and when he fell out of favour it was devised to Sir William de Arsick, who owned other estates in the area.

In 1146, Philip and Michael de Laibron, two brothers of Breton descent, living in Leyburn in Yorkshire's Wensleydale, came into possession of the castle, and twenty years later erected what was known as Lillebourne Castle on the site. Sometime before Philip's death in 1195, the family name and that of the castle changed to Leyburn and then Leybourne.

Philip left the castle and estates to his son, Sir Robert de Leybourne, who had fought alongside Richard I at Acre in the Crusades, but Robert was not to enjoy them for long, dying in 1199 and passing them on to his son, Sir Roger de Leybourne, the first of two to bear that Christian name.

Sir Roger (1) was one of the barons who forced King John to sign the Magna Carta at Runnymede and defended Rochester Castle against the king's followers in 1215–16. When the castle was taken, the rebel barons were punished and Sir Roger lost his Leybourne estate but the family bought it back for 250 marks in 1216.

On Sir Roger (1)'s death (c.1250), he was succeeded by his son, Sir Roger (2), whose exploits could fill an entire book. Sir Roger (2) was one of the 'turbulent barons', and according to the *Oxford Dictionary of National Biography* he was 'one of the most stirring and distinguished warriors of the day whose whole life was passed between tilting and the battlefield.' It was he who built the stone castle in around 1260, largely replacing the earlier construction effected by Philip de Laibron, utilizing Kentish ragstone with Caen stone dressings. He was made the Constable of Rochester Castle, which he defended in 1264 against Simon de Montfort and died in 1271 at the age of 51.

The next Leybourne, William, the first Lord Leybourne, was made the Constable of Pevensey Castle and the King's Admiral, and sometime early in the thirteenth century, William conferred Leybourne to his eldest son, Thomas. However, Thomas died in 1307, predeceasing his father, who lived

The remains of Leybourne Castle. (Illustration courtesy of L2F1 Photos)

The remains of Leybourne Castle. (Illustration courtesy of L2F1 Photos)

until 1310, and William was therefore succeeded by William's daughter, Juliana.

Juliana was but an infant when her father and grandfather died, and when she was old enough she was married off to Sir John Hastings and bore him a son. Her marriage was short lived as Sir John died soon after the marriage, but she married twice more, and although she bore no further issue, she increased her personal wealth over the years. By the time she died in 1367 she was a very wealthy woman, known locally as the 'Infanta of Kent'. Following her death the property passed, through her son, into the Pembroke family, the family line dying out with the death of her great-great grandson.

The castle then reverted to the king, Edward III, who granted the castle, together with Leybourne church, to the Abbey of St Mary's Graces in London, which stood where the Royal Mint now stands. Following the Dissolution, Henry VIII passed the castle to his Chancellor, Sir Edward North, and the castle stayed in private hands, eventually being converted into a farmhouse and gradually falling into ruins.

In 1930 a house was built within the remains of the castle, replacing an earlier one that was destroyed by fire many years earlier. Not a great deal of the original castle remains, although a large part of the rather impressive gatehouse has survived, including the unusual channel for the portcullis that is to be found on the external wall of the gatehouse, rather than inside it.

An important property, Leybourne Castle never suffered any serious assaults, and like so many others was essentially a fortified dwelling rather than a purely military fortification.

Rochester occupies an important strategic position on the River Medway and it was at this point that the Roman Watling Street route from Richborough, via Canterbury, crossed the river. The Roman town and garrison was protected by stout walls, parts of which remain to this day, being protected and classified as a Grade I listed building. Nothing remains of the Roman bridge, believed to have been of wooden construction, a stone bridge being built in the late fourteenth century.

Equally there is no trace of the Saxon fort that undoubtedly stood here to protect the town and crossing, possibly on the prehistoric mound at Boley Hill where there was certainly once some form of fortification, and which was also the site of a short-lived motte-and-bailey castle, probably erected by the Normans to assail and subdue the town, prior to the building of the more substantial stone castle by the river.

What is much clearer is that the existing castle shares with Canterbury the distinction of being one of the few stone castles that were not built on the site of an earlier motte-and-bailey castle. In 1087, the great ecclesiastical architect, Gundulph, the Bishop of Rochester, began building his castle alongside the existing motte-and-bailey construction, using the latter to provide protection during the course of construction. It was a simple fortress, consisting of a single stone enclosure erected within the city walls, using this to form two sides of the bailey wall, with the river providing a further defence and feeding the moat. This castle had the first stone curtain wall and at least one of the first mural towers in England. It boasts the tallest tower keep in England (still reaching 113 feet high to this day) that was added by Archbishop William de Corbeil around 1130. With walls up to 12 feet thick, it rises 4 stories – although the roof and floors have long since disappeared – and is divided into two almost equal halves by a cross wall. There is also a small forebuilding.

The importance of Rochester as a fortress may be gauged by the fact that the castle was besieged at least three times in its history. In 1087, following the death of William I, the eldest son, Robert, was named as his successor to the Normandy dukedom, the English crown going to the second son, William II (Rufus), much to the displeasure of certain Norman barons who saw the feckless and weaker Robert as much more malleable and likely to accede to their various demands. William countered the barons' revolt by successfully appealing to the English for their aid, promising them a greatly improved standard of living if they helped him put down the barons.

Amongst the Norman dissenters was the belligerent Bishop Odo of Bayeux, the owner of vast estates in Kent, who garrisoned the original motte-and-bailey castle at Rochester with 500 men-at-arms before prudently slipping off to Pevensey, which, like Tonbridge, was also held by the rebels. William besieged the castle at Rochester with a strong force that prevented any movement into or out of it and he built two powerful forts nearby. The castle fell without too much trouble, being beset by disease and a biblical plague of exceptionally vicious flies that covered everything and everyone. William II continued his reign over England, banishing Odo from the country forever and stripping him finally of his earldom. In the meantime he ordered Gundulph to begin the building of his stone castle nearby.

The second siege took place more than a century later. As soon as the barons returned to their own lands after forcing King John to sign the Magna

Rochester Castle.

Carta in 1215, the king set about assembling a mercenary army and set out to discipline the dissident nobles one by one. Well aware of this situation, the barons decided to take the initiative, and as a preliminary, to quickly occupy Rochester Castle which was held by Stephen Langton, the Archbishop of Canterbury, an opponent of the king. Accordingly, William d'Albini was sent to the castle with a small body of men, where he was welcomed by the castellan and all seemed to be going to plan. However, there was very little time to provision the castle before it was subjected to a siege by the king and his highly capable force of foreign troops.

The seven-week siege was to prove no run-of-the-mill event but one of those rare battles in which the opponents fight on until all are killed or disabled; simply fighting until they drop. The crafty and militarily astute John ordered a tunnel to be dug, running under the curtain wall to the tower on the south-east corner of the keep to which the beleaguered garrison had retreated. He then used the fat of forty pig carcases to burn through the tunnel's timber supports, causing it to collapse, taking the huge tower above with it. The poorly provisioned defenders, who had been forced to withdraw into the keep, had to resort to butchering and eating their own horses, but they continued to hold out, aided by the fact that the keep had been divided into two sections by a cross-wall. But starvation eventually brought an end to the siege and it was all over. A contemporary chronicler wrote, 'Our age has not known a siege so hard pressed nor so strongly resisted,' adding that, henceforth, 'Few cared to put their trust in castles.' William d'Albini was ordered to be executed, but his life was spared because of the repercussions this was likely to provoke. Other members of the garrison were not so fortunate.

It was as a result of this siege that the first substantial alterations were made to the castle, including the building of a cylindrical tower to replace the square one destroyed by the king's men.

The third siege occurred in 1263/4 during the conflict between Henry III and his barons, the latter led by Simon de Montfort. This time it was the king's troops under the Earl of Surrey (one of the celebrated Warenne family) who were within the castle, and in the course of nine days, the barons had taken the bridge and the first gate of the castle. The hard-pressed garrison withdrew to the last tower, but when all seemed lost the king arrived with a strong relieving force and the besiegers fled. The castle only suffered slight damage – so slight that repairs were not carried out until over a century later when Edward III, in the latter part of the fourteenth century and in response to a new threat from France, ordered their completion, together with the building of the remainder of the towers in the curtain wall.

Rochester Castle in 1836.

This era was to signal the end of Rochester Castle's importance, and it gradually declined and deteriorated. Much of the bailey buildings and a large part of the curtain wall were demolished and the materials shipped to Upnor for use in the construction of the new castle there. Over the ensuing years much of the fabric of the castle was sold off, and only the colossal challenge represented by the immense walls prevented the castle from being totally destroyed. It was purchased by the Rochester Corporation in 1884 and repaired and made safe, while the bailey was turned into a public park. In 1964 it was taken over by the Department of the Environment, who continue to maintain this invaluable relic of the last millennium.

As noted in the previous chapter, **Saltwood** Castle owes its origins to Æsc, the son of Hengist, who built the first castle there in 488. The earthworks he put up subsequently formed the inner bailey of the Norman fortress built by Hugh de Montfort, and the early Saxon works were cleverly assimilated into the newer, Norman ones. For example, the stone curtain wall of the inner bailey built by Henry de Essex, Henry I's standard bearer, follows the oval course of the Saxon earthworks. (The outer bailey was not built until the late fourteenth century.)

Saltwood Castle.

Standing on a bluff overlooking Hythe and with a view of the sea beyond, which used to lap the foot of the very heights which it dominates, Saltwood is one of the most complete castles to survive and remains in an excellent state of repair and perfectly habitable.

A deed, now held in the British Museum, signed in 1026 by Cnut and a number of bishops and nobles, including Earl Godwin of Kent, conveyed the manor of Saltwood and Hythe to the Church, since when the castle has enjoyed an uneasy joint occupation by both priests and noblemen, both Saxon and Norman.

Henry de Essex progressed from Standard Bearer to become the Warden of the Cinque Ports and Constable of England under Stephen, but during the reign of King Henry II he was accused of casting down the standard during an ambush at Counsylth in Wales and fleeing the scene. Impugned with cowardice and challenged to a judicial combat by Robert de Montfort some years later, the ageing Henry de Essex was defeated and sorely wounded. He spent the rest of his life in a monastery, relieved of all his wealth and belongings, including Saltwood Castle, reputed to be the strongest in the south of England.

This incident set the scene for one of the most celebrated and serious incidents in English history. With the removal of Henry de Essex, Archbishop Thomas Becket petitioned the king to return the castle to the Church in accordance with the 1026 deed, but Henry was already at loggerheads with this archbishop, archdeacon and royal chancellor and instead made the disreputable Sir Ranulf de Broc the castellan. Some writers refer to this archenemy of the Church turning Saltwood into a den of thieves.

When, on Christmas Day 1170, Henry II made his historic tirade against this 'turbulent priest', three of the knights present saw an opportunity of getting into the king's good books. Cronies of de Broc, they made their way to Saltwood from whence, on 29 December, they set forth for Canterbury where, as is well known, they murdered Becket in the cathedral.

Saltwood
Castle gateway.

It was around this time, or shortly thereafter, that de Broc erected the substantial tower keep, but the remorseful Henry II soon handed the castle over to the Church and it remained in ecclesiastical hands for over three hundred years. The archbishop had a suite of rooms at his disposal in the main gatehouse, but the priests, who resided there permanently, were accommodated on the south and west sides, where the existing Great Hall, Library and the Secret Garden are currently situated.

Between 1370 and 1380, during Archbishop William Courtenay's tenancy, the castle was greatly improved and strengthened, partly in response to the Lollard uprisings during which Archbishop Sudbury was murdered, and partly as a result of an earthquake that caused considerable damage to the castle. Sentries were posted on top of Thorpe's Tower, on the West Tower and on the high southern tower overlooking the lake. In times of trouble, a gong would sound the alarm and the garrison in the gate-house would quickly man the walls, using the doors which lead directly onto the Battlement Walk from the first floor. There was a further battlement walk on the walls of the outer bailey which could be reached by the small section of men that was permanently stationed in the barbican gate.

Consequent upon the Dissolution, Archbishop Cranmer handed the castle back to the king in 1540, after which it passed through a succession of secular hands. A Tudor wing was added on the south side of the gate-house, but a further earthquake caused a great deal of damage, rendering the

Saltwood Castle bailey.

castle virtually uninhabitable. Nevertheless, the main structure remained sound, and as a result of repairs carried out in the late nineteenth and early twentieth centuries, the castle was restored to a habitable condition. Much of the restoration is due to Lady Conway from Allington Castle and was effected between 1934 and 1949. When she died, the castle was purchased by Sir Kenneth Clark (later Lord Clark) of 'Civilisation' fame. In 1970 it passed in turn to his son, Alan Clark MP, the flamboyant Member of Parliament and controversial military historian who died of a brain tumour in 1999 and is buried at the castle.

Regretfully, this magnificent and historically important castle is no longer open to the public.

Until its access to the sea via the River Stour became silted up, **Sandwich** was a thriving town and port – one of the original Cinque Ports – and was understandably fortified with a stout town wall and a castle. Sadly, nothing remains of either and little is known about them.

The first recorded reference to a castle appears during the reign of Edward III (1327–1377), who was apparently very fond of the town. Just where this castle stood is unknown; Hasted mentions seeing some remains in a field known as Castle Mead, but these have since vanished. Other accounts refer to it being within the town walls, in the south-west corner. Both of these proposed sites were surrounded by the river and a wet moat and are credible. The town wall was erected somewhat later and is covered in a subsequent chapter.

Little remains of what was once the small castle at **Sutton Valence**. High on the southern slopes of a hill overlooking the Weald, it held a commanding view and would have offered a strong defence against invaders from the south. Built from the local ragstone, it was always of modest size, the keep being externally around 38 feet square with walls 8 feet thick, giving an internal dimension of just 22 feet square. Now standing around 30 feet high, it was once probably around twice this height. The keep is the only part that remains, the outer defences and buildings having long been erased by hop gardens, as have the defensive ditch and earthworks.

The design of the castle suggests that it was built in the mid-twelfth century, during the reign of Henry II, but there is no record of a licence to crenellate having been granted, which would have assisted in the dating of the building.

By the beginning of the thirteenth century, the castle was in the hands of the Mareschal family, the earls of Pembroke, before passing to Eleanor, King John's daughter. After her first husband, William Marshal, died while she was still only sixteen, she earned her father's displeasure by marrying his arch-enemy, the rebel Simon de Montfort. When de Montfort was defeated and his lands forfeited, Sutton (as it was then simply called) was given by Henry III to William de Valence (the king's half brother), and the village henceforth added his name.

The castle had a very peaceful existence, and by the beginning of the fifteenth century had already begun to fall into decay, eventually becoming, like so many others, a simple farm.

Thurnham Castle was built on the site of a Saxon fortress and this, in turn, may have replaced a Roman watch tower, as a number of Roman artefacts have been discovered in the area. Of typical early Norman motte-and-bailey design, it was once part of Bishop Odo's vast holdings in the county. It consists of a conical motte around 80 yards across with a flattened top, on which there are a few remains of an early flint-built keep. The original deep ditch is still visible, although it is now only 3 or 4 feet deep.

To the west of the motte the remains of the thick flint wall that surrounded the bailey have completely disappeared. However, on the north side, despite the depredations of subsequent years, the wall is still around 10 feet high in parts, and one can still see the remains of a gatehouse beside the ditch.

All that remains of Thurnham Castle.

The castle has been acquired by Kent County Council, which has done much to clear the area of the invasive undergrowth and open it up to the public.

Tonbridge is a medium-sized market town, strategically located around a ford on the River Medway, probably of late Saxon origin although there are no records of any Saxon fortifications. Following the Norman Conquest the whole area around the town was granted to Richard FitzGilbert (later known as Richard de Clare or Richard de Tonbridge), and it was he who built the first motte-and-bailey castle on a bend in the river in 1068/70. This greatly influenced the growth and prosperity of the town which, by the end of the century, had become a thriving settlement, its economy based on agriculture, textiles and iron working.

The FitzGilbert/Clare family were a warlike and belligerent lot, with Richard being killed in a battle in Normandy in 1091 and his grandson, also Richard, killed in Wales in 1176. The end of the eleventh century saw the conflict between William II and the recently rehabilitated Odo, Earl of Kent, the latter being supported by Gilbert de Clare. While Gilbert was hosting a number of Odo's men and according to the *Anglo-Saxon Chronicle*, 'many others who meant to support him against the king', the castle was assailed by William and taken in just two days, resulting in the destruction by fire of the original wooden castle and much of the town. For the remainder of William's reign the de Clares kept their heads down, but their fortunes were restored following the death of the king in a hunting accident in the New Forest in 1100, to be succeeded by his brother, Henry I. (Conspiracy theorists have remarked that the fatal arrow was coincidentally fired by William Tyrell, Gilbert de Clare's son-in-law!)

On the death of Henry there arose a civil war over the accession of Stephen of Boulogne (Henry's nephew) to the throne rather than Henry's daughter, Matilda, during which, in 1139, Tonbridge Castle was once more attacked and quickly fell.

In 1152 the castle passed to Roger, Earl of Hertford and Clare, a close acquaintance of Matilda's son, Henry II, and an enemy of Archbishop Thomas Becket, who actively supported the king's ill-fated dispute with his prelate. Roger's son, Richard (the fourth Earl of Gloucester), succeeded in 1173. It was Richard's son Gilbert and grandson, also Richard (the fifth and sixth Earls of Gloucester), who played a major part in the rebellion against King John, forcing him to sign the Magna Carta. John was not prepared to take this treasonable action lying down and he besieged and took Tonbridge Castle in 1215. Although it is believed that the wooden keep was replaced by a stone one quite early on, possibly in the eleventh century, the castle does not seem to have presented much of an obstacle to John, and it probably still relied to a large extent on the original wooden outer walls at this time.

Over the years the much-damaged castle was repaired, enlarged and improved, the work culminating in the construction of the curtain wall and gatehouse and the strengthening of the stone keep. The ovoid shell keep, sited on top of the mound, was never a particularly strong one, its walls being little more than 4 or 5 feet thick at the base, whereas the curtain wall is of double this thickness. The sandstone gatehouse is of particular interest, originally rising three storeys with the entrance guarded by a deep moat, a drawbridge and a portcullis, the ground floor containing the guardrooms with storerooms beneath. The first floor provided private quarters and rooms for the garrison, while the whole of the second floor was taken up by a great hall.

It was Henry III who gave Gilbert de Clare, the 7th Earl of Gloucester (known as the Red Earl because of his auburn hair), permission to build the gatehouse in the mid-thirteenth century, but such was the nature of politics at the time that the loyalty of the very powerful and influential Gilbert de Clare soon shifted, and he was to play a leading role in the rebellion, siding with the rebel Simon de Montfort against the king. In 1264 the castle was stormed and taken by Henry, and the town put to the torch with Gilbert being declared a traitor.

Model of Tonbridge Castle, showing the keep on its motte on the extreme right.

It was not until the next generation of de Clares had shown their loyalty to Henry's son, Edward I, that they regained possession of the castle. This royal patronage was demonstrated by the fact that Edward and Queen Eleanor stayed at Tonbridge Castle in 1275, *en voyage* from France to London. In 1290, Edward I gave 47-year-old Gilbert the hand of his teenage daughter Joan of Acre (1272–1397), but Gilbert died in 1295.

Gilbert the Red's only son and successor, Gilbert de Clare, the 8th Earl of Gloucester, was killed at the Battle of Bannockburn in 1314 at the age of 24, and the castle then passed through the female line to his sister Eleanor and his brother-in-law, the fearsome Hugh de Despenser. Frustrated by the delay in settling the inheritance, Despenser seized an opportunity to take the castle by force. But, as the true ownership was vested in the archbishopric of Canterbury, he was unable to hold on to it. Although close to Edward II (some claim they had a homosexual relationship), Hugh Despenser's dastardly exploits eventually resulted in his execution by being hung, drawn and quartered.

In due course the castle passed into the hands of the de Audleys and then the Stafford family, who added the Stafford Tower and the Water Tower, among other improvements. One of the many wall towers and bastions, the Water Tower, of which little now remains, was reputed to have been almost as grand as the magnificent gatehouse. The Staffords remained in control for a couple of relatively peaceful centuries until 1520, when, Edward Stafford,

The hanging, drawing and quartering of Hugh de Despenser.

the Duke of Buckingham, having been accused of high treason, the castle was once more taken by force by the monarch (Henry VIII). It was described at the time as 'a strong fortress' and its gatehouse to be 'as strong a fortress as few be in England.'

From 1551 until the Civil War, the castle changed hands on numerous occasions and was finally held by one Thomas Weller, a staunch Parliamentarian who appears to have used the castle simply for storage and leased out the dependent farmland. Upon the commencement of the Civil War, the Kent Committee rented the property from him and proceeded to strengthen the fortifications with 'several provisions of timber, platforms, planks etc'. It withstood a Royalist assault in July 1643, but, once the war was over, the timber structures were sold to Weller for £140 and he was instructed to 'take them down, thereby to slight and dismantle the fortifications.'

Weller was a lawyer and kept meticulous records that show the significant and extensive timber defensive structures erected within the castle and the bailey, justifying the considerable sum he had to pay to purchase the reclaimed timber. Although the actual stone castle was not slighted in the ordinary sense of the word, it rapidly fell into decline, the stones being purloined for the construction of other buildings. As a result, much of the curtain wall and keep, as well as the domestic apartments within the bailey, have vanished.

After passing through various hands and being used as a school and a military academy amongst other purposes, the castle was purchased by the local authority towards the end of the nineteenth century.

Tonbridge Castle: the impressive gateway.

Standing as it does on the banks of the River Medway, the castle always made the maximum use of water in its defence system. The river-fed moat surrounded the castle on those sides that the river itself did not protect, while the dense Wealden forest additionally protected the three landward sides.

In 1999 the gatehouse was closed to visitors and the floors on the ground and first floors replaced and the spiral staircase in the East Tower repaired. The gatehouse was reopened the following year in celebration of the millennium, the reroofing being completed by 2003.

Perhaps in these more modern times, **West Malling** is better remembered for its role in the defence of England in the Second World War, when many fighter aircraft took off from its airfield during the Battle of Britain and later. But its history goes back at least a millennium. Although the airfield has long since been covered by a vast, sprawling housing estate and office blocks, the town's Norman heritage still stands proud on the southern outskirts of the present town.

St Leonard's Tower is something of an enigma. It is known that it was built around 1080 and was therefore one of the earliest stone Norman buildings. Its architect is held to be the great Norman architect, Bishop Gundulph, who was responsible for Rochester's castle and cathedral, as well as the White Tower of the Tower of London. The purpose for which St Leonard's Tower was built, however, is something strongly disputed by historians.

Unusually, the tower was not built on a motte or mound; it had no bailey or defensive curtain wall. It was a simple, stand-alone tower keep, or perhaps nothing more than a substantial church tower or even simply a store. There was once a nearby church or chapel of St Leonard's, hence the name of the tower, and one suggestion is that it was built simply as a document store for the church.

Some sources point to the unusually large windows and the fact that there is no well inside the tower, nor any latrine or fireplace, and suggest that it would have been of limited use as a siege-withstanding defence, although it could have provided protection for a limited period of time for the priests and their acolytes. Others say that, although slight compared with the keeps at Dover or Rochester, St Leonard's Tower was too substantial to have been simply a Norman church tower and point to Gundulph's Tower in Rochester as an example of an ecclesiastic castle-like shelter.

In fact, the ornate St Leonard's Tower stands between 60 and 70 feet high, rising from a sloping rock shelf, and is 32 feet square at its base. It was made of coarse Kentish ragstone with tufa stone dressings. It would seem

St Leonard's Tower, West Malling.

that there were just two floors, plus a basement. Unusually, the only entrance is on the ground floor rather than the first floor, although there are no windows at ground floor level (a defensive 'plus'). Curiously, although the tower sits at the corner of two medieval walls that could have partly enclosed a bailey, the tower entrance is on the outside of the wall, meaning one would have had to leave the security of the walls to enter the tower. It is, of course, always possible that this wall is a later addition and was never part of any defences.

The unfortunate lack of documentary evidence about the tower's history and ownership leaves these questions unanswered and subject to conjecture and inspired guesswork. There is a vast gap of knowledge between the

St Leonard's Tower, West Malling.

eleventh century and the seventeenth, when the Rainey family, followed by the Honeywoods, owned the tower. At one time it was relegated to use as the town gaol and later became a store for locally produced hops, but fortunately it is now a Grade 1 listed building in the care of English Heritage.

Chapter 5

Late Medieval Kent (1300–1450)

By the fourteenth century, the Plantagenet kings, starting with Henry II, had replaced the Norman line more than a century ago, and the country had become much more unified than it was when the Normans first arrived to impose their rule on the unwelcoming Anglo-Saxons. In 1307 Edward I (Longshanks) died and his son, Edward II (Caernarfon), ascended to the throne of England. National unity was upset in 1314 when Robert Bruce beat Edward's men at Bannockburn and so relaxed the grip of England on the Scottish lowlands and thus secured Scottish independence.

Edward II was a weak and unpopular ruler and there were rumours of homosexual leanings, fostered by his excessive generosity to certain young men in his inner circle. He was eventually overthrown by his own wife, Queen Isabella, who installed their son, Edward III, on the throne in 1327. King Edward II met a suspicious death shortly afterwards.

Whilst there were still occasional uprisings and civil unrest in England, generally speaking the defences of the country were now beginning to be directed outwards, in particular towards France, rather than remaining just a means of defence against unruly locals. In 1338 French privateers burned Portsmouth, marking the commencement of the Hundred Years War, and by the second half of the fourteenth century, after a long period of English supremacy, the French had gained the upper hand and their raiding parties were beginning to inflict severe damage on the coastal towns in the south-east, especially Dover, Folkestone and Sandwich. Whether these raids were the precursors to an invasion or whether they were a means to a discrete end – such as the destruction of English maritime trade or the infliction of material and psychological damage – is not known, but we do know that the French drew up plans in 1339 for an invasion.

This led England to look closely at its defences and to embark on a phase that involved the modernization and strengthening of existing castles and the erection of a number of newer and more modern ones. The use of explosives and cannon had begun to supplant the lance and the sword, the arrow and the axe, and a whole new style of warfare was arriving. The arrow slits on some castles were enlarged or new apertures, known as gun loops, were created to accommodate these new weapons that were to change the whole art of warfare.

It was also necessary to ensure that the populace was aware of the enemy's presence if he should come ashore and also to warn them of impending invasion. By long tradition, news of a hostile landing was disseminated by

Dane John Tower, erected on the Canterbury city walls in the late 14th century, showing the keyhole gun ports. (The floor on which the guns and gunners stood is missing.)

means of a system of hilltop beacons. So far as the coastal regions were concerned the control and manning of these was entrusted to the 'keepers of the maritime lands'. In times of danger, each beacon was to be manned by a 'watch' of around half a dozen men, one of whom would always be seated at the beacon on a roster basis, keeping a sharp lookout for signals from other beacons. The material to be burnt varied: in Kent, pitch was preferred, as it showed better and lasted longer. In addition, churches in Kent were ordinarily to ring one bell only and only in case of attack were all the bells to be rung – an arrangement similar to that which was to be used to signal an invasion six hundred years later.

But the most important measures taken were those for general defence. Men of the coastal counties such as Kent were called upon to meet their military obligations and defend their area (according to the Calendar of Close Rolls, 1337–9, '... all men should be compelled to repel enemies if they invade the realm').This militia operated in a coastal strip of land called 'the maritime lands' which extended inland for six leagues (eighteen miles), the boundaries of which were determined conventionally and traditionally. Men living within this strip were not liable to be called upon for service abroad, but on the other hand were not permitted to leave their strip. Men living outside this strip could be conscripted to serve within it, and together, these men formed the *Garde de la Mer*. They were formed into constabularies, centaines (hundreds) and vingtaines (scores), and controlled by two or three local magnates in each county known as the 'keepers of the maritime lands'. The keepers of the Kentish maritime lands at this time were John de Warenne, the 7th Earl of Surrey, and William de Clinton, the 1st Earl of Huntingdon – the latter also being the constable of Dover Castle. The Warennes were a very old Norman family, the name being derived from the Old Norse word, *varangi*, which meant warrior-band, and the town of Varenne in the Seine-Inférieure derives its name from the same source. John's forebear, William de Warenne, the 1st Earl of Surrey, was the first secular owner of Allington Castle, having come over to England with William I, and another successfully defended Rochester Castle in the reign of Henry III.

All those who lived in the maritime lands were required to remain there and defend it 'while danger is imminent'. In addition, those who owned property in a maritime land but lived elsewhere had to up sticks and go and live in the maritime land concerned for the duration of the threat. This presented a number of problems for those, particularly the nobility, who owned land scattered in various places all over the country.

Sandwich was one of the busiest ports in the south of England, much more so than Dover. The port provided ships for the king and the shipping of large quantities of hurdles to the port of Orwell, where the king was massing his forces. However, this did not prevent a number of the inhabitants leaving the town in order to avoid having to pay the taxes for the defence of the town against invasion. The mayor and bailiffs of Sandwich were directed to proclaim that men who had left the town must return and bear their share of the expense or lose their lands and goods. In all, Kent was required in 1339 to have arrayed (mustered) 35 men-at-arms, 140 armed men and 140 archers.

These precautions appear to have had some effect, since, despite the detailed plans, no invasion was attempted by the French and King Edward felt able to go overseas, taking a considerable force with him. However, from around 1345, the defences were once more put on an anti-invasion footing, with the fencibles arrayed and the beacons manned. This period also heralded the inclusion of canons among the English weapons and the beginning of true artillery to replace the *artilleria* that hitherto had consisted of various engines such as springalds and arbalests that projected stones at the enemy fortifications.

The precautions were reinforced in March 1360 due to a large French raiding force having attacked Winchelsea whilst Edward III was in France. Although they only stayed one night, they were reported as 'riding over the country, slaying, burning, destroying and doing other mischief', and fearing an all-out invasion, the men of London and the south-east, including Kent, were mobilized to repel them.

The Enemy Within

It must have been very confusing in the fourteenth century to determine who was friend and who was foe, given that the two nations, France and England, were so closely assimilated. Many Englishmen at that time had strong Gallic or Norman roots – especially among the aristocracy and in the Church – and regarded French as their native tongue. England had extensive possessions in France, many of the inhabitants of which regarded the king of England as their true sovereign. Even in times of war, there was regular two-way traffic across the English Channel. But whose side were these travellers on? Six hundred years later England would be concerned with so-called Fifth Columnists, spies and saboteurs, but, even in those medieval days, Edward III was expressing concern about military 'secrets' being passed to the French. Prime suspects were the French monks who had come to stay in various priories such as Lewes and who had made periodic pilgrimages to their native land, taking with them knowledge of the military preparations being made for the movement and equipping of troops bound for France. So strong was this fear that, in 1353, the authorities at the ports of London and the Cinque Ports were ordered to stop anyone leaving the country without a special licence from the king. It appears that this measure was not entirely successful since, seven years later, the king had 'learned that great numbers of letters and credences prejudicial to him and the realm are brought into England by merchants and aliens', and he instructed the port authorities and sheriffs to carry out rigorous searches of all foreigners.

By the middle of the fifteenth century the picture had changed once more. The Hundred Years War finally ended in 1453 and it was once again domestic quarrels that took centre stage. In 1455 a series of civil wars broke out between the supporters of the opposing Houses of Lancaster and York that were dubbed the Wars of the Roses in reference to the red and white roses borne by either side as the symbol of their allegiance. Both Houses were direct descendants of Edward III, but the ruling Lancastrian king, Henry VI (the son of the hero of Agincourt, Henry V), had mental health problems and surrounded himself with unpopular cronies leading to public unrest. A number of dissatisfied nobles looked to Edward, the son of Richard Plantagenet, Duke of York, to replace this unpopular king. The success of the Yorkists in a number of battles in 1461 led to Edward being crowned King Edward IV, and apart from a brief restoration of Henry VI in 1470–71, the House of York, represented by Edward IV, Edward V and (briefly) Richard III, occupied the throne (not without difficulty) until Edmund Tudor's son ascended to the throne in 1485 as Henry VII, thus establishing the House of Tudor.

Despite the tendency to look across the Channel for likely problems in the first part of the period under review, it was the Peasants' Revolt in 1381, during which Archbishop Sudbury was murdered, that led to the city walls of **Canterbury** being repaired and strengthened and the new West Gate tower being built to protect the citizens of the city from such uprisings.

The work was directed by Archbishop Courtenay and the cost borne by the Church and the burghers rather than the crown. It is a tribute to the workers involved in the construction of the walls, and those who maintained them throughout the years, that a large part of the walls remains to this day, so that it is still possible to walk along nearly two-thirds of the original ramparts. The open-backed towers located at intervals along its length are notable for the incorporation of gun-loops rather than arrow-slits – some of the earliest uses of such 'modern' improvements. These later fortifications seem to have accelerated the decline of the Norman castle.

Despite the considerable refurbishment of the city's defences towards the end of the fourteenth century, much of the castle's by then dilapidated structure was demolished in the eighteenth and nineteenth centuries. In 1792 the Roman Worthgate, which had been blocked in 1548, was completely

The approach to the West Gate Tower, Canterbury, from the north, circa 1890.

The southern (internal) approach to the West Gate Tower, Canterbury, today.

Canterbury Castle today.

Interior of the keep at Canterbury Castle.

destroyed and the gateway opened up and widened to allow access to Castle Street through the bailey, with much of the outer bailey walls demolished. This desecration culminated in 1825 when the newly created Gas, Light & Coke Company was allowed to demolish two internal cross walls in the keep and use it as a coal and coke store. A hundred years were to pass before the city acquired the keep and embarked on its preservation.

Despite its present condition, Canterbury Castle keep is a fine example of its type and remains of great interest to historians and castle-lovers. Because of its lack of tourist interest – especially compared with the cathedral and the many other fine historical buildings in the city – the castle has remained largely unknown to all but a few outsiders.

The West Gate straddles the Roman road from Dover to London and replaced Canterbury Castle as the local gaol. It was originally protected by a drawbridge and has the same gun-loops as the city walls. The gate is constructed from Kentish rag stone, unlike the city walls that were built mainly of flint. It has been described as a self-contained fortress in its own right, with its own drawbridge and a row of machicolations over the gate. Courtenay's influence can be seen in the gate's similarity to the inner gate-house at Saltwood Castle, which he owned.

Cooling lies at the extreme north of the county, on the Hoo Peninsular between Rochester and Gravesend, where the Cliffe and Cooling Marshes run out to the River Thames. Originally much closer to the river than is now the case, the area had been defended since Roman times and traces of Saxon settlements have also been located there. It had been an ideal spot on the river for Viking and other raiders to land and undoubtedly had seen its share of plundering and pillaging, but the impertinent raids by the French in the fourteenth century gave the area a whole new importance.

In the first part of the thirteenth century, Sir John de Cobham was lord of the manor when it was known as Coolyngg. Richard II granted his descendant, also Sir John, a licence to crenellate in 1379, following a particularly annoy-ing series of raids by French and Spanish ships the previous year, and he began building immediately. The intention was for a castle to be built to provide a point of resistance against invaders and to also be a place of refuge for the scattered peasants who worked the manorial land. The king's master mason, Henry Yevelle, was employed in a supervisory capacity, but, he being much involved at the time in the building of Bodiam Castle as well as Canterbury West Gate tower and the nave of the cathedral, the actual building work was carried out by local labour under several master masons, including William Sharnall, Thomas Wrek and Thomas Crompe and their personal teams. The whole process from start to finish took around five years according to surviving building accounts.

Due to the exigencies of the marshy surroundings, the design was unusual in that, instead of the usual arrangement of a system of inner wards or court-yards surrounded by one or more outer wards, Cooling Castle had two wards arranged side by side, each on a small mound to raise it above the water level and surrounded by a figure of eight moat. However, such was the design that it would have been necessary to take the larger outer ward before attacking the inner one.

The rectangular outer ward, to the east, was completely surrounded by a high stone wall with the main gatehouse in the south-east corner. At each of the other corners there was a protruding D-shaped tower, open to the inside. The western wall ran northwards from the gatehouse, and halfway along, there was a gateway and drawbridge providing access to the gatehouse for the inner ward.

The outer gatehouse, consisting of two D-shaped towers linked by a crenellated wall, survives largely intact and the Cobham arms can be seen on the wall above the gate. The tops of the towers are crenellated and have huge machicolations, the eastern one bearing a copper plate on which is inscribed the following rhyming reason for the building of the castle:

> *Knouwyth that beth and schul be*
> *That I am mad in help of the cuntre*
> *In knowing of whyche thing*
> *Thys is chartre and wytnessyng.*

It seems probable that this inscription had a two-fold aim: to proclaim the allegiance of the Cobhams to the monarch and also to reassure the local population that it was not intended to compromise their interests.

The inner ward, smaller than the outer one, was raised much higher, giving a commanding view over the outer ward and the surrounding country-side. Roughly square in shape, each corner of the inner ward's stone wall had a tower, reaching up as high as 40 feet. Within this compound were the living quarters of the family and the central defences of the castle. Surrounded by its own moat, the only access to the inner ward was through the external gateway to the outer ward, then through the outer ward to the two gateways, one on either side of the separating section of the moat, and then across the heavily defended drawbridge and past the portcullis.

The castle's defences, especially the various towers, were provided with inverted keyhole or plain round gun ports to make use of this new form of warfare – a development that was ironically to make such castles obsolete.

The outer gatehouse at Cooling Castle.

Shortly after the completion of the castle, Sir John was in dispute with his king and suffered a period of exile, but he returned to reclaim the estates and died at Cooling in 1408. Sir John was succeeded by his granddaughter Joan who survived four husbands, the last, Sir John Oldcastle, Lord Cobham, being hanged over a burning fire for heresy in 1417. Although the title remained extant, the castle and estates passed to other families through the female line.

The castle experienced a further, brief claim to fame in the mid-sixteenth century, when rebels under Sir Thomas Wyatt, a wealthy Kentish land owner, seeking to place the (then) Princess Elizabeth on the throne in place of the detested Queen Mary, attacked the castle with two great cannon he had captured in an earlier engagement at Strood. In the besieged castle, Lord George Cobham (Wyatt's brother-in-law) was desperately short of both men and weapons; some reports say he had only eight men to defend the castle and his later report on the incident to Queen Mary refers to his men having 'only four or five handguns, four pikes and some blakbylls'. The castle gates and drawbridges soon succumbed to the power of the cannon and the castle surrendered after a mere eight hours' siege.

Ostensibly on their way to London, it is not entirely clear why Wyatt and his party made the detour to Cooling and wasted a day in besieging the castle, thus giving Mary more time to rally her own troops. The revolt was defeated and Sir Thomas paid the ultimate penalty. Suspected of having sympathy with his brother-in-law and thus failing to put up a sufficiently spirited defence of his castle, Cobham and his son were imprisoned in the Tower of London, but they were soon released and their lands restored to them.

The short-lived siege clearly demonstrated how such castles were ineffective against the might of gunpowder, and Cooling Castle was abandoned, the family repairing to Cobham Hall, which remained their principal place of residence. The castle remains unrepaired to this day, although a house has been built in its grounds and is still inhabited, the last recorded occupant being the musician Jools Holland.

Most of the post-Norman castles that were built in the south-east were constructed to prevent the French from getting a foot-hold in England during the reign of Edward III (1327–77), but a few came later, in response to a threat from a different quarter.

In 1415 the Battle of Agincourt marked the collapse of the organized French resistance, and the Treaty of Troyes five years later recognized the English claims to the French throne. Subsequent uprisings, such as that led by Joan of Arc, were crushed, but Burgundy's withdrawal of support for England and the Flemish transfer of loyalty from England to France gave grave cause for concern in 1435. For the first time for many years, England was facing the very real possibility of an attack by powerful armies from Flanders, and so Kent's coastal defences were revised and strengthened. In addition to refortifying places such as Sandwich, some manors were fortified and made ready to resist any invasion.

One such manor was **Garlinge**, near Margate, owned at the time by a disreputable Kentish gentleman by the name of John Dent de Lion (aka Daundelyon or Dandelion). Although ostensibly fortified in 1440 in response to the Flemish threat, John undoubtedly had an eye to the main chance since, besides being a fairly prosperous farmer, he was also much implicated in the smuggling trade, and a fortified manor could resist the revenue men as much as the Flemish military. To what extent these fortifications proved efficacious is not known, but, in any event, John died in 1445, so his use of them was somewhat limited. He was duly buried in the Margate churchyard and the castle (as it was now known) passed to his only daughter and thence, through marriage, to the Petit family from Shalmsford.

When the Hundred Years War finally ended in 1453, the military value of the building ceased and it remained with the Petit family until the eighteenth century, when it passed through various hands. The building was gradually altered over the years and reverted back to being a country house and for a time, a hotel. Sometime in the nineteenth century, virtually the whole of the original house was demolished and the site became once more a farm. Most of the extensive fortifications were torn down and today only the impressive gatehouse remains more or less intact.

The gatehouse, although now uncomfortably squashed between a modern housing estate and the farmland, is still impressive. Roughly square in shape, with four towers made from alternate courses of brick and flint with dressed stone arches and quoins, it has two gateways, side by side, one very much larger than the other. The existing arrow slits and gun loops provide testimony of its defensive purpose although the portcullis is no longer there.

As we have seen, **Lympne** was regarded as an important location by the Romans who built Stutfall Castle, one of their Saxon Shore forts, there. After their departure, around AD 410, the fort fell into disuse and the once busy and prosperous town declined until it was little more than a small settlement. The Saxons ignored it and concentrated their defensive measures elsewhere, but the Norman archdeacons built themselves a small, two-storeyed castle, or fortified and castellated manor house, close to Lympne church, to complement the archbishops' castle at Saltwood.

The principal features were the impressive great hall, flanked at either end by a great chamber, with other accommodation in the towers. The

Lympne Castle.

Lympne castle, with the ruins of the Roman Stutfall Castle in the foreground.

structure was extensively rebuilt and fortified around 1360, during one of the rare moments of relative tranquillity during the Hundred Years War.

Despite its ecclesiastical ownership, it should not be thought that the castle was just for show. The Church in the Middle Ages was a significant political power and was prepared to do its bit in the defence of the country, and perhaps more to the point, to safeguard its extensive possessions and properties. As it happened, the castle was never put to the test and its fortifications remained entirely unused, although, like certain other Kentish fortified buildings, it was actively involved in smuggling activities during the eighteenth and nineteenth centuries, when it was no doubt felt that it provided a degree of protection from the revenue men.

Although the castle remained in the hands of the Church until the middle of the nineteenth century, it was leased to various tenants who, for the most part, farmed the land. This change of use resulted, as was so often the case, in the actual fortifications being sorely neglected and the property becoming dilapidated. Much of the curtain wall disappeared, as did most of the outer buildings. Once the castle passed into private hands (a Major Lawes of Old Park, Dover), the great hall was converted into a two-storey house and divided into a number of smaller rooms, and it was not until 1905 that a new owner, a Mr Tennent, set about restoring the castle. Under the direction of the architect, Sir Robert Lorimer, the partitions and false floor in the great hall were removed and windows sympathetically installed in the two towers. Fireplaces were provided in the towers and the great hall, dating from 1420, was restored.

Despite the restoration, much of the original castle remains and the newer additions have been harmoniously made. It is not open to the general public but is extensively used as a wedding venue and for corporate entertaining.

According to the Domesday Book, there has been a manor at **Penshurst** since at least the eleventh century, but the first recorded owner was Sir Stephen de Penchester of Allington Castle, early in the fourteenth century. In 1338, the manor was sold to Sir John de Pulteney, the Mayor of London on four occasions, who received a licence to crenellate the manor house in 1341 but failed to proceed with this and built a range of buildings that still form the basis of the present Penshurst Place. When Pulteney died of the Black Death in 1349, the manor passed through various descendants and finally to Sir John Devereux, later the Warden of the Cinque Ports and Constable of Dover Castle.

Devereux applied for and was granted a second licence to crenellate in 1392, upon which he proceeded to erect a rectangular curtain wall around the house, with towers on each corner and mid-way along each side, those on the north and south sides being in the form of a small gatehouse. The hall block at Penshurst is a particularly fine example of a medieval hall and is well preserved, and the whole building is largely constructed, unusually for Kent, from a delightful, pale cream sandstone, although there are some Tudor brick additions. At the heart of the medieval manor house is the Baron's Hall with a

Penshurst Place with the great hall on the right.

magnificent 60-foot high chestnut roof, supported by satirical representations of contemporary peasants and estate workers. In the centre is one of the very rare central hearths, the smoke from which simply escaped through the roof.

In the fifteenth century the castle passed from the Devereux family into royal ownership, being successively owned by John, Duke of Bedford, and Humphrey, Duke of Gloucester, the brothers of Henry V. These were succeeded by Humphrey Stafford, the First Duke of Buckingham, who, in 1519, entertained Henry VIII to a lavish banquet. This, however, did not prevent him from being beheaded for treason in 1521, and the castle became the property of the Crown.

It was Henry's young son, Edward VI, who died of tuberculosis in 1553 at the tender age of sixteen, who gave Penshurst Place to Sir William Sidney, the grandfather of the famed Elizabethan poet, Sir Philip Sidney, who wrote much of his works there. It was Sir Philip's successor, the wealthy Robert Sidney, who created the Long Gallery in addition to the state rooms. A great favourite with the Tudor monarchs, the house has remained with the family ever since, but fell into decline in the last half of the eighteenth century. It was revived in the early nineteenth century by Sir John Shelley-Sidney, whose son, Philip Charles Sidney, was created the first Lord de L'Isle and Dudley in 1835.

A little more than a century later, William Philip Sidney, the son of the fifth Baron de L'Isle and Dudley, serving with the Grenadier Guards during

Penshurst Place, showing the Tudor additions to the fourteenth century manor house.

the Second World War, was awarded the Victoria Cross for extreme courage during the Italian campaign at Anzio. He succeeded to the title in 1945, and the building having suffered greatly through neglect during the war, commenced a long and arduous programme of repair and restoration at a time when building materials and skilled labour were scarce and costly.

In 1956, following a distinguished political and diplomatic career, William Sidney was elevated to the rank of viscount and dropped the 'and Dudley' part of the title, being henceforth referred to as simply 'the Viscount de L'Isle, VC'. When he died in 1991 he was succeeded by his son and Penshurst Place continues to remain with the family who have done so much over the years to maintain and restore this thousand-year-old building. Having begun its existence as a manor house, been converted to a fortified castle and reverted to its original purpose over the centuries, Penshurst Place is still one of the finest examples of this type of building in the county, if not the country.

In Anglo-Saxon times, a tiny settlement became established on a small islet by the name of Bynne, just off the coast of what we now know as the Isle of Sheppey, at the point where the confluence of the rivers Medway and Swale debouched into the Thames Estuary. This settlement went by the name of Cyningburgh or 'King's Borough'. Owned by the monastery of St Sexburgha, the site was of both mercantile and strategic importance, and in AD 893, the Danish Prince Hoesten reputedly built a fort there, although there is little or no archaeological evidence of this. The site seems to have declined over the ensuing years, and it was not until a lull in the Hundred Years' War that Edward III decided to build a castle on what was probably a prehistoric mound there and the probable site of the earlier fortress.

The construction of what was to be the last royal castle of the medieval period took from 1361 to 1377. It appears that the site was a hive of industry in summer and winter, both by day and by night, there being references to candles being transported there so that work on the new royal castle could continue through 24 hours. Whether this castle was built for purely defensive purposes or simply a bolt-hole for the king and his retinue to escape the plague is the subject of dispute between historians.

Simultaneously, a whole town sprang up around the castle, built according to a classic medieval design, which so delighted Edward that he named it **Queenborough** after his queen, Philippa of Hainault. He conferred upon it the rights of a free borough, administered by a mayor and two 'jurats', and in 1388 it was declared a royal borough. Queenborough swiftly became an important town for the flourishing wool trade, so much so that, in 1368, Edward issued a Royal Decree transferring the Wool Staple from Canterbury to Queenborough, meaning that the latter, together with Sandwich, became the only two places in Kent through which any wool exports were to be made.

Despite the size and importance of Queenborough Castle, nothing remains of it today apart from the original mound and a few scattered stones. Our knowledge of the castle is limited to an old plan, some drawings, a few eighteenth- and nineteenth-century etchings and the results of a Channel Four *Time Team* archaeological dig in 2005. The latter discovered that none of the documentary or pictorial sources were entirely reliable. The fact that practically all the stonework had been purloined over the years and the soil conditions at the time of the dig were not conducive to a geophysical survey added to the Time Team's problems.

It is known that Edward's castle was an unusual circular one, possibly modelled on the contemporary French chateaux, and may have influenced the design of the later castles in Deal and Walmer. It probably contained some forty rooms, although some estimates go as high as seventy. It was a castle built for the age of gunpowder and cannons.

At the centre of the fortification there was a circular keep or rotunda that was completed by 1368 – three years after the appointment of John de Foxley as the first constable of the castle. Fear of a French invasion was obviously running high at the time, as John de Foxley was instructed to immediately arm the castle and place it on a high state of alert. Fortunately, this threat never materialized and the castle's subsequent depredations were more at the hands of the locals rather than any foreign invader.

Queenborough Castle has been described as 'the ultimate in concentricity', being based wholly on a circular plan. At its centre there was the rotunda, rather like a very large shell keep, consisting of a central courtyard encircled by two high concentric walls. Spaced along the outer wall were six circular towers, two of which were placed close to each other on either side of an eastern entrance to the rotunda, forming a gatehouse. Some 30 yards out from the rotunda there was a further, plain curtain wall, also circular, with just a single entrance on the western side, protected by two towers, the entire outer wall being surrounded by a wide and deep moat. This design meant that any attackers who managed to force their way across the moat and through this outer entrance into the bailey would have to fight their way round to the opposite side of the castle in order to be in a position to assail the entrance to the rotunda, exposed all the time to intensive and deadly fire from the rotunda and the curtain wall.

The castle's importance as a royal residence is evident from the records that show that there was a garden and a fish pond, and one of the towers was furnished with a mechanical, weight-driven clock with a large bell. To judge

Artist's impression of Queenborough Castle.

by the amount of lead piping that is mentioned in the records, the plumbing and sanitary arrangements must have been of a very high standard.

The castle contemptuously repelled a half-hearted attack in 1558 by a bunch of Kentish peasants under Jack Cade and including the mayor of Queenborough, during which they were all captured and sent for trial, but, apart from this, the castle never had any militaristic role to play. The castle was adapted over the ensuing years to further render it suitable for modern warfare. It was equipped with cannon at a very early date, with references in the 1365 Wardrobe Account to nine hand guns and two larger guns being made in the Tower of London for use at Queenborough.

The castle was in Royalist hands during the Civil War but was captured by the Parliamentarians in 1650 and was slighted before being sold for £1,792.12.0½ for demolition. The new owner, John Wilkinson, demolished much of the castle, selling the recovered materials for re-use. Some of the timbers found their way into the church tower to restore the belfry, and what remained of the buildings were converted to use as barns, stables and coach houses, and in the nineteenth century, the newly arrived railway company found a use for the well and installed a pump house over it. But gradually all vestiges of this great royal castle disappeared and all that was left was the prehistoric mound.

One might be forgiven for thinking that the destruction of this magnificent building in the seventeenth century was somewhat premature when one considers that, just seventeen years afterwards, the Dutch sailed up the Thames Estuary, captured the unfinished Sheerness fort and invaded Queenborough for a short time.

As mentioned in the previous chapter, the pretty, medieval town and port of **Sandwich** once had a defensive wall and a castle. All trace of the castle has long since disappeared and only the earthen ramparts of the wall now remain.

Originally, the wall consisted of these ramparts, surmounted by a wooden palisade, but, after the French sacked the town in 1438 and 1450, the worthy burghers decided to construct a stout wall on the ramparts. The dimensions and construction of this are unknown, although it seems there were five gates, of which only one, Fisher Gate, remains to this day. Later a stone bridge was built across the River Stour, defended by a Barbican Gate that also survives.

In 1451 a two-storey Great Bulwark was built just to the north of the Sandown Gate (roughly where the Salutation grounds now are) and was equipped with cannons, but it was stormed and taken by the French in 1457. It has been suggested that this bulwark was constructed using stone from the castle, hence its rapid and complete disappearance. Others believe that it was in fact the castle itself, altered to meet contemporary military requirements.

During the Wars of the Roses, the Great Bulwark (or perhaps the castle) was held by Sir Thomas Neville, the illegitimate son of William Neville of Fauconberg, the Earl of Kent, on behalf of his cousin the Earl of Warwick (Warwick the Kingmaker). Thomas, who was known as 'The Bastard of Fauconberg', or simply as 'Thomas the Bastard', was an accomplished sailor, and in 1471 sailed up the Thames from Sandwich to assail the city. He was repulsed and returned to Sandwich where he surrendered to Edward IV, who had arrived to lay siege to the town. He was executed the same year and the Great Bulwark was destroyed.

The manor of **Scotney**, close to Lamberhurst in West Kent, originally lay in East Sussex alongside the River Beult that formed the boundary between the two counties, but the diversion of the river to feed the castle moat led to some confusion, and it was eventually settled that Scotney was in Kent.

The first recorded holder of the manor of Scotney was one Lambert de Scoteni, who held it in 1137 under the barony of Leeds Castle. One of Lambert's descendants, Walter de Scoteni, was alleged to have poisoned Gilbert de Clare, the Earl of Gloucester, and his brother William de Clare. William died but Gilbert, who was the Lord of Tonbridge Castle, survived, and Walter de Scoteni was hanged in Winchester.

By 1310 the manor was in the hands of John de Grofhurst of Horsmonden, whose widow later married John de Ashburnham, but any manor house that

Scotney Old Castle.

they may have occupied has long since disappeared, together with any record of what form it took.

Their son, Roger de Ashburnham, became a prominent local admini-strator and one of the joint Conservators of the Peace for Kent and Sussex. It was he who, between 1378 and 1380, was responsible for building the fortified, moated castle in response to the French sackings of Hastings, Rye and Winchelsea in 1377. His fellow Conservator, Sir Edward Dallingrigge, later built Bodiam Castle in East Sussex and modelled it on Scotney, although he made it much larger and stronger.

Ashburnham's castle at Scotney was constructed under the supervision of Stephen Lambhurst, who had just finished work at Boxley Abbey. It was rhombus shaped with a tower on each of the four corners, only one of which still stands. The castle stands on an island that was revetted in stone, the approach to which was across another, smaller island that acted as a kind of barbican, the two islands being joined by a drawbridge and surrounded by a figure-of-eight moat fed from the River Beult. There was a central gatehouse on the south-west side with a drawbridge and a surrounding curtain wall.

On the death of Roger Ashburnham's childless son, William, the castle passed through various hands, one of whom was Archbishop Henry Chichele. Ultimately it came into the possession of the Darell family, a loyal Roman Catholic dynasty, who held it for 360 years.

The castle had apparently become indefensible by the middle of the six-teenth century, with three of the four towers having tumbled into ruins, and so, in 1580, Thomas Darell set about building the Elizabethan wing close to the remaining tower. The castle had its own chapel, and in the course of the reconstruction work he had a number of secret rooms and a priest hole incorporated – a decision which was to prove fortuitous. The priest hole was a small cell reached by a sloping shaft, the entrance to which was cunningly concealed under a section of the flooring between two small rooms hidden within the structure of an oak staircase.

Richard Blount was a Protestant from Leicestershire who converted to the Roman Church at a time when England had broken with Rome and Catholics were suffering from persecution. Having been ordained in Rome, he returned to England via Spain in 1591 at the age of 26, in the guise of a seaman who had been taken prisoner by the Spanish. He made his way to Scotney where he knew the sympathetic Darells would shelter him, and during the course of the next few years he had recourse to the various hiding places on a number of occasions.

In 1598, the justices of the peace raided Scotney Castle, and the whole adult household, including the servants, were taken into custody while the building was thoroughly searched. Blount and his servant, Bray, were already quietly occupying the priest hole, but there was not time for them to take more than a few scraps of food with them, and after a week in hiding and with their victuals long-since exhausted, their very survival was in peril. Eventually, Blount's servant slipped out of the hidey-hole and was soon apprehended. However, he was able to convince the justices that he had been hiding in one of the other secret rooms, and he was taken into custody in the belief that he was Father Blount. By the time the mistake was discovered, Blount had found other hiding places and so escaped the dire fate that undoubtedly awaited him.

Blount and Bray returned to Scotney, and around Christmastide the justices made a further raid in the dead of night. The fugitive pair managed to get to one of the other hiding places, taking with them their Bibles, some other books, a bottle of wine and a loaf of bread. In the absence of Thomas Darell, his wife and children were locked in the gatehouse for ten days while yet another thorough search of the premises was carried out. Despite almost being accidentally betrayed by Mrs Darell, the pair evaded discovery and finally broke out one evening while the searchers were dining. Barefoot, the fugitives clambered over two 10-foot walls to the tower, from the top of which, Blount jumped into the frozen, 80-foot-wide moat and swam to safety. As Bray was too weak to follow his master's example, it was agreed that they would meet later at the home of one of the castle's servants. Bray then made his way to the dining hall, where he burst in, crying that thieves were trying to steal the horses belonging to the magistrates, and whilst they hurried to the stables, Bray made good his escape. He joined the priest and they made their way to London, where Blount enjoyed a perilous existence pursuing his religious beliefs and ministering to fellow Catholics until his natural death in 1638.

Scotney Old Castle with the 19th century 'New Castle' in the background.

Although William Darell rebuilt much of the castle in 1630, his death in 1639, increasing debts and the start of the Civil War, prevented the full rebuilding programme from being realized. His widow arranged for guns to be installed at the castle to protect herself and her children from the Protestant soldiers – perhaps the only time the castle was put on a defensive position. In fact, the castle was only attacked on one occasion: in the late eighteenth century, the Darells became involved in the widespread contraband business, and one night the castle was attacked by the Revenue officers. There was a fierce fight, during which one of the government men was killed and his body thrown into the moat.

Not long after this affair, the Darell family got itself embroiled in a number of lawsuits in which, as was so often the case, the only winners were the lawyers, and the estates had to be sold off to meet the crushing family debts. In 1778 the property was sold to Edward Hussey, a well-known Kent, England and MCC cricketer. By this time a number of attractive Georgian additions had been made and the conical roof and cupola added to the top of the tower.

A later owner, Edward Hussey III, decided to build a new Scotney Castle in the Tudor style on the high ground overlooking the medieval castle. This building work was completed and the romantic gardens landscaped between 1836 and 1843, while the later additions to the original castle were also removed to reveal the ruins of the original medieval and Elizabethan building.

The estate was left to the National Trust in 1970 on the death of the then owner and the medieval castle ruins opened to the public, but the new 'castle' remained occupied by the Hussey family until 2006 when, with the death of Mrs Betty Hussey, the new 'castle' was vacated and this too is now open to the public.

The **Westenhanger** estate dates back to before the Norman Conquest, when it was owned by King Cnut, but little is known of its early history. According to the St Augustine's Abbey registry, in the early twelfth century the area went by the name of Le Hangre and was comprised of Westenhanger and Ostenhanger (West Hangre and East Hangre) and was divided between two great medieval personages: Hugh de Montfort and William de Eddesham (or Addisham). By the early thirteenth century it was in the hands of the de Auberville and the de Criol families and the two parts of the estate seem to have become confused, probably through intermarriage.

In 1242, Sir Bertram de Criol was referred to as being of Ostenhanger when he rebuilt a major part of the 'ancient mansion'. His importance may be judged by the fact that, in that year, in addition to being the Sheriff of Kent, he was made the Constable of Dover Castle and Lord Warden of the

Cinque ports, posts he held until 1255. His son, Sir Nicholas, was similarly honoured and held these twin posts from 1260 to 1263.

It is said that, in the twelfth century, Rosamund Clifford, one of Henry II's mistresses, used the manor house, and one of the towers was named after her (although that tower clearly post-dates her lifetime). Indeed, over the years the castle was to receive a great many royal and other noble guests within its walls.

Sir John de Criol was given a licence to crenellate his manor in 1343, during Edward III's reign. This was at the height of the fears of a French invasion, and de Criol was responsible for building the first permanent structure on the site – a fortified manor house, built in quadrangular form on land between what is now the railway and Folkestone racecourse. According to the Kentish historian, Hasted, writing at the end of the eighteenth century, this edifice contained no less than 126 rooms and had 365 windows, the whole being surrounded by a moat formed by a diversion of the River Stour.

The design of this new castle owed much to that of Scotney and Cooling, and even more to Bodiam. The central courtyard, some 130 feet by 90 feet, was enclosed by the domestic apartments. There was a tower on each of the four corners, three round and one square, with further, shallow rectangular towers along three walls. On the remaining side these towers were replaced by a gatehouse with two towers.

The de Criol family retained possession of the castle until 1461 when Sir Thomas de Criol, who sided with the future Edward IV in his contest for the throne of England, was executed on the orders of Queen Margaret of Anjou, the consort of the mentally unbalanced Henry VI who was deposed that year. Since Sir Thomas had no sons, the castle went to his son-in-law, Sir John Fogge.

By 1503 the castle was back in the hands of one of de Criol's descendants, Sir Edward Poynings, an important soldier, administrator and diplomat who was a great favourite of Henry VII. Once again, the occupant of Westenhanger was appointed Constable of Dover Castle and Warden of the Cinque Ports. Poynings was responsible for making a number of significant Tudor additions to the castle, virtually all of which have since fallen down or been demolished. Sir Edward did not live to see his plans reach fruition and he died in 1521, leaving seven illegitimate children. His only legitimate son, John, had predeceased him, and so his three illegitimate sons and four daughters were the beneficiaries under his will. The Westenhanger estate was passed on to the eldest of these, Thomas, who was to go on to have a distinguished career himself, being elevated to the peerage as Baron Poynings and made Lieutenant of Boulogne.

In 1540 Lord Thomas Poynings exchanged Westenhanger for certain crown lands in Dorset, and the castle became crown property, being rented to various, and comparatively short-term, tenants. Queen Elizabeth I entrusted it to Thomas Smythe, known as 'Customer' Smythe, with him having purchased the office of Customer (collector of customs and taxes) from a Mr Cocker for £2,500 – a sum which indicates the value of this office. During his occupation of Westenhanger, the castle was used by the Queen as her command centre for the 14,000 troops in Kent whose role it was to defend the south coast from the Spanish Armada.

Westenhanger's importance declined rapidly after the defeat of the Spaniards and became a simple farmhouse. A disastrous fire in 1701 gutted the building, and all the Tudor additions were destroyed, apart from a brick fireplace in the west wall near the gatehouse, and the owner, a Mr Finch, sold the remaining materials to Justinian Champneys, who, sometime between 1701 and 1748, had much of the rest of the fabric ripped out and used to build another farmhouse nearby, described as a 'small neat edifice'.

After Champneys' death the property passed to his granddaughter, Harriott, who, marrying a John Burt, took the surname of Burt-Champneys. In 1796, Justinian Champneys' house was demolished and the Georgian building erected in its stead remains to this day, attached to the north-eastern tower. The tower itself was partially converted into a dovecote and covered by a conical roof, giving it the appearance of a truncated oast house. Little remains of the other eight towers, and the moat, originally 50 feet wide, is now dry and overgrown.

For most of the twentieth century, the company that ran the adjacent racecourse owned the castle, and the course manager occupied the house until around 1965, after which the owners seem to have lost all interest in this ancient monument. Fortunately, the racecourse people continued to use the magnificent Tudor barn for fodder and straw, as well as the manufacture of brushwood jumps. Situated outside the castle walls, the barn was probably built on the instructions of Customer Smythe in the late sixteenth century and boasts what is possibly the finest oak hammer-beam roof in Kent, and has four, full-height wagon doors. Although it remained in reasonable condition while under the care of the racecourse owners, it suffered considerable damage during the great storm of 1987.

Happily, after many years of neglect and decay, the castle and associated medieval buildings and barns are currently being tidied up and steps taken by the new owners to consolidate the stonework to prevent further deterioration. When the Forge family bought this scheduled ancient monument in 1996 it was on the 'Buildings at Risk' register and they decided to endeavour to preserve the remains of the ruins for future generations. It quickly became

Westenhanger Castle.

apparent that this would be a monumental task and financial assistance and the advice of experts in the field would be necessary. English Heritage, well aware of the importance of this monument, agreed to assist in its restoration. Much has already been done, and the castle is now a popular venue for weddings and other events.

The new owners took possession of the Tudor barn in 2003 and took immediate steps to protect this important and beautiful building from the weather. Work on restoration began in 2007 and will continue as funds permit. The castle is now open to the public during the summer months.

Chapter 6

Tudor and Stuart Kent (1450–1700)

This period in history is notable for the development of gunpowder and artillery as a means of attack and defence. The use of heavy artillery in Italy by the French army under Charles VII in 1483 and the Battle of Bosworth (1485) highlighted the arrival of a new dynasty of heavy weaponry and greatly improved small arms. Both Henry VII and Henry VIII showed a great interest in ordnance, and the Weald was soon producing guns to replace the trebuchets and other siege instruments of medieval times. This new era meant that no longer would fortresses be subjected to the mere 'slings and arrows' of earlier years and the unassailability of the medieval castles was no longer a problem. The value of castles like that at Dover had diminished, and the forts and castles now being built were of a different design and concept. The castles at Sandown, Deal and Walmer were specifically designed as artillery fortresses to protect the coastline fronting the Goodwin Sands, while that at Sandgate covered the coastal route across the Romney Marsh.

To begin with, there were no significant changes to the design of the county's fortresses, and it was largely a matter of converting the narrow arrow slits to gun loops, usually resembling an inverted keyhole. Some of the earliest conversions are to be seen at Cooling and Saltwood castles and in the West Gate at Canterbury, which date as far back as the fourteenth century. Queenborough Castle on the Isle of Sheppey was specifically built in the latter half of the fourteenth century with provision for artillery.

However, by the time Henry Tudor came to the throne, such fortifications were no longer seen as an end in themselves but as part of a wider and grander scheme involving a large number of trained men-at-arms – the beginnings of a standing army – to meet any invader and force him back into the sea.

With England at loggerheads with the Vatican as a result of the Dissolution of the Monasteries, and the combined might of France and the Holy Roman

Sandgate Castle in the 18th century.

Empire preparing to enforce the Pope's Bull of Excommunication, Henry VIII was compelled to embark on a series of important projects for the defence of the realm. His main plan was to build a series of specially designed fortresses to guard the Thames Estuary and the Medway River, and the vulnerable points on the coast where an invasion might take place and a beachhead be established. Equipped with guns firing from specially made emplacements, these were lower in profile than the old, medieval castles, and the bastions were built with curved walls to deflect shot. In just two years, between 1538 and 1540, Henry built a chain of forts from Hull to Cornwall, together with a number of bulwarks and blockhouses, few of which now remain. Some of the older castles were also adapted and strengthened.

As a result of its unparalleled strategic position, Kent found itself hosting more of these new-style fortifications than anywhere else in England, with fine examples at Deal, Walmer, Sandown and Sandgate. Thus armed, the county was once more ready to repel Johnny Foreigner.

One by one, the various edifices that had been erected on the **Allington** Castle site since the Bronze Age had been destroyed, culminating in that of the unlicensed motte-and-bailey castle which was pulled down on the orders of Henry II. This was replaced by a manor house, and it was not until the end of the thirteenth century that Stephen de Penchester was given permission by Edward I to crenellate it. Penchester set about surrounding his property by a stout curtain wall with eight towers and a gatehouse. But, although classified as one of the royal castles of Kent, it was always primarily a dwelling rather than a fortress.

Penchester's daughter inherited the castle, and when she married into the Cobham family, the castle passed into their hands and remained so until the end of the fifteenth century. In 1492 (while Columbus was busy discovering America) the castle was acquired by Sir Henry Wyatt, following which it took on a new lease of life.

Wyatt was a Yorkshireman and a fervent supporter of Henry VII (ruled 1485–1509), the first Tudor monarch, for whom he acted as a spy. It was Wyatt who, on taking on the ownership of this ancient castle, added the Long Gallery (the first in England) and the delightful little lath and plaster house that replaced a redundant tower in the south-east corner. The early English windows were replaced with modern (Tudor) ones, and contemporary fireplaces installed. Many of the plain, cold, internal walls were panelled with wood and there was a new kitchen, as well as two solars or drawing rooms.

The castle's royal connection continued with Henry VII and Henry VIII, as well as numerous other personages from the royal court, such as Anne Boleyn, Katharine Parr and Cardinal Wolsey. Henry VIII, who stayed at the castle many times, was so obsessed with his personal safety that he caused himself to be walled in to his chamber in the north-east tower whenever he stayed there. The room, now referred to unsurprisingly as the Royal Room, was accessible only by a spiral staircase, and the entry door was blocked with a dry stone wall each night, after the king retired.

Sir Henry's son and successor, Sir Thomas Wyatt the Elder, was born in the castle in 1503 and inherited it in 1537. A great man of letters, poet, courtier and diplomat, he too was a great favourite at court, at least to begin with, although his star waned somewhat when Henry VIII discovered that he was rumoured to have had an affair with his childhood friend, Anne Boleyn – albeit prior to the royal marriage. A brief (but no doubt worrying) stay in the Tower of London was followed by a much more amenable banishment to Allington. His return to favour was demonstrated by the gift to him of the estates belonging to the abbeys of Boxley, Malling and Aylesford following their dissolution. Sir Thomas was only thirty-nine when he died in 1542.

Sir Thomas's son, another Thomas, was not so lucky. More soldierly than his father, he was created Earl of Kent by Edward VI (ruled 1547–1553), and after a distinguished military career in the wars against the French, he retired in 1550 to live the life of a wealthy country gentleman as the Sheriff of Kent. Only a very short while later, however, he heard the news of Queen Mary I's plans to marry Philip II of Spain, and as a staunch Protestant, he was appalled at the thought of what he perceived as a revival of Catholicism in England. He was therefore among the leaders of the rebellion against Queen Mary in protest of her proposed marriage. It was planned that the revolt would spark off in four places simultaneously, and Wyatt was responsible for that which was to occur in Kent. As it happened, the other three never really took off and Wyatt was at the helm of the only real uprising. The Kentish plotters held their first meeting at Allington before marching on London and reached Potter's Bar, where the revolutionaries were overpowered by the Queen's loyal troops. The so-called Wyatt Rebellion was thus short-lived, and Sir Thomas Wyatt the Younger followed his father's example by being taken to the Tower, where he, less happily, was executed on 11 April 1554 for treason. Ironically, many of the other revolutionaries were imprisoned in Allington Castle.

The Wyatts' possessions, including Allington, were confiscated and the family emigrated to America. The castle's fortunes declined from that moment, and around the latter half of the sixteenth century, there was a disastrous fire that destroyed most of the Great Hall and the north-east wing. Early in the seventeenth century, the castle was leased to a John Best who, to compensate for the fire damage, took down the battlements and added a half-timbered, gabled second storey to the north and west wings. A distant relative of the Wyatts, Sir Robert Marsham, the first Lord Romney, bought the castle in 1720, but never lived there and allowed it to fall into disrepair. Another fire destroyed the top of the Long Gallery, and only strong local opposition prevented the castle from being totally demolished by the fifth Lord Romney in the nineteenth century. By now Allington was only fit for an impoverished farmer to inhabit, living in the present Tudor House.

Things looked very black for the castle until, in 1895, a retired London barrister, a Mr Falke, rented it from Lord Romney and began to restore it. But it was a monumental and very expensive task, and he was delighted to read in his newspaper in 1905 that Sir Martin Conway was looking to buy an old castle or manor house. Falke contacted Sir Martin, suggesting that he might be interested in Allington, so he and his American wife came to visit it. They were apparently enchanted by the romantic ruins and bought the freehold from the castle's owner, Lord Romney, for the sum of £4,800.

Sir Martin first spent a year researching the history of Allington with his daughter, Agnes, an archaeologist, and clearing the ivy and undergrowth that were covering the ruins. He then began the major restoration work and spent the next thirty years and a small fortune on restoring the castle to its former glory. Raised to the peerage in 1931, Lord Conway died in 1936 and his daughter inherited the castle. When she too died in 1950, the castle was sold to the Carmelite Order of nearby Aylesford Priory, an ironic twist, given that Sir Thomas Wyatt took possession of the Priory's estates following the Dissolution, and now the priory owned his old home and birthplace. When the Carmelites decided to go secular and left the castle in 1958, their work was continued by the former prior of Aylesford as the resident priest. In 1967 Allington became a Community of Friars within the English Carmelite Province and remained so until recently. A Grade I listed building, the castle has been a private residence since 1999 and is not open to the public.

Always a strategically important site, **Dover** has undergone considerable alterations over the years, especially at times when invasion by the French or other near neighbours was expected. Henry VIII's 1534 Act of Supremacy, which removed England from the authority of Rome, created a new fear of invasion, and to meet this latest threat, and the contemporary problems posed by the use of cannons and gunpowder, a new harbour was built at Dover, protected by three bulwarks or gun batteries that were constructed in 1539. Moat's Bulwark and Archcliffe Fort were strategically placed either side of the harbour entrance, while a third, the 'bulwark under the cliff going to Wyke', which was cut into the cliff face overlooking the old pier, was a very short-lived affair and was disused by 1568. Following the king's inspection in 1542, a further, fourth bulwark was built, consisting of a rectangular two-storey timber building with gun ports. Erected in the sea off the south jetty and coated with black tar, this 'Black Bulwark at the Pier' quickly succumbed to the depredations of the sea, and despite extensive repairs, by the end of the century, it was merely a heap of sea-washed rocks.

It was the clear intention in 1539 that any potential invader would be destroyed by gunfire while still at sea or while striving to establish a beach-head in the town. To the east of the harbour, Moat's Bulwark (named after its second captain, Stephen Mote) was cut into the cliff beneath the castle and was originally built of turf, reinforced with stout timbers. Parts of this still remain, high up overlooking the present-day Eastern Docks, although most of the existing structure dates from around 1735.

To the west of the valley, through which the River Dour runs to debouche into Dover harbour, there is a headland known as Archcliffe Point, from which one has a commanding view over the town and harbour. This was an obvious site on which Henry VIII should erect one of the forts or bulwarks that were destined to control the seaborne approach to the town. Its strategic value had not been lost on earlier occupants of the town, and in 1370 a tall watchtower had been erected there, surrounded by a chalk bank and ditch. This was removed in 1539 when Henry commenced his grand plan for the fortification of Dover that included the construction of a bulwark at the same point.

This bulwark, which later became **Archcliffe Fort**, was a rectangular complex, comprising the Gunner's house and other buildings behind a timber-revetted earth platform. It was originally manned by a captain and two soldiers, and its armament consisted of one demi-culverin (a medium-sized cannon), 2 brass sakers (similar to, but slightly smaller than a demi-culverin), one iron fowler, three single serpentines and a dozen bases – the latter weapons being various types of small cannon.

Once it was felt that the threat no longer existed, the fort quickly fell into a state of disrepair, and the guns were left to rust and rot until 1588 when, despite its substantial construction, Archcliffe Fort had to be restored and further strengthened by Queen Elizabeth I in response to the threat from Catholic Spain's Armada.

In the early seventeenth century, during the war in the Netherlands, James I spent more money on repairing the fort, since Dover was the main port of embarkation for the thousands of troops heading for the Low Countries. When Charles I came to the throne, the cliff below the fort was cut away in order to prevent an enemy scaling it, and in 1639, exactly one hundred years since its original construction, Archcliffe Fort was completely rebuilt at a cost of £4,300. In 1641, further repairs were carried out and an additional 20-foot high brick wall was built around the fort, dominating a 7-foot deep and 18-foot wide ditch. The wall was poorly constructed, however, and needed major repairs within a year.

The fort did not figure significantly during the Civil War, but with the Restoration of the Monarchy in 1660 it was fully garrisoned with a captain, a lieutenant, an ensign, a sergeant, two corporals, 'sixtie souldiers each at eight pence per diem', one drummer, one gunner and two assistant gunners, or 'matrosses'. This establishment was reduced to two officers and four gunners once King Charles II was firmly ensconced on the throne of England. In 1666, with the Great Plague at its height, the terrified garrison lit fires, fired guns and rang bells to keep the dreaded disease at bay.

More repairs were called for towards the end of the seventeenth century, when the defensive walls and the platforms for the thirteen heavy iron cannons all needed urgent attention. These helped the fort to survive another hundred years, and the role of Archcliffe Fort in the run-up to and during the Napoleonic Wars will be covered in the next chapter.

Despite the fact that **Dover Castle** was largely demilitarized and effectively obsolete by Tudor times, considerable sums of money continued to be spent, mainly in relation to its use as a royal palace by Henry VIII and Elizabeth I, although Henry VIII did adapt the defences to carry cannon and built the Tudor Bulwark. The castle still displays the beautiful brass cannon, cast in

Utrecht in 1514 and presented to Queen Elizabeth I by the States of Holland. Referred to as 'Queen Elizabeth's Pocket Pistol', it carried a 12-pound shot, but is now quite unfit for use. Indeed, only a century or so later, the castle was described as being 'ruinous and all its guns useless'. By the end of the seventeenth century the principal purpose to which the castle was put was as a debtors' prison, and occasionally, to hold prisoners of war. The castle was not to become a significant military installation for yet another century, when the threat posed by Napoleon Bonaparte prompted a complete rethink about the county's coastal defences.

Described as an 'example of a Henrician castle *par excellence*', the new **Deal** Castle was built in just eighteen months. Surrounded by a dry moat and constructed from stone-clad brick in the form of a rose, it has remained virtually intact over the years. The central circular tower or keep surmounts two tiers of six semi-circular bastions, each of which, like the central tower, housed heavy cannon. This tiered system provided an excellent and un-interrupted clear field of fire from all three levels. The sole entrance is from the most westerly outer bastion, protected by a stout oak door, a portcullis and a drawbridge. There are also a number of *muertrières* – apertures in the vault above – through which the defenders could fire, or inflict other damage, on anyone attempting to gain entrance. Although it was once thought that

Deal Castle. One of Henry VIII's typical fortresses. (Photo: Lisa Letheren)

the design was based on the Tudor rose, this is pure fantasy, as the design was already in use in Europe some twenty years earlier, the brainchild of Albrecht Dürer. Despite the haste with which they were built, these castles contain a high degree of workmanship.

Although built to repel a sixteenth-century invasion, the castle was not called upon to take any war-like action, other than firing a few warning shots across the bows of passing ships. It was not until the Civil War a century later that it saw any real action. Although initially in Parliamentary hands, as a result of a Royalist uprising in the south-east, in 1648 the three castles at Deal, Walmer and Sandown declared themselves to be Royalist supporters. The Roundheads under Colonel Nathanial Rich soon put down the rebellion and then turned their attention to the castles. Despite a grave lack of artillery, they soon succeeded in taking Walmer and Deal, and Sandown quickly surrendered.

Notwithstanding their role in the Civil War, the castles were not slighted, as they were seen to be a useful means of defence for the fleet. But Deal was not to escape depredation entirely: in the 1730s a house was built partly on top of one of the outer bastions and partly into the courtyard, for the use of the Captain of the Cinque Ports Volunteers, and became known as 'The Governor's Lodgings'. This was replaced in 1802 by another unprepossessing house, but a lucky bomb, dropped by a Luftwaffe aeroplane in the Second World War, succeeded in destroying this carbuncle, without causing any real damage to the ancient fabric of the castle.

The keep now houses an interesting collection of arms and armour, and a display of Henry VIII's entire coastal defence system. There is also a curious double spiral staircase in the keep, by means of which defenders were supposed to be able to descend unobserved by anyone who tried to gain access to the upper floors of the keep, and so surprise them from behind. Perhaps fortunately, this ingenious concept was never put to the test.

Folkestone is not generally seen as a defensive stronghold, despite the Roman and pre-Roman vestiges and the now-disappeared Norman fort on Castle Hill, but a significant coastal fort existed in the town at least as far back as Tudor times. Local tradition has it that a fort was 'traced out' by Sir Anthony Archer during the reign of Henry VIII and it is certain that this was already old by the end of the seventeenth century. Located on the cliff-top area known as The Bayle (pronounced 'bail'), the name would suggest possible Norman origins and it is possible that The Bayle was the site of the bailey of another Norman stronghold, but no trace of this now exists.

A 'True map of the Towne of Folkestone' by Abraham Waller, dated 1698, in fact shows three forts existing at that time, all of which were probably a century old by the time the map was drawn up: the 'Bayl' Fort, the 'Durlocks' (on East Hill) and Church Fort (near the parish church and where Priory Gardens now stand). The Bayle Fort is shown as having four guns while the other two had three each.

After (or possibly before) this time, the forts appear to have been neglected and rundown like the other coastal batteries, and it was not until 1756, when another invasion fear arose, that the forts were dusted off and prepared (as far as their condition would allow) for action. The Board of Ordnance purchased The Bayle from the Viscount Folkestone in 1759 and the fort was garrisoned and the guns and their carriages repaired. A house (now called 'The Battery') was built inside the fort for the Master Gunner and has a brick bearing the date 1760 incorporated into the chimney.

The Bayle Fort's only action appears to have been in 1800 when a French privateer captured a British brig close inshore, under the noses of the fort's garrison. The sentry, mistakenly thinking the incident was the crew of a customs cutter boarding a smuggler, failed to call out the gunners who were stationed at the fort, and any action was confined to some desultory and ineffective small arms fire.

The ensuing history of the Bayle Fort seems to have been one of quiet decay. The town was becoming an attractive seaside resort, and the thought of the guns firing over the newly built Royal Pavilion Hotel was deemed to be most undesirable, and the growth of residential properties in the area rendered the noise of artillery very unwelcome. And so the battery was dismantled in 1887, the land being sold off by the War Department for £3,425 and used for the construction of a number of elegant houses.

Gravesend, strategically sited on the southern bank of the Thames where it flows into the Estuary, has always been an important port and a key component of the defence of London. Better protected against the wind and weather than anywhere further out into the Estuary, it was for centuries the port at which royalty and nobility disembarked on their way to the capital and it boasted a royal palace by the 1360s. But it was also vulnerable to sea-borne raids, and a beacon had been set up on Windmill Hill by 1377. This did not, however, prevent a French force from landing and burning the town in 1380, during the Hundred Years War. But Gravesend recovered and strengthened its defences, ready for the next onslaught.

Situated where the river is just 800 metres wide, Gravesend was selected in 1539–40 to be the site for two artillery blockhouses, the fire from their guns crossing with that from the Essex fort at Tilbury on the other side of the river, thus denying river access to London for any intruder. Two further blockhouses 3 miles downstream at Higham Marshes in Kent and East Tilbury in Essex provided an outer line of defence. At the time of the Great Armada scare in 1588, these defences were supplemented by a boom, consisting of boats and hulks, linked by ropes and chains and anchored to the river bed. A similar arrangement was brought into use in 1667 when the Dutch fleet penetrated up the Thames and Medway rivers.

The modest D-shaped bastion in front of present Clarendon Royal Hotel was altered in the late 1540s to include an angular bastion, but only the foundations of these Tudor blockhouses remain, the site having been excavated in 1981, but these are no longer visible.

By the end of the seventeenth century, the Gravesend defences had been effectively abandoned and left to decay for almost a hundred years until the threat from France was once more a matter of concern. This will be covered in the next chapter.

The conurbation we now know as **Medway** comprises essentially the towns of Chatham, Rochester and Gillingham, all of which have been very much involved over the years in the protection of the county and the nation. Rochester, as we have already seen, has been an important strategic site since at least Roman times, and its great Norman castle still testifies to the ancient city's military history. Chatham encloses within its boundaries a number of fortresses and forts, largely provided to protect its incomparable historic naval dockyard, sadly no longer active, while Gillingham contains other military installations and several barracks and camps. It is difficult to describe the features to be found in any one of these towns without cross-reference to at least one other and so, for the purposes of this and the ensuing chapters, it is proposed to deal with the area as a single entity: Medway.

During the reign of Henry VIII, the River Medway's role as a (comparatively) safe anchorage for the Royal Navy increased greatly, and it was around this time that the dockyards at Chatham and Sheerness were inaugurated, greatly influencing the demographic status of the area.

Principal among the Tudor fortresses on the Medway was the castle built at **Upnor**, the history of which is synonymous with that of the Chatham dockyard, which grew from its modest beginnings under Henry to a greatly expanded enterprise during the reign of Elizabeth I. On coming to the throne in 1558 she ordered that a blockhouse be built on the bank of the River Medway, opposite but slightly downstream from the dockyard, and the following year work on Upnor Castle began. The architect was Sir Richard Lee, the foremost military engineer of the day, who handed over the actual construction to his assistant, Humphrey Locke, although it was the celebrated

Upnor Castle on the River Medway.

benefactor and mayor of Rochester, Richard Watts, who actually oversaw most of the work. Unlike the astonishingly rapid construction of Henry's castles at Deal, Walmer and Sandown, Upnor took some eight years to build, even though some of the stonework was filched from Rochester Castle and much of the timber came from Sir Thomas Wyatt's confiscated land at Allington.

The original blockhouse (as this edifice is more correctly called) consisted of a main rectangular building with a pointed bastion projecting out into the river and two small towers at either end of the wall fronting on the river. It departed from the rounded walls design of the castles constructed during her father's reign by adopting the growing continental preference for angular bastions that provided better flanking fire and close defence.

This blockhouse was soon made larger and stronger, and by the end of the sixteenth century, the bastion had been raised and protected by a wooden palisade in the water. The twin towers were replaced by larger ones, and a wall with a gatehouse surrounded the courtyard on the landward side. A ditch surrounded the whole emplacement.

In addition to the castle at Upnor, the river's defences were augmented by a series of small blockhouses and bulwarks built during the Tudor and Stuart periods. However, these all proved ineffective when, in 1667, the Dutch fleet stormed and destroyed the fort at Sheerness and then brazenly sailed up the River Medway. On arriving at Gillingham Reach (between the Hoo Salt Marshes and what is now Gillingham Strand), their passage was blocked by a chain stretched across the river with gun batteries at either end, guarded by English ships of the line. Undeterred, the Dutch broke through, destroying or capturing a number of English vessels, including the flagship. The next day they continued upriver, leaving a trail of destruction. It was only the decision by the English commanders to sink several of their own ships in mid-channel that prevented the Dutch from reaching and seizing the all-important Royal Dockyard at Chatham. Reliance on the castle at Upnor had proved misplaced, one of the castle's failings being the fact that, sited directly opposite the dockyard, only half of its guns could be brought to bear on an approaching enemy vessel. Having failed in its supreme test, Upnor Castle was relegated to the role of store and magazine.

This humiliating defeat and destruction of the greater part of the English fleet made it clear that new fortifications were needed along the River Medway, and the services of the great (Dutch-born) military engineer Sir Bernard de Gomme were employed to advise on this and also on the defences of Portsmouth and Harwich. His recommendations were for two batteries to be installed on the bend in the river at Gillingham Reach; one near Gillingham and another at **Cockham Wood**. The Gillingham battery would be able to engage any enemy shipping sailing up the river before it reached the bend and also rake it from the rear if they managed to get past. At this point the Cockham Wood fort would add its firepower to the defences. The Cockham Wood fort was a significant construction, built in 1669, with two tiers of gun platforms built into the hillside on the north side of the river, opposite

All that is left of Cockham Wood Fort.

the little town of Gillingham. The lower tier held twenty-one guns and the upper tier a further twenty. The fort was surrounded by earthworks and a dry ditch, and to the rear there rose up a ravelin-type structure and a guard tower. It was already reported as falling into ruin by 1794, and today, only parts of the lower gun platform and the ramparts, together with a small section of the guard tower, remain. The other fort, built on the opposite (south) side of the river at Gillingham, has now completely disappeared.

In addition to the castles at Deal, Walmer and Sandown, Henry VIII built another, smaller one at **Sandgate**, but this time to a different design. Instead of the cinquefoil or Tudor Rose pattern, Sandgate's castle is more triangular, with elliptical rather than straight sides. It comprised a three-storeyed central tower or keep, surrounded by two outer walls or chemises, the outer one being lower than the inner, thus providing the defenders on the keep or the inner wall with a clear field of fire over the heads of those on the lower levels. The three corners of the inner wall each contained a circular tower or bastion, with a D-shaped tower on the north-west outer wall providing the only entrance.

Huddled between the sea and a row of cottages, and suffering the ravages of nearly five centuries of erosion, the castle was built over eighteen months between 1539/40 by the great German fortifications expert Stephan von Haschenperg and cost just over £5,500. Queen Elizabeth I was lodged and entertained here in 1588 on her way to Dover.

Sandgate Castle today, with modern adaptations.

Today only about half of the original building exists and this has been changed and adapted to suit contemporary demands. In 1806, the central circular keep was lowered and altered to make it conform to the design of the Martello Towers (see next chapter). All the walls were reduced in height and their battlements removed while, on the seaward side, the outer wall bastions were completely removed, as was part of the inner wall. These modifications were carried out with scant regard for the structure of the building, and the edges of the breaches were left rough and unprotected. Further deterioration through weather and erosion has occurred since – especially during a great storm in 1950, and the castle has been partly undercut by the sea and the Napoleonic alterations.

In his book, *A Journey Round the Coast of Kent* (1819), L Fussell describes the castle in the following terms:

> Descending a steep hill into Sandgate, the castle there built by Henry VIII (and part of it recently converted into a Martello Tower, of larger size than usual, and built with stone instead of brick) is the first object which presents itself. It stands on the beach, and so near the water's edge that its walls are frequently washed by the surf. Whether this building was originally more extensive than at present, may be doubted [sic]; for here there are no vestiges of its ancient walls to be traced.

The castle is now privately owned and not open to the public. In recent years a distinctive stainless steel cap has been fitted to the top of the keep with windows all round to give a 360-degree view over both the Straits of Dover and the landward hills.

Walmer Castle is virtually identical to Deal Castle and the now virtually disappeared Sandown Castle, lost to the sea, although it is rather smaller than Deal. These three fortresses were collectively known as 'the Three Castles which keep the Downs' (the safe anchorage that lies between the land and the treacherous Goodwin Sands). It was built between 1538 and 1540 in view of an invasion threat by the combined French and German forces, but saw no action of any kind until the Civil War (see the entry above for Deal Castle).

The castle consists of a two-storey central tower or keep, circular in design, standing alone in the centre of a round courtyard which is surrounded by an outer wall with four, semi-circular bastions or single-storey towers. The northernmost bastion doubles as a gatehouse, access to which is via a bridge and a drawbridge. Running round the castle at basement level there is a gallery provided with gun loops and there are three further gun position levels. The usual moat outside the outer wall completes the defences.

Over the years, Walmer Castle increasingly became a place of residence rather than one of defence, and in addition to a number of internal alterations, some buildings were constructed over the outer bastions and in the courtyard. During the eighteenth century, the castle was adapted to provide accommodation for the Warden of the Cinque Ports (synonymous with the post of Constable of Dover Castle) and is still used as such today. The great Duke of Wellington, Lord Warden from 1829 until his death in 1852, died in the castle and his room has been preserved for visitors to see, with his famous Wellington boots and the chair in which he died being on display in the small museum. It is evident that each Lord Warden left his or her mark on the building, often with a view to making it more comfortable to live in.

It was during Wellington's tenancy, in November 1842, that Queen Victoria decided she wanted to spend some time there with Prince Albert and their first two infants. Wellington had to move out and complained of having to 'pull the building to pieces' to accommodate her requirements, and the visit was fraught with all kinds of problems.

When the queen arrived, her carriage got stuck in the mud, and she and her children had to be carried over the bridge into the castle. Inside the castle chaos reigned: 'The place was a scene of the most utter confusion with trunks and baggage in every room and maids and nurses of every description running about,' wrote the Duke. Despite this, Victoria was not happy, complaining that the 'bedroom was small, dreadfully cold and draughty',

The entrance to Walmer Castle.

and both she and the children went down with severe colds during their short stay.

A later queen who was much more content with the (no doubt greatly improved) facilities was Queen Elizabeth the Queen Mother, who spent a lot of time at the castle during the time she held the position of Warden. In 1997, a garden designed by Penelope Hobhouse was presented to her to celebrate her 95th birthday and to commemorate her tenancy of the post. The castle and delightful gardens are managed by English Heritage and are usually open to the public.

Chapter 7

Napoleonic wars and thereafter (1700–1900)

The entire period between 1700 and 1900 was overshadowed by conflict between Britain and France, leading once more to fear of a French invasion. The period opened with the War of the Spanish Succession and Marlborough's great victories at Blenheim, Ramillies and Oudenarde, followed by the advantageous but uneasy peace brokered between Queen Anne of Great Britain and Louis XIV of France in the 1713 Peace of Utrecht.

The War of the Austrian Succession brought Britain into conflict with France once more, culminating in the Battle of Dettingen in 1743, in which George II personally led his troops into victorious action against the French army, the last British king to command his army in the field.

The Seven Years War brought the British and the Prussians into conflict with France and Austria in 1756. Battles were fought on a wide number of fronts, including Quebec, Minden, Lagos, Quiberon Bay, Bengal and India. The Peace of Paris, signed in 1763, brought this war to an end, with both Britain and Prussia gaining a number of colonies and other territorial gains, forming the beginnings of the first British Empire. However, the Treaty of Versailles in 1783 saw the loss of America following the War of Independence.

And things were not entirely peaceful on the Home front. A Jacobite Rising was put down in 1715, the Scottish rebels under Bonnie Prince Charlie being ultimately and definitively destroyed at Culloden in 1746, after an initial success in the Battle of Prestonpans.

However, great as these overseas conflicts and their associated victories and losses were, the population safely tucked up in their beds in Britain were not directly affected, nor did they fear any serious invasion of their tight little island. But this was all about to change; scarcely had the British recovered from the loss of America when a further and much more pertinent threat arose. In 1789, the citizens of France rose up against their decadent monarchy and George III came to the defence of the French aristocracy, declaring war on the revolutionaries – who were too busy fighting amongst themselves to worry too much about the blockading British ships and possible interference from across the Channel.

But out of the turmoil of this bloody revolution there rose a figure that was to strike fear into the hearts of many people throughout Europe, including Great Britain: Napoleon Bonaparte.

Napoleon Bonaparte was the second of six children born in Ajaccio, Corsica, of noble parents of Italian descent. He had dreams of a military or naval career and entered the French military academy in 1779, graduating as a lieutenant of artillery in 1785. He came to prominence during the First Republic in the turmoil that followed the revolution, especially through his brilliant Italian campaign of 1796/97. The French government, the *Directoire*, mistrusting this brilliant strategist and military mind, sent him to Egypt, where his role was to deny to the British the route to India. But when he learned of the problems that were arising back home in France, he returned and led a coup d'état against the government, forming a consulat with himself as Premier Consul. Reassuring the troubled middle classes, he stabilized the revolutionary conquests and proved himself to be a brilliant and gifted administrator. He made peace with Austria in 1801 and with Great Britain at the 1802 Treaty of Amiens that brought to an end nearly ten years of war. This was not to last long, however, as on 18 May 1803, faced with clear evidence of Napoleon's expansionist aims and unwilling to tolerate French control of Holland, England declared war once more on its ancient foe.

A royalist plot gave Napoleon the opportunity to have himself made Emperor of the French, being crowned by the pope in Paris in 1804. He promptly surrounded himself with the trappings of royalty and appointed members of his family and close friends to the thrones of conquered nations or other important governmental posts. Taking up once more his policy of conquest, he embarked upon campaigns against the great European Powers, of which Great Britain was the most significant. In alliance with Russia, he set up a continental blockade, with a view of bringing Britain to its knees through lack of supply of essential military equipment and the starvation of its populace. With Napoleon massing 100,000 troops and 2,000 invasion barges on the northern coast of France in 1803, it is not surprising that a great many steps were taken to prevent 'Boney' from landing a military force on English soil or, failing this, to deny him the opportunity of creating one or more beachheads or any chance to progress further inland.

A 6-pounder cannon, circa 1796, as used extensively during the Peninsular War. For the Battle of Waterloo and henceforth it was replaced by the heavier 9 pounder. (Royal Artillery Museum)

Thanks to the Royal Navy, however, this blockade was not entirely effective, and British troops and their allies fought the French in the Iberian Peninsula and in France, where Napoleon was defeated and exiled.

Even once Napoleon had returned to power and been definitively beaten at Waterloo in 1815, Anglo-French relations remained extremely sensitive, and it was not long before another very real threat of invasion was perceived.

The New Threat

By the middle of the nineteenth century, the major European countries were busy entering into pacts and treaties, with a view to surrounding themselves with a protective mantle of allies and colonies. Britain even entered into an uneasy alliance with France to prevent Russia's encroachment on their possessions, culminating in the Crimean War.

Like Great Britain, France in particular was actively engaged in expanding her territories, and the competition between the two countries was rife. The once-dominant Royal Navy now had a very real rival in its French counterpart that was being equipped with modern iron-clad ships. The opening of the Suez Canal led to the possibility of France increasing its foothold in the Far East and even being in a position to blockade the Mediterranean, forcing

Great Britain to continue to use the much longer and more expensive Cape route to India and her other eastern colonies.

At the same time, tension was rising between France, Italy and Austria, resulting in war between France and Austria being declared (the Second Italian War of Independence) in April 1859. This prompted fears of another European war and the possibility of an invasion of Great Britain and so, that same year, a Royal Commission was set up to 'consider the defences of the United Kingdom' in the light of this new threat.

This chapter is therefore devoted to those measures that were taken in Kent to achieve the defence of the nation during two distinct threats that were nevertheless closely allied, inasmuch as many of the defences installed around the turn of the eighteenth/nineteenth centuries were updated and utilized to confront the second threat fifty years later. These adaptations were a complement to the other steps that were being taken in the light of advances in military and naval capacity.

Unlike, for example, the Norman and Medieval precautions, in the late eighteenth and early nineteenth century it was not sufficient simply to build castles or other fortresses to repel the invader; a whole complex of obstacles was devised and built, a single town boasting four or five entirely different defensive structures. In medieval Rochester, for example, a single castle had sufficed to defend the town and district, but now a whole chain of forts, castles, batteries, barracks, earthworks and other obstacles needed to be planned, designed, built and manned, ready for the expected invasion. Some of these defences, like the Martello Towers, were built right along the county's Channel coast whilst, to the north, other measures were taken to prevent a waterborne assault via the Thames or the Medway rivers. It is therefore more practical for this chapter to list the defences at three locations – the Channel, the Thames and the Medway, rather than by individual fortress or town, whether they were erected to repel Napoleon I or Napoleon III.

Dover and the English Channel

Dover's strategic importance was summed up in the report of the 1859 Royal Commission 'into the Present State, Condition and Sufficiency of the Fortifications existing for the Defence of Our United Kingdom':

- It was the nearest point to France, and would be an excellent bridge-head for an invading army;
- An [British] army based at Dover would be able to attack the communications of an invading army that had landed elsewhere and was advancing on London. Dover would have to be besieged to contain

its garrison, thus keeping a considerable portion of the invading force tied up; and

- Dover harbour was in the process of being considerably enlarged and there was already a good pier for disembarkations.

The core of the town's defences over the centuries had been the great Norman castle, but, by the beginning of the eighteenth century, Dover Castle had become a place of residence and a prison rather than a significant fortress. The Constable had moved out and taken up residence in the much more comfortable Walmer Castle (to which he had a right in his role as the Warden of the Cinque Ports) and the castle was occupied by the Deputy Constable with his staff and household.

However, the threat facing the country from France and Spain around the middle of the eighteenth century meant that considerable work was done to the castle to render it suitable for modern warfare. Any invading army would need a port to land its heavy equipment and supplies, and fearing the power of the Royal Navy, the shortest sea crossing possible was to be favoured – such as from Northern France or the Netherlands to Dover or Thanet. And so a vast construction project was commenced in order to make Dover invincible, and this continued throughout the rest of the eighteenth century, culminating with the declaration of war with France in 1793.

From 1792 to 1809 the defence works at Dover were under the control of Lieutenant Colonel William Twiss, an extremely competent military engineer, aided closely by Captain William Ford, the latter being responsible for the design and construction of the numerous Martello Towers built along the Kentish coastline.

At the castle, the thirteenth-century underground works were extended and various outworks were constructed (mainly on the north and west sides) and more than 200 large guns were mounted in the castle ditch. In order to mount guns on top of the towers, many of these were reduced in height, as was the curtain wall. A number of underground casemates and batteries were constructed within these embankments. Many of the medieval buildings within the castle walls were destroyed and the battlements were lost; the medieval keep was used as a powder magazine and the roof replaced by the present 'bomb-proof' brick vault.

The Napoleonic threat meant that there was a pressing need for accommodation for a large number of troops in the south-east, where any invasion could be expected to take place. A novel solution was arrived at by creating a series of subterranean barracks underneath the castle. Chalk is much easier and safer to work with than clay or sand, and the military engineers were quick to appreciate this and to take advantage of its possibilities. And so, between 1793 and 1815, seven tunnels were dug by hand in the soft chalk, using picks and shovels. Two groups of three substantial parallel tunnels, each about 100 feet long, were dug into the cliff face and later lined with bricks, forming an unusual and extraordinary underground barracks for the town's garrison. These tunnels were subsequently referred to as casemates and each terminated in a vertical air shaft at the landward side and was furnished with fireplaces for heating. Access to these casemates was provided by a further, smaller and unlined tunnel that linked them at the landside end and contained the latrines, and a well for water. At their peak, the tunnels housed some 2,000 officers and men. It was intended that the entrances in the cliff face would be used to mount large guns, but by the time the tunnels and the access were completed the threat had passed, and there is no record of any guns having been mounted there.

Outside the castle, the Tudor strongpoints built in the sixteenth century at Archcliffe Fort under the Western Heights to the west, and Moat's Battery below the castle to the east, were reinforced in the invasion scares of the mid-eighteenth century and brought up to date to cover the harbour and its approaches.

The east side of the castle

An account written around 1772 describes the Moat Battery (or bulwark) in the following terms:

> Although dependent on the castle, it has its own peculiar officers; there are a captain, lieutenant, and master-gunner. It consists of a gate, having rooms over and on both sides of it, a house for the gunner, and a circular stone battery, to which there is a descent by a flight of steps. The entrance is on the east side, by a gradual ascent formed out of the chalk. A gunner, who formerly resided there, with great industry embellished the sides of the cliff with several parterres of flowers, which had a very pleasing effect: indeed, both the forms and the situation of these buildings conspire to render the view extremely picturesque and romantick.

It is difficult to reconcile such a description with an emplacement built solely for the purpose of causing death to anyone who presumed to attempt an invasion. Indeed, the site is much less attractive today, having been altered over the years, and very little of the original structure remains. In any event, the botanical displays were undoubtedly destroyed a couple of years later, since the Bulwark was updated and completely overhauled between 1775 and 1783. This included the building of the Guilford Battery in front of the Bulwark, equipped with four 32-pounder guns and a number of carronades. Three other separate emplacements, the North, Townsend and Amherst batteries, were also built at this time and similarly armed, but virtually no trace of these now exists.

In the middle of the nineteenth century, the Guilford Battery and Moat's Bulwark were modernized and a spiral stairway was carved inside the cliff to link them to the castle. To prevent any invader using this stairway, it was designed with defensible landings at intervals, protected by doors with firing slits. Short passages were cut between the stairs and the cliff face to provide light, and these were used around a hundred years later as observation posts during the Second World War.

According to a sixteenth-century map, the bulwark consisted of a timber revetted platform, with a roughly circular front, approached by tunnels in the cliff, although the large semi-circular battery, which is its current most obvious feature, dates from around 1740.

Between 1794 and 1805, Colonel Twiss built the massive Horseshoe (or Avranches) and Hudson's Bastions on the high ground to the east of the castle, together with East Arrow and East Demi Bastions below. The East Arrow Bastion was effectively destroyed when the East Arrow Barracks were built in the 1930s (which were in turn demolished in the late 1960s), and the other three are all in a generally poor condition and not open to the public. A tunnel was created between the East Demi Bastion and the castle during the nineteenth century so that mines could be detonated under it in the event of it being overrun.

There are, in fact, relics and remains of a number of nineteenth-century batteries in the Dover area, such as the Hospital, Shotyard and Shoulder of Mutton batteries – most of which are derelict, overgrown and often inaccessible to the public. Others, like the Guilford and South Front batteries, have completely disappeared, having been destroyed to make way for roads and houses in the name of 'progress'.

Western Heights

In 1779, with great urgency, a number of simple earthwork batteries were constructed on the opposite side of the Dour valley on what is known as the Western Heights. England was at war with America, and her European allies, France, Spain and the Netherlands, had an army, 50,000 strong, poised across the Channel from Dover ready to invade. Once the threatened invasion had failed to materialize, these defences were effectively abandoned for a quarter of a century until the Napoleonic threat became apparent. And so, in the early nineteenth century, these simple earthworks were replaced by an extensive complex of bastions and forts and barracks under the direction of Lieutenant Colonel William Twiss, who was given the task of overseeing the entire defensive arrangements in the Dover area.

Situated on a promontory, overlooking the important Folkestone road to the north and perched high on the cliffs overlooking the sea to the south, the Western Heights defences consisted principally of two forts and two batteries or bastions, all linked together by a series of dry moats (the 'lines') extending four miles in all and encompassing barracks, a church and a Grand Shaft, giving direct access to the beach below. These lines were not just a small ditch but a significant barrier, being some 30 feet across and between 30 and 50 feet deep, and usually revetted with brick or flint coursed with brick. Since these forts and bastions were built on the summit of a high and precipitous cliff, the guns were mostly aimed inland to deal with any approach from the north, aimed at taking Dover from the rear. There is one battery within the complex, St Martin's Battery, which is situated right on the edge of the cliff and was built during the subsequent invasion scare in the mid-nineteenth century. It had emplacements for three guns but is scarcely recognizable, a Second World War emergency battery having been built on top of it. It is, however, accessible by the public.

On the eastern extremity of the Heights, the brick-walled Drop Redoubt was built as a detached fort between 1804 and 1808, replacing an earlier, eighteenth-century structure. It is probably the most impressive and instantly noticeable feature on the Western Heights. It has been partially restored and remains in a reasonable condition. The name 'Drop' refers to the remains of Dover's second Roman lighthouse, known by the locals as the 'Devil's Drop of Mortar'. Originally the Redoubt was a simple pentagon created by digging trenches and revetting them with brickwork. As such, it formed an autonomous fort with its own guns and magazine and barracks for 200 soldiers within it. The Soldiers' Quarters consisted of five bomb-proof casemates in parabola form on the roof of the redoubt, covered with a thick layer of earth to withstand shells and mortar bombs. Access was by way of a swing bridge and gatehouse. The redoubt was improved some fifty years later by the provision of caponiers to serve as gun rooms and the reinforcement of the powder magazine. The guardroom, cells and officers' quarters were also added at this time. Now owned by English Heritage, the Drop Redoubt is occasionally open to the public.

At the western end of the complex, some 1,000 yards west of the Drop Redoubt, stands the other, larger fort, the Citadel, which was the heart of the defences. This great, irregularly shaped fortress was surrounded by a dry moat and contained within its confines a range of mortar-proof underground

The Drop Redoubt on the Western Heights, Dover.

barracks, while galleries along the sides of the moat made it possible to rake the moat with gunfire. Having started around 1804, it was still under construction (albeit in an advanced state) in 1815 when the end of hostilities rendered it redundant. It was revitalized in the mid-1850s to meet the new threat when it was provided with a bomb-proof officers' mess, intended as a 'keep of last resort' and protected from the west by the now overgrown and dilapidated Western Outworks, and beyond these, a further Citadel Battery with emplacements for three guns. An Outer Bastion guarded the north side of the Citadel.

The Citadel was garrisoned until the 1950s (David Niven was stationed there during the Second World War). Since 1957 it has been used as a young offenders' institution and is therefore not open to the public.

Sited between the Citadel and the Drop Redoubt, the North Centre Bastion is a small detached fort with four, irregular-sized walls, something like a triangle with the peak removed. There is a caponier on one corner and the intention was that this bastion could provide enfilading fire along the lines connecting the Citadel to the Drop Redoubt. Work began in 1804, but, like the Citadel, was not finished by the time the war ended in 1815. The plans were revised and the bastion completed between 1859 and 1867, linking it with a Detached Bastion. The bastion is now very overgrown but remains an impressive sight.

Less substantial and therefore easier to build, a block of barracks was built in 1804 to provide accommodation for fifty-nine officers, 1,300 other ranks and eight horses. These were exceptionally light and airy, overlooking the English Channel. Nearby, a military hospital was built around the same time with 180 beds.

One problem facing Colonel Twiss in the design of the Western Heights defences was the lack of access to the beach and town. He reported that:

> the new barracks . . . are little more than 300 yards horizontally from the beach . . . and about 180 feet above the high-water mark, but in order to communicate with them from the centre of the town, on horseback, the distance is nearly a mile and a half and to walk it about three-quarters of a mile, and all the roads unavoidably pass over ground more than 100 feet above the barracks, besides the footpaths are so steep and chalky that a number of accidents will unavoidably happen during the wet weather and more especially after floods. I am therefore induced to recommend the construction of a shaft, with a triple staircase . . . the chief objective of which is the convenience and safety of the troops . . . and may eventually be useful in sending reinforcements to troops or in affording them a secure retreat.

Twiss's plan was approved and the Grand Shaft, 26 feet in diameter, was sunk 140 feet deep, terminating in a tunnel, 180 feet long, connecting it at sea level with Snargate Street. There were in fact two brick-lined shafts, one inside the other, the outer one containing a triple staircase of Purbeck limestone while the inner shaft acted as a light-well with 'windows' to illuminate the staircases. There are 200 steps in each staircase, separated by a number of landings.

An impressive work of engineering, even by modern standards, the construction of the Shaft was not without its problems, not least of which was the exceptionally inclement weather towards the end of 1806, when continuous rain made the site a chalky mud bath. Captain Ford, who had been put in charge of the works, wrote to Major General (as he had by now become) William Twiss, saying:

> The Grand Shaft has become so dangerous that I forbid all working there till 24 hours after the Rain ceases; we have as yet had but one accident by the fall of a piece of about two tons weight which broke the stages all to atoms and carried one man to the bottom; he be very much bruised, but (miraculously) doing well; we have got about 25 feet of the Steering up, and 20ft more will I think make us quite secure.

But Captain Ford's prognostication proved erroneous and his efforts thwarted, as a further missive described a fortnight later:

> So large a quantity fell last night that the scaffolding is entirely demolished, and I really think it is not safe to risk the lives of men in attempting to re-establish it . . . it appears to me almost miraculous that every great fall has happened when the men were not at work.

Nevertheless, despite the difficulties, the Grand Shaft was completed in 1809, two years after the adjacent barracks. As it was built to enable the maximum number of troops to ascend or descend as quickly as possible, once the Shaft was opened it was tested by a whole regiment filing down it to assemble in the town's market place. It took them eleven and a half minutes

The interior of the Grand Shaft, Dover.

but caused great concern to the local inhabitants, as this trial run was carried out around midnight and without notice. A further 'test' was conducted by a Mr Leath from Walmer who rode his horse up the staircase to win a bet in 1812. To crown it all, in 1860, the band of the 47th Regiment marched up it, no doubt much to the dismay of those who needed plenty of wind to play their instruments as they climbed the stairs.

Once the immediate fear of invasion passed with the defeat of Napoleon, the three staircases were segregated by rank; one was reserved for the use of 'officers and their ladies', another for 'sergeants and their wives', while the third could be used by 'soldiers and their women'. After the Second World War, the Grand Shaft became increasingly derelict, and a great deal of rubbish, including cars, was dumped down the centre of the Shaft. Fortunately, the Grand Shaft staircase was restored in the 1980s by Dover District Council and the Department of the Environment, and is now in good condition and open to the public in the summer months. However, only the foundations now remain of the Grand Shaft Barracks that were demolished in the 1950s. A further set of barracks was built on the Western Heights in the 1860s, known as the South Front Barracks. These were curiously constructed in an enormous trench and facing the sea, the various floor levels being linked to the hill behind by galleries and iron bridges. Unlike the Grand Shaft Barracks, these newer buildings were unpleasantly dark and cold and unpopular with the occupants.

Entrance to the Grand Shaft, Dover.

The construction of this whole complex of defences on Dover's Western Heights was both time consuming and very costly, and the virtual cessation of work on the still-uncompleted works, following Napoleon's defeat in 1815, led many people to question the wisdom of the project. William Cobbett visited the uncompleted works in the course of one of his 'Rides' having wanted to:

> ... see with my own eyes, something of the sorts of means that had been made use of to squander away countless millions of money. Here is a hill ... hollowed like a honeycomb. Here are line upon line, trench upon trench, cavern upon cavern, bomb-proof upon bomb-proof; in short, the very sight of the thing convinces you that either madness the most humiliating, or profligacy the most scandalous must have been at work here for years ... more brick and stone are buried in this hill than would go to build a neat new cottage for every labouring man in the counties of Kent and Sussex.

It is a curious fact that the Western Heights defences were never intended to repel an invasion but were designed as a base for a large military force that would attack the enemy *after* they had landed. The concept was entirely alien to William Cobbett, a one-time sergeant major in the West Norfolk Regiment:

> This is, perhaps, the only set of fortifications in the world ever framed for mere *hiding*. It is a parcel of holes made in a hill, to hide Englishmen from Frenchmen. Just as if the Frenchmen would come to this hill!

North of the castle
In November 1855, General Sir John Fox Burgoyne submitted a Memorandum on the General Principles of Standing Defences Suggested for Great Britain, in which he opined that France was the only power likely to attempt to invade Britain and that the whole coastline from the Solent to the Thames was in danger. He felt that there was 'a great deal still wanting to make [Dover] a respectable place'. This Memorandum was largely responsible for the renewed work on the Western Heights, and in August 1869, the Royal Commission looking into the state of the fortifications for the defence of the United Kingdom was advised by General Burgoyne that any attacker able to take the high ground to the north of Dover Castle would be able to dominate the whole of the castle's defences. In accordance with the general's recommendations, between 1861 and 1868 a fort was built on this high ground to protect the castle and was named **Fort Burgoyne** in his honour. Some 700 metres from Dover Castle, the new fort was 700 years apart in time.

Like many of the forts built around this time, it was polygonal in shape, about 280 metres from north to south and 260 metres east to west. The fort was surrounded by a 35-foot wide dry ditch in the centre of the northern aspect, of which was concealed a double caponier that provided flanking fire along the ditch in both directions. Other, single caponiers were provided on the north-east and north-west corners and on the west flank. Connected to the main fort by ditches there are two wing redoubts with gun emplacements, one on each side. The parade ground in the centre of the fort is enclosed on three sides by bomb-proof barrack rooms with a thick covering of earth over the roofs on which the main guns were sited.

The fort was designed to house thirty-five guns on the terreplein, twenty-four in the caponiers and gun rooms, and nine in the outworks. Its two main magazines could each hold 1,296 barrels of gunpowder, with further, smaller supplies in the expense magazines. During the Second World War, a battery of 25-pounder field guns was mounted on the fort in reinforced concrete shelters. The fort is currently within a former military barracks and not normally open to the public – a factor that has undoubtedly contributed to its excellent condition and state of preservation.

Archcliffe Fort and Barracks

The bulwark built on the orders of Henry VIII under the cliffs on the western side of the town and known as Archcliffe Fort enjoyed a new lease of life in 1745, when barracks were built there with two guard houses, and the parapet was raised in height. In 1757 there arose a need for more accommodation and so new barracks were completed as a matter of urgency. This, however, did not prevent a number of complaints being lodged when, in 1793, the 1st Devon Militia arrived to relieve the 2nd Queens Regiment. Apparently, although the barracks had been built to accommodate sixty men, the Ordnance officers had taken over the whole of the premises for their own use – the other ranks presumably having to sleep under canvas.

The fort was badly damaged in 1794 in an explosion, when engineers at the fort were proving some cannons destined for an armed cutter. Fortunately, the engineers escaped relatively unharmed.

On 21 July 1803, 125 citizens of Dover formed themselves into a company of volunteers or 'fencibles' (forerunners of the 1940s Home Guard) and were instructed in the use of the guns at the coastal forts and at the castle should an invasion occur. A second company of volunteers later joined them.

Later that same year, Colonel William Twiss described Archcliffe Fort as being inadequate to prevent a landing at Dover, as its field of fire was obscured by houses that had sprung up in the town, and certain improvements were made.

The fort was often required to engage French privateers who boldly entered the harbour to attack the shipping there. On 20 January 1804, *The Times* wrote:

> The enemy's privateers constantly at low water infest our coast, and so daring are they that two of them came to anchor abreast of our harbour. The sea fencibles went to the batteries but were prevented from going to the guns by the sentinels who alleged that no persons should touch the guns without an order from Lord Forbes, the commanding general, who unfortunately was in Canterbury.

In 1808, when the gunners did finally engage the enemy ships, one of the guns blew up, injuring two of the gun crew.

A military report in 1830 described the fort as: '. . . an irregular enclosed work, situated above the cliffs. To the landward two bastions and a ditch protect it, with a demi-bastion on the eastern side. On the seaward side was a faussebray to facilitate four guns on garrison carriages and for musketry. In the main work there were sixty-five curbs for traversing platforms, all of which are reported as being unserviceable.' However, by 1847 there were reported to be six 32-pounder smooth bore muzzle loading guns there, mounted on traversing platforms, so presumably the necessary repairs had been effected.

By 1859 this 'old work constructed in the time of Henry VIII and very much obstructed by houses' was deemed only useful as a sea battery, although it was in great demand by the local volunteer artillery companies (the forerunners of the Territorial Army) for practice purposes. It was during one such training session that one of the sixty-year old guns blew up, killing two gunners and injuring a number of others. When the smoke cleared, Lieutenant George Thompson of the 1st Cinque Ports Artillery Volunteers, aged 51, was seen to be bleeding from a wound in his back, but he stood up and said, 'I'm not hurt; let's see to the others.' As he turned, he fell to the ground and died without saying another word.

In his everyday life, George Thompson was a much-respected Dover solicitor. He was the Harbour Registrar and the coroner for the town, and in this latter capacity his death in this incident created a number of problems. It was not usual for a coroner to be the subject of an inquest in his own town, and on the advice of the Lord Chief Justice, a new coroner had to be appointed by the Borough Corporation. Lieutenant Thompson was, in accordance with his wishes, quietly interred in the family vault in Shepherdswell churchyard.

The second man was Sergeant John Monger, 32 years of age, who was rendered unconscious by the blast although there were no obvious injuries. He, and another soldier, was taken to the nearby military hospital, where

Entrance to Archcliffe Fort, Dover.

he died on arrival. Sergeant Monger, who kept a small tobacconist shop in Snargate Street, was buried with full military honours in Cowgate cemetery, Dover.

The fort was little used during the First World War, other than for the mounting of some small-calibre, quick-firing guns for use against any landing parties taking advantage of the shelter afforded by the cliff face. In the 1920s, the southern half of the fort was demolished to allow a railway track to be laid. The fort was largely ignored during the Second World War, apart from some training purposes and use as a medical centre. It was demilitarized by 1956, and in 1979 passed into the hands of the Department of the Environment and scheduled as an Ancient Monument. Part of the entrance and the dry moat were destroyed in the 1990s to make way for the new A20 road. In 1995, work started to convert the fort into accommodation and workshops for the Emmaus Community, a charitable body for the aid of the homeless.

The Dover Turret

Admiralty Pier, stretching out into the Straights of Dover and shielding the safe anchorage from both natural and man-made assault, was not begun until 1848 and so was not present during the Napoleonic wars. Its purpose was primarily to provide a calm anchorage for the ever-increasing cross-Channel and other maritime traffic, and it was not built with any specific defensive role in mind. In fact, it seems the builders had no clear plan and no decision as to how the pier should terminate. The initial contract was for a stone pier, 800 feet long, and this was duly completed by the end of 1864, but it was not until 1871 that the authorities decided to add a further 300 feet and terminate the structure with a substantial pierhead. The pier was finally completed in 1875 at a total cost of £639,077.

Coincidentally, the Admiralty had been investigating the matter of armour plating and the armour-piercing capabilities of its guns. The days of Nelson's 'wooden walls' were long gone and we were entering the era of the iron-clad dreadnoughts. The Royal Navy's principal battleships of the time were equipped with 12-inch guns, each weighing 38 tons, but the Admiralty wanted to experiment with an 80-ton gun, which was as large as was felt could be operated on-board ship and which would pierce 20 inches of armour plating from a distance of over half a mile. The gun was to have a calibre of 14 inches but be capable of being bored out to 15 or even 16 inches, which-ever proved the best. A prototype was completed in 1876 at a cost of £8,000 and following extensive trials, the Admiralty settled on an 81-ton rifled muzzle-loading gun with a 16-inch bore. This was nearly 27 feet long with a 20-foot barrel and had a range of nearly 7 miles.

Up until that point, this fearsome weapon had been conceived solely as a weapon to be enclosed in a turret on board a battleship, but thoughts began to turn towards the question of shore defences. Consequently it was decided to mount two of these great guns in a turret on the end of the newly constructed Admiralty Pier. The pierhead was modified to accept these monstrous weapons, and a turret, 37 feet in diameter, was installed over a magazine and with an engine room below. This had two steam engines to provide the power to turn the turret, hoist the ammunition, and power a lighting generator, while a pump was to provide the means of washing out the barrels. The turret was protected by three layers of 7-inch steel with two 2-inch intermediate layers in between.

The guns were manufactured at Woolwich and conveyed to Dover by lighter, where they were hoisted into position by means of ropes and tackle. Power was old-fashioned muscle power, provided by a thousand soldiers, drawn from the town's three garrisons and stretching the whole length of the pier. It is said that the orders, given verbally by the Garrison Sergeant Major, were so loud and clear that the guards at the castle, a good mile away, sprang to attention!

The work completed, the first test took place in July 1883, but the Channel was so full of shipping crowded with spectators that 'a course could not be found for the projectile.' Eventually, perhaps because of the delay, the shipping began to slip away and there was room for the first shell to be fired. Further rounds of increasing charge, rising to 450 pounds, were fired over the next few hours. The installation was now fully installed and ready for action. But little action came; apart from a few further test firings, these great guns remained unused, and in 1902 the Dover Turret was declared obsolete. The guns were run in and the huge barrels greased and depressed to the loading position where they remain, slowly rusting away, to this day.

Martello Towers

The brief cessation of hostilities between France and Great Britain following the signing of the Treaty of Amiens in 1802 was swiftly followed by a resumption of the war the following year. During the first two years of the war, Napoleon's main aim was the invasion and subjugation of Britain, and to this end he massed three army corps of seasoned veterans in the Pas de Calais department, mainly between Calais and Etaples, and embarked on the construction of a fleet of barges and other small craft to carry them to England. This prompted the British to take yet another look at the country's defences against an invasion from across the English Channel – or *La Manche* as the French preferred to call it.

The shortest crossing was between Calais and Dover, but it was not expected that Napoleon would be so foolhardy as to attempt a frontal attack on the most stoutly defended town in the country. However, it would be reasonably practical to follow the example of both the Romans and the Normans by effecting a landing anywhere between Ramsgate and Beachy Head. As such, a line of various types of defence was needed along the entire Kent and Sussex shoreline.

It was Captain William Ford of the Royal Engineers (who was later to take charge of the construction of the Grand Shaft at Dover, amongst other projects), who put forward a suggestion to his superior, Colonel (as he then was) William Twiss, sometime in early 1803. His plan, which was for a series of Martello Towers stretching along the Kent and Sussex coastline, was not an entirely novel one, as similar towers had been built as watch towers around the Mediterranean Sea centuries before. One of the best known of these was the tower at Mortella Point on the island of Corsica, the scene of a combined naval and military battle in 1793, and there is little doubt that the name 'Martello' is a corruption of 'Mortella'. Similar towers had already been built in the Channel Islands, Ireland, Canada and other British possessions.

Ford's plan was that the towers should be built at regular intervals along the coast, sufficiently close so that the fire from their guns, mounted on the roofs, would cross. They should be of simple but sturdy build to keep construction and maintenance costs to a minimum, and in peacetime, their guns could be moved inside for storage while the tower itself was closed and 'mothballed'. Only a small garrison would be needed for each tower and they should be capable of withstanding a lengthy siege.

Colonel Twiss was impressed by the concept and passed the proposal on to the Master of Ordnance, General Sir David Dundas (who had been in charge of the troops that assailed and captured the tower at Mortella Point), with the recommendation that it be adopted but not on the scale envisaged by Captain Ford. Twiss proposed that the towers be used simply to support gun batteries and only at obvious landing places. Thus amended, the plan wound its tortuous way through the political and military bureaucracies, emerging after fifteen months only slightly altered. Only the design remained to be determined and this was to take some time.

In the meantime, William Twiss, now a brigadier, embarked on a survey of the whole coastline from Dover to Beachy Head – some 66 miles by road but considerably further following the coast. This resulted in a report to the Inspector General of Fortifications, Lieutenant General Robert Morse, proposing a total of fifty-eight towers, plus the building of bomb-proof arches over parts of Henry VIII's castle at Sandgate to turn it into a secure sea battery.

Brigadier Twiss and two other officers then submitted a joint report setting out their recommendations for the construction of a series of 'Bomb Proof Towers', each having an internal diameter of 26 feet and a roof designed for the mounting of one 24-pounder gun and two carronades of the same calibre, all mounted on traversing platforms, firing over a parapet, the crest of which was to be about 33 feet above the foundations. The ground floor should house a magazine and other stores, while the middle floor would house the garrison of one officer and twenty-four men. Like the medieval castles, the entrance would be 20 feet above the ground, and although Captain Ford had envisaged square towers, it was agreed that they should be circular, as this would cost less to build (and presumably be better able to deflect missiles).

In the end three types of tower were proposed: the largest, holding around 350 men, were really more like independent forts and were never referred to as Martellos when that name came into common usage. One fort of this type was built at the eastern end of the sea wall at Dymchurch. A middle-sized fort was proposed, but none was ever built. Eighty-three of the remainder, the very-recognizable Martello Towers, were proposed. These were to be of the type suggested by Twiss and his colleagues, other than that they were to be equipped with one 18-pounder in addition to the two carronades. However, the number was amended on several occasions, as was the armament, and the actual construction was lamentably protracted through the usual

nineteenth-century bureaucracy and the failure to place the necessary con-
tracts with suitable builders. The intense rivalry between the Board of
Ordnance, the Royal Staff Corps and the Committee of Engineers, and their
respective empire-building machinations, did not help matters. And so it
was not until the spring of 1805 that work actually commenced – almost two
years since Ford had first mooted the idea, despite the fact that Napoleon's
Armée d'Angleterre was poised just over 20 miles away, ready to attack. Back
in August 1804, when Napoleon had just been celebrating being awarded
the title of Emperor of the French, Lord Hawkesbury (the future prime
minister) had written to his father, the Earl of Liverpool:

> From the intelligence which has lately reached us we are included to
> believe that the attempt of invasion will soon be made. Their prepara-
> tions are very great and they have stopped building, which looks as
> if they considered them complete. They have about 3,000 vessels of
> different descriptions and 180,000 men between Ostend and Cherbourg.

It is perhaps fortunate for England that Napoleon procrastinated (much as
Hitler did in 1940), and in the summer of 1805 he had a change of mind and
moved his army to Austria, leaving England with a shambles of partly built
forts, barracks, batteries and towers but relieved of the imminent danger of
invasion.

Despite the Royal Navy's great success at Trafalgar in October 1805,
work continued on the construction of the Martello Towers. However, by
the end of 1806 only six had been completed, and it took another two years
before the whole seventy-three had been built on the South Coast. These all
followed the general design, being small, round, built of rendered brickwork,
around 33 feet high with a solid, circular supporting pillar of brick in the
centre of the tower. The only entrance was on the landward side, and like
the medieval castles, 20 feet above the ground, access through the wooden
door being gained by a removable wooden ladder.

The thickness of the outer walls decreased towards the rear (landward
side) and towards the top, giving the towers their characteristic 'inverted
flower-pot' shape. The walls, which incorporated around 500,000 bricks
(enough to build some thirty modern houses), were immensely strong, the
bricks being laid with a mixture of lime, ash and hot tallow, known as hot
lime mortar which, once set, was as hard as iron. People who have bought
and moved into one of these towers have found that the strength of this
mortar was such that any structural alterations were virtually impossible.
When the Kent County Council decided to demolish Tower 22 at Dymchurch
in 1956, they found that modern demolition equipment was not up to the
task and they had to resort to explosives. Some, but not all, towers had a dry

A Martello Tower.

ditch or moat around them, but there is no apparent policy as to which were so protected and which were not.

In true military style, each of the towers was numbered, the number being incised on a small stucco tablet in Roman numerals. Only No. 25 does not appear to have its number displayed, although it may have originally been painted on and since eroded away. The numbering ran from east to west, Tower No. 1 being on the East Cliff at Folkestone and No. 73 being at Eastbourne, now commonly referred to as the Wish Tower. A seventy-fourth tower was built in 1810 at Seaford.

The distribution of the towers in Kent falls into three groups. The cliff-top towers, numbering from 1 to 9, ran from East Wear Bay, Folkestone to Shorncliffe Camp. The lower-level towers, from 10 to 21, were equally spaced in front of the highly defended town of Hythe, terminating with the redoubt at the beginning of the sea wall at Dymchurch. These towers supplemented the barracks, batteries and blockhouses already springing up around here.

Numbers 10 (near the present Imperial Hotel), 11 (near Saltwood Gardens) and 12 (Stade Street) were all destroyed towards the end of the nineteenth century when the Hythe promenade was constructed. Numbers 16, 17 and 18 (Hythe firing ranges) were largely eroded by the sea in the early twentieth century, and only a few ruins are now visible. Numbers 20 and 21 followed a similar fate and have completely disappeared.

Thirdly, there were the towers guarding the Romney Marsh sluice gates, numbered 22 to 27. As mentioned earlier, No. 22 was demolished to facilitate roadworks in 1956. Numbers 26 and 27 (St Mary's) were demolished in the nineteenth century. Probably the best preserved of these towers today is No. 24 at Dymchurch, owned by English Heritage, which has been fully restored and is open to the public. It is dominated by an original 24-pounder gun bearing the cipher of George III.

With the changes in Napoleon Bonaparte's fortunes, the Martello Towers were never employed to resist an invasion, and once more, the erudite and caustic William Cobbett had something to say on the subject in 1823, when the country was once more at peace:

> Here has been the squandering! Here has been the pauper-making! . . . To think that I should be destined to behold these monuments of Pitt! . . . Here they are, piles of bricks in circular form . . . Cannons were to be fired from the top of these things, in order to defend the country from the French Jacobins! I think I counted along here upwards of thirty of these ridiculous things, which I daresay cost five, perhaps ten, thousand pounds each . . . I daresay they cost millions.

With the final defeat of Napoleon and the end of the war in 1815, the Martello Towers became redundant and were put to a number of uses. Some became homes for retired soldiers, others were used as signal relay stations and had semaphore apparatus installed. A large number were allocated to another war – that against smuggling – and were occupied by coastguards. The towers had a limited renaissance in the 1850s when a fresh threat arose, but their military usefulness declined with the changes in artillery – the new guns being breech-loading and firing explosive shells rather than solid shot, for which the towers were unsuitable.

The Royal Military Canal

Whilst the building of the chain of Martello Towers along the Kent coast was under consideration, other defensive measures were being considered and Prime Minister William Pitt commissioned the Assistant Quartermaster-General, Lieutenant Colonel John Brown (commandant of the short-lived Royal Staff Corps and later major general), to carry out a survey of the whole coastal region. The invasion of this country was expected at any moment and one place that lent itself to a possible landing was the low-lying and sparsely populated Dungeness promontory, long the haunt of smugglers. Ambleteuse was only 28 miles from Hythe and 37 miles from Rye, and as Admiral Lord

Keith wrote to the Duke of York (Commander in Chief of the British Army) in October 1803:

> Between these two points stretched a thinly populated flat coastline to Dungeness, which offered an easy landing at most states of the wind and tide. The beach was sandy and from whichever quarter the wind might blow, Dungeness Point usually offered a sheltered tide where small boats could safely be brought to shore.

This view was shared by the French General, Charles Dumouriez, who had defected to the British and who wrote a paper in 1804 that highlighted the ease with which an enemy might land on the Dungeness promontory. This disturbing report was undoubtedly influential in the unusual speed with which the authority to build a new form of defence was given.

One solution was to flood the whole of the Romney Marsh, most of which was below sea level and was criss-crossed by dykes and drainage channels. However, this would take time and would be subject to the state of the tides at the crucial moment. General Sir John Moore, the officer commanding the troops in the area, was sceptical and believed he would need at least ten days notice of invasion for such a plan to be put into action, something that

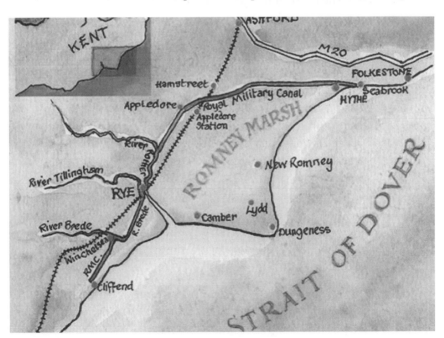

Route of the Royal Military Canal from Hythe to Cliffend, via Rye. (Image courtesy of the Romney Marsh Countryside Partnership 2010 and John Cann – www.arccreativedesign.com)

was clearly impossible. Others believed that it would take 36 to 48 hours to inundate the area, and since covering the fields with seawater would sterilize them for several years, the local landowners would be reluctant to allow the flooding of hundreds of acres of very valuable agricultural land unless the French had actually set foot on English soil. The associated matter of compensation to the landowners was another factor to be considered.

Within the space of a few days from being entrusted with his mission, Colonel Brown came up with the idea of constructing a canal, 60 feet wide and 9 feet deep, running from Seabrook in Kent via Appledore to join the River Rother at Rye in Sussex (later extended to Cliff End near Hastings). It was suggested that this would make the dubious plan of flooding the marshes unnecessary, as it would divide the whole of the Marshes from the higher ground to the north. For once, there were no dissenting voices to the idea, and government approval was given in September 1804.

The project was very clearly set out in a report made by General Sir David Dundas, the General Officer Commanding the Southern District, to the Duke of York, the Commander in Chief of the British Army, on 15 October 1804:

> Romney Marsh may be considered as a quadrant of a circle of which Dungeness is the centre and equidistant from Rye and Hythe along the coast, the circumference bounded by the heights of Lympne, Aldington, Appledore, Isle of Oxney and Playden and the water of the River Rother. The country behind is wooded and intricate and ... difficult for the passage of a large corps.
>
> Every effort on the certainty of an enemy attack should be made to clear and excavate the marsh, destroying whatever could be useful to the enemy ... One arch of all the bridges must be easily removed.
>
> It is supposed that this kind of work can only be carried out in the dry and good season, and the quantity of tools, planks, wheelbarrows, ropes, pumps, etc. required is a great expensive article ...
>
> The troops at Hythe and Playden Heights are well placed in support of the flanks of this line. Those at Brabourne, Ashford and Reading Street are well situated for the centre of the line and would arrive at Aldington, Horton and Appledore [with] the accumulating force of the surrounding country.

The commander-in-chief was well aware of the delays likely to be occasioned if the work were entrusted to the engineers under the Board of Ordnance (which was responsible for permanent works), and so decided to treat the canal as a field-work and not as a fortification. As such, the work was placed in the hands of the Royal Staff Corps under the Quartermaster-General,

Robert Brownrigg. With Lieutenant Colonel John Brown in day-to-day command, construction started in October 1804.

Unlike most canals, this was not designed principally for the conveyance of goods but almost solely as a water-filled ditch that would cut off virtually the whole of the Romney Marsh from the higher ground to the north. Transport was catered for by a military road constructed on the landward side of what was to become known as the Royal Military Canal, although the movement of certain supplies and men could obviously be effected using the canal as well. There is little doubt that the politicians also saw the commercial possibilities of this venture once its military use was concluded, and it was this possibility, plus the canal's use for drainage purposes, that won over the local landowners and facilitated the acquisition of the necessary land.

This considerable feat of engineering was carried out mainly by civilian 'navigators' and labourers under John Rennie, the builder of London and Waterloo Bridges, as the consulting engineer, and with the capable Lieutenant Colonel Brown as the Director of Works. It proved to be a much less simple task than anticipated, as bad weather held up work for most of that winter and there were a number of complaints about the standard of the work performed by the contractors. In fact, by May 1804, less than 6 miles had been started, 'not a twentieth part of the whole was executed and that in a slovenly manner' according to Rennie, and the work was abandoned. The services of John Rennie and the contractors were dispensed with and Lieutenant Colonel Brown appointed in sole charge of the project. Brown wasted no time resuming work, using the materials and equipment purchased from the previous contractors, and employing soldiers and casual labour as required. A great many civilian workers, previously employed by the original contractors, had remained in the area and were taken on, with well over 1,000 workers being employed at times.

The huge labour force, drawn from all over the country, placed a heavy burden on the local facilities, and accommodation was in very short supply, especially for wives. On 15 March 1805, the *Kentish Gazette* reported that one 'navvy' solved the problem by selling his young and attractive wife in Hythe market to a mulatto soldier for sixpence! According to the *Kentish Gazette*, '. . . her face, however, exhibited evident marks of incompatibility of temper; vulgarly, she had a pair of black eyes.' Whether Thomas Hardy was influenced by this tale when writing *The Mayor of Casterbridge* many years later, or whether it was a not unusual occurrence, is not known.

The imminent threat of invasion passed in August 1805, when Napoleon altered his plans and sent the *Grande Armée* to Austria. The defeat of his fleet at Trafalgar in that October added to the sense of relief felt in England. The defeat also added to the complaints about the cost of various defensive works carried out in the South East of England in response to what the former foreign secretary Charles Fox described as 'a groundless alarm of invasion, raised for some political purpose by the ministers.' Lord Ellenborough wrote of 'the great dyke or canal near Hythe, of which about fourteen miles are completed out of thirty-six' and opined that 'It will cost an enormous sum of money, and be, in my poor judgement, of no adequate use. An invading enemy will, by means of fascines [brushwood faggots used to fill ditches and trenches], get over it in any part they please in a very short time.'

Nevertheless, work continued on the canal for most of that winter despite continual flooding, and by the end of August 1806, it was possible for the Royal Dukes of York and Cambridge to travel some 18 miles along the canal in a small, horse-towed boat to inspect the work, which had been completed in less than two years (the Sussex portion being completed between 1807 and 1809).

The shortcomings of this delightful waterway as a piece of military field-work were soon realized and the canal was stocked with fish in 1806. If William Cobbett was critical of the costly defences built on Dover's Western Heights and the Martello Towers, it comes as no surprise to find that he was similarly scathing about this project in his *Rural Rides* entry in 1823:

> Here is a canal ... made for the length of thirty miles ... *to keep out the French*; for those armies that had so often crossed the Rhine and the Danube, were to be kept back by a canal, made by Pitt, thirty feet wide at the most.

Of course, it is always easy to be critical of any precautions taken where the anticipated calamity fails to materialize, and one wonders whether the facile criticisms would have been voiced had Napoleon carried out his avowed intention to invade England in those dark days of the early nineteenth century.

Following the Royal Navy's victory at Trafalgar, the defensive require-ments eased and both the canal and military road were used for transporting troops by barge and by wagon between Rye and Shorncliffe Camp, as well as carrying some commercial traffic. The tolls paid by civilian barges and wagons, which, together with property rents, exceeded an average of £1,200 per annum, went towards the cost of maintenance between 1810 and 1877. In the latter year, the War Department leased part of the canal to the Lords of Romney Marsh and to Hythe Corporation, with the last barge passing through Iden Lock in 1909.

As early as 1807, permission was granted for licensed pleasure boats to use the canal, and the first recorded excursion by a private individual dates from 1851 when the vicar of Iden was granted permission by the Board of

The Royal Military Canal at West Hythe Dam today.

Ordnance to sail up to Hythe and back in a small boat. Other applications to go boating on the canal soon followed, as did applications for fishing licences. In 1860, the first Hythe Venetian Fete was held and has continued with only occasional breaks up until the present day.

The Hythe Battery

The Royal Military Canal and the Martello Towers were not the only defences along this stretch of the shore, as Hythe town had its own battery, as did a number of towns such as Folkestone. Hythe's battery seems to have been set up as long ago as 1413 when eighteen 'gonney stonnys' were purchased, but by 1627 these had long since rotted away. A petition to the king in this year eventually resulted in the supply of two new guns, and by 1684, the simple earthwork platform on which four guns were now mounted was being described as Hythe's 'forte'. In accordance with common practice at the time, local volunteers probably manned these guns as and when required.

The high state of alert that existed in the middle of the nineteenth century prompted the Board of Ordnance to refurbish the coastal batteries at seven towns, including that at Hythe, and post a Master Gunner and an assistant at each of them. The Woolwich Royal Arsenal supplied six brand new 18-pounders, but the town and port was already suffering from the effects of erosion and shifting beaches. Around the end of the eighteenth century, the historian Edward Hasted wrote in his *History of Kent*:

Here is a small fort, of six guns, for the protection of the town and fishery, which till lately belonged to the town, which was bought by the Government but now rendered useless by its distance from the sea (somewhat more than half a mile) from the land continuing to gain upon it: the guns have been taken out.

Nevertheless, the Napoleonic threat resulted in the Hythe battery, like the nearby Moncrieff, Sutherland, Saltwood Heights, Shorncliffe, Twiss and Dungeness batteries, being restored and placed on a war footing. These, together with the Seabrook Redoubt and the modernized Sandgate Castle, presented a close-knit and powerful line of defence between the west of Folkestone and the Romney Marsh, supplementing the new Martello Towers. It was the introduction of these more efficient and sturdy towers that led to the coastal forts being gradually abandoned, none sooner than that at Hythe because of its increasingly remote position with regard to the sea. Nature soon overwhelmed the abandoned fort and its precise site is not known, although certain remains unearthed during building work on the corner of Mount Street and Prospect Road suggest this might have been its location.

The Medway Defences

On the other side of the county the Medway River debouched into the Thames Estuary, providing hostile ships with a means of accessing the dock-yard and the anchorages at Chatham. The great prize of the Medway was the Royal Dockyard itself which since the time of Henry VIII had been building and repairing naval vessels, being located on the present site since 1613. Central to any of the Royal Dockyards were the dry docks, essential for the repair and maintenance of wooden-walled men-of-war and unique to the naval yards. No civilian dockyard would boast such facilities until well into the nineteenth century, by which time the Royal Yards were employing thousands of workers, skilled in a variety of trades and callings. The Royal Yards combined represented the largest industrial organization in the world. Small wonder that many foreign powers were casting covetous eyes on these invaluable complexes, especially those at Chatham and Sheerness.

There were two ways an enemy might assail the dockyard at Chatham: directly from the river or by landing an army elsewhere and attacking from the landward side. The British government was well aware of this, and during the various wars with France – both before and after the Napoleonic era – the whole area became littered with forts and batteries and other defensive structures.

Ships intending to adopt the first alternative would have to pass through the narrows between the Isles of Grain and Sheppey in order to gain the wider estuary of the Medway before they could get anywhere near Chatham Reach and the dockyard. And this journey through treacherous shallow waters, beset with numerous islets and salt marshes, was rendered all the more difficult by a number of defences constructed to provide protection for the anchorages. The main protective fortress was built by Henry's daughter, Elizabeth I, in 1559 at **Upnor** (see previous chapter). This castle – or blockhouse as it is more correctly described – was situated on the opposite side of the River Medway to the burgeoning naval dockyard at Chatham and was adapted by the Georgian military engineers to form part of the network of forts and batteries along the Medway. However, having proved ineffective against a raid by the Dutch fleet some one hundred and fifty years earlier, it was destined for a very minor role in comparison with the new forts being built in the area. In the nineteenth century, the waterborne approach to Chatham was protected by a series of forts, either erected on the river bank or isolated on the river itself.

The entrance to the Medway lies between Garrison Point, Sheerness and the village of Grain on the Isle of Grain. Until the 1860s, it was protected by gun batteries at Sheerness, but, as a result of recommendations made by a Royal Commission into the defence of the country, the Garrison Point Fort at Sheerness and its counterpart, the Grain Tower, built in the shallows of the Isle of Grain Flats, were commissioned.

The **Garrison Point Fort** was a substantial building that replaced a series of batteries and blockhouses that had defended this historically strategic point, the more recent being the Half Moon Battery and the Cavalier Battery. Completed by 1872, it is a granite-faced, semi-circular building with two tiers of casemates and underground magazines. It was equipped with thirty-six 9-inch and 10-inch Rifled Muzzle Loader guns (RMLs), protected behind iron shields in the casemates. These weapons were supplemented by 11-inch and 12.5-inch guns in 1880. In 1909 two 6-inch breech loaders were installed on the roof and four 12-pounder quick-firing guns on the lower level. Like Cliffe Fort (see later), the Garrison Point Fort was equipped with the means of launching the Brennan Torpedo, the launching rails for which are still visible. The remains of the Admiralty Signal Station are also to be seen on the roof.

Opposite Sheerness, a tower was erected in 1855 on the western side of the entrance to the river itself, known as the **Grain Tower**. Originally built as an off-shore Martello Tower, it was designed to replace the earlier Grain Fort (finally demolished in 1962) that served as the counterpart to the impressive Garrison Point Fort. The three smooth-barrelled roof-top guns were designed to fire *en barbette*, that is to say, over a parapet rather than through an embrasure. The tower was, and still is, accessible on foot at low

Garrison Point Fort, Sheerness.

tide, via a paved pathway: otherwise access is only by boat. The fort, which has been much altered and added to over the years, is in a fair state of preservation. It is in private hands, and proving too much of a task for the then owner, was offered for sale in 2010, the address being given as 'No. 1 The Thames'.

Shortly afterwards, a further fort was built on the edge of the Isle of Grain, between the eastern edge of the present village of Grain and the shoreline, and referred to as the **Grain Fort**. Its heptagonal keep was surrounded by an inner ditch with three caponiers and two demi-caponiers, which was in turn enclosed within a further ditch with four caponiers. Beneath the fort there were underground magazines, linked to the caponiers by brick-lined tunnels. Accommodation for the garrison was provided in the keep. Various modifications were made over the years and the fort remained in use until 1956 and was almost completely demolished in the 1960s, leaving just the earthen rampart and the underground passages. The ditches became a repository for all kinds of rubbish and the site became overgrown.

From the estuary, the river winds though treacherous shallows and mud-flats. As enemy vessels came round the Long Reach and into Pinup Reach they would have to pass between **Fort Darnet** and **Hoo Fort**, built as replacements for the seventeenth-century Cockham Wood and Gillingham forts, little of which now remain (see previous chapter). The construction of these paired forts was commissioned following the recommendations of

Grain Tower.

the Royal Commission on the Defence of the Country. It was originally intended that one of the forts should be built further downstream at Oakham Ness Marsh, on the site of an earlier battery. However, the terrain proved unsuitable and Fort Darnet, a circular fort, was built between 1861 and 1872 on a small island on the southern side of the navigable channel, where Long Reach meets Pinup Reach. Its 'twin', Hoo Fort, was built on very similar lines about one kilometre further upstream on the opposite side of the channel, on the south-eastern corner of the insular Hoo Salt Marshes. Between them, these two modern forts were ideally placed to deny access upstream to any unfriendly shipping, using both gunnery and a boom.

Hoo Fort. (Image courtesy of Nick Catford)

Unfortunately, the marshy ground was not entirely suitable for such constructions and the design had to be altered several times. The magazines had to be moved from the centre of Fort Darnet to the edges, to better distribute the weight, and 3,000 tons of ballast had to be poured into the centre to stabilize it. The bases of both forts were encased in an iron belt, 8 inches wide and 1 inch thick, and a concrete skirt was added to prevent flooding during spring tides. Nevertheless, bad weather in December 1863 resulted in the foundations of Fort Darnet being flooded to a depth of over a metre. The original plan for there to be two casemated gun floors for the twenty-five guns, with a further casemated tier beneath for accommodation and storage, was abandoned. In the end only one gun floor was provided for eleven 7- and 9-inch RMLs (rifled muzzle-loaders) above the accommodation for a hundred men and stores. The gun shields consisted of alternate layers of wood and wrought iron, 14 centimetres thick, while thick rope curtains, known as mantlets, protected the gunners from splinters in the event of a direct hit on the emplacement. The penetrative force of the 9-inch RMLs was such that it was considered that they would force any enemy ironclads to withdraw before they could attack the fort itself.

The fort is only accessible by boat and the main entrance was through two gates, separated by a drawbridge. Both forts remained manned and gunned up until and including the Second World War, being used mainly as mine observation posts. Fort Darnet is now the property of the Medway Ports

Authority and has been deliberately flooded to deter vandals, while Hoo Fort remains the property of the Ministry of Defence. Most of the comments that apply to Fort Darnet also apply to Hoo Fort, since the design and armament was essentially the same and the constructional problems were very similar. The constructional difficulties are vividly described in the *Report of the Committee Appointed to Enquire* ... which states that the 'pile was driven by a monkey weighing seventeen hundredweight, at an average of nearly seven inches to each blow ...', conjuring up visions of some King Kong type of creature driving the pile in with its mighty fists. In fact, a monkey is simply 'a drop hammer' (*Penguin Dictionary of Civil Engineering*), which is something of a disillusion.

If the enemy succeeded in getting past both pairs of forts (Grain/ Garrison Point and Darnet/Hoo), they would round St Mary's Island, only to be confronted by Upnor Fort on the Upnor Reach, the last river defence before the dockyard, which would then be in sight. But so would the land-based batteries around the dockyard, which would then be within range.

The realistic likelihood of any significant enemy penetration of the River Medway as far as the dockyard was negligible, but this critical target could also be approached overland from a landing or beachhead established else-where. Such a possibility had been mooted in the early eighteenth century, but nothing concrete was done to prevent it until 1756 when the possibility of invasion was very much in the minds of the government and the people of Great Britain. Once more it was a Dutchman, Hugh de Beigg, who was called upon to design a territorial system of defence for Chatham and who came up with the proposal to create a bastioned line of fortification some 2 kilometres in length, running roughly north/south around the dockyard and the village of Brompton. This continuous line would have two redoubts, one at each end, the northernmost being the **Townsend Redoubt** and the southernmost the **Amherst Redoubt**.

Taking advantage of the high ground to the landward (eastern) side of the dockyard and town, the lines (known as the **Cumberland** or Chatham Lines) consisted of unlined earthen ditches, 27 feet wide and 8 feet deep, with a parapet of 9 feet. Such was the length of the lines that an arsenal of a thousand cannons was required to defend them, manned by a large garrison of artillerymen. Despite the cost and labour involved in creating this line of defence, within a decade they were being described as overgrown and 'rendered almost defenceless by Cattle grazing thereon.' In 1770, a plan was drawn up by Lieutenant General Skinner that would restore and upgrade the lines, extending them beyond the Townsend Redoubt to run as far as

St Mary's Creek. The Amherst Redoubt at the southern end of the lines was remodelled to become **Fort Amherst**.

Matters came to a head when the Napoleonic War broke out and a great deal of money was spent between 1803 and 1811 in improving and modernizing the lines. This included the lining of all ditches with brick and the creation of magazines and a series of bastions: Right and Left Demi-Bastions, Prince Edward's Bastion, Kings Bastion, Prince William's Bastion, etc. Apart from Fort Amherst, little or nothing remains of these fortifications, the area having been subjected to considerable building operations since 1820, although there are some remnants within the nearby military barracks and installations. During the period of the Napoleonic threat, the dockyard defences were greatly reinforced and enlarged, and a whole network of tunnels and under- ground magazines and stores were dug. Some sources hold that French prisoners of war made these, but it is more probable that British convicts from the St Mary's Island Prison were employed on this back-breaking work, under the supervision of experienced Welsh and Cornish miners whose knowledge and experience would have been invaluable. (It is known that the bricks used to build the dockyard and probably to revet the defensive ditches were made at the prison.)

The main stronghold on the Cumberland Lines was the redoubt built between 1756 and 1758 at the southern end and which ultimately became known as Fort Amherst. Its armament comprised fourteen 42-pounders, ten 9-pounders, eight 6-pounders and two 4-pounders.

The fort has been greatly restored in recent years and has been described by English Heritage as the most complete Napoleonic fortification in Britain. As such, it is of great national historical importance and is now owned by the Fort Amherst Heritage Trust, who open it to the public on Sundays during the summer and also arrange ghost tours. Often used by re-enactment groups who occasionally fire the cannon, the fort had the honour of firing what is claimed to be the country's only 21-gun salute on the occasion of the wedding of Prince William and Catherine Middleton on 29 April 2011.

The other redoubt on the Cumberland Lines, the Townsend Redoubt, was never upgraded to a fort like Amherst and eventually disintegrated. It has now been built over by houses. However, two other forts, built on the Chatham/Rochester borders, were also completed during the period 1805–15 to protect the southern approaches to the dockyard. Upstream from St Mary's Island to just past the dockyard, the river runs in a generally southerly direction until it suddenly takes a sharp bend to the right round the Frindsbury Peninsula, changing direction to run north-westerly. It is here that the river runs within the boundaries of the ancient city of Rochester, and between 1805 and 1819 a fort was built on the high ground to the south of

Re-enactment group training at Fort Amherst, Chatham.

the river and overlooking this bend where ships would have to reduce speed and change tack in order to navigate round it. Known as **Fort Pitt**, it was also well placed to counter any land-based approach from the south and so protect the dockyard that lay some thousand yards north as the crow flies across what was then largely open countryside.

This was not the first fort to be named after William Pitt, the 1st Earl of Chatham: in North America in 1758, General John Forbes took Fort Duquesne from the French and renamed it Fort Pitt. It is now known as Pittsburg, Pennsylvania. Fort Pitt, Chatham, Kent, England, was not to have such a distinguished future and was always to be just a part of the urban landscape on the boundary between Chatham and Rochester. Indeed, with the fading of the perceived threats from France, Fort Pitt became a military hospital in 1828 and it was here that Florence Nightingale set up the first Army Medical School in 1860, as a result of her experiences in the Crimean War. The hospital was last in use during the First World War and closed in the 1920s, being demolished in the early 1930s to make way for a school. Just a few pieces of brickwork are all that are left of this once substantial casemated and bastioned fort, although some of the outer defences remain visible. From this strategic point, it is still possible to look across the great conurbation of the Medway towns and see Fort Amherst to the north-east and Fort Clarence to the west – the three forts that made up the southern (landward) defences of the dockyard at that time.

Chatham Dockyard from Fort Pitt, Rochester.

From the Frindsbury Peninsula, the River Medway turns once more, sharply to the left around Gas House Point, to flow once more south-westwards, under Rochester Bridge and following a course which today is echoed by Rochester Esplanade. It was along this stretch, at a point where the river narrows somewhat, due to the projection of Temple Marsh into these somewhat polluted waters, that **Fort Clarence** was constructed on an extensive site (over 23 acres), requisitioned from the cathedral and one private person in 1808. Stretching westwards from the Maidstone Road (B2097) to the riverbank (now the Esplanade) and crossing the Borstal Road, the fort was not completed until 1812. It was essentially a line of ditches and ramparts, furnished with magazines and strongpoints along its length, intended to perform the dual role of defending the area from a land-based attack from the south and also to prevent a river-borne landing in that locality. There was a tower at each end and a larger one in the centre, of which just one large brick tower overlooking the Medway now remains at the junction of St Margaret's Street and Borstal Road. This central tower, known as the Fort Clarence Tower, was the heart of the fortifications and was built over a series of magazines and stores, with a network of tunnels linking it to the other parts of the defences, some of which still exist. The fort had a sally port at the Medway end of the ditch, through which the fort could be provisioned unseen by the enemy in the event of hostilities. The sally port and a small section of the adjacent ditch still remain, although the port has been sealed.

Where the Borstal Road was severed by the deep ditch, a swing bridge was provided to enable traffic of all kinds to cross to the other side – the bridge being protected on the northern side by a sturdy brick archway and an adjoining gatehouse. According to an inventory dated January 1819, the central tower (Fort Clarence Tower) was equipped with twelve 12-pounder guns and six 18-pounder carronades. The Maidstone Road (eastern) Tower had four 18-pounder carronades while, at the other end of the fortification, the Medway (western) Tower had two 12-pounder guns and two 12-pounder carronades. Despite all the money and time spent on this fort, it was regarded as obsolete by the military authorities even before it was completed. When the above inventory was taken, a mere seven years after its completion, the fort was being taken over by the Medical Department for use as a Naval Lunatic Asylum and Hospital.

In 1845 the fort was adapted to become a military prison, with Fort Clarence House being built on the Borstal Road for the governor's use, and accommodation for the warders and cells for the inmates provided within the confines of the fort. At its peak, the prison could take over 200 prisoners, but this diminished until, in 1879, it accommodated a mere twenty-two

Fort Clarence Tower, Rochester.

prisoners, attended by a staff of nine. Any soldier stationed in the area whose misbehaviour was deemed to have earned him a flogging (and this was the punishment for many comparatively minor offences) would be marched through the town down to the fort to receive his punishment. On his return he would be permitted to simply slip his tunic over his shoulders for the return to his barracks, as his back would be too lacerated and sore to bear the rub of the rough serge.

In 1924, the bridge and gatehouse taking the Borstal Road over the ditch were demolished in order to allow the road to be widened, and the ditch at this point filled in with the rubble to replace the bridge. The fort ceased to be used as a 'glasshouse' in the early 1930s and became a Territorial Army centre. In 1940 the 33rd Battalion (Short Brothers) Kent Home Guard moved in for the duration of the Second World War.

After many years lying derelict, the fort was taken over by the GPO. However, Fort Clarence House was used to house senior army officers until 1974, when the GPO took over this as well. Most of the fort was demolished to make room for a new British Telecoms engineering works, although a bid to demolish the house as well failed, as this was a listed building. The tower passed into the hands of English Heritage, who transferred ownership to a firm of private developers who converted the tower into flats, although the site remains a scheduled ancient monument.

When the next invasion fear arose in the mid-nineteenth century, the government, under Prime Minister Lord 'Firebrand' Palmerstone, embarked on yet another extensive review of the nation's defences, with the result that a further ring of five forts was built in the Medway Towns, generally looping around the southern approaches to the conurbation and outside the existing Napoleonic defences. These comprised forts Borstal, Bridgewood, Horsted, Luton and Darland. Military opinion as to the usefulness of these forts was divided, leading to these, and other similar defensive structures, being referred to as 'Palmerstone's Follies'. It would seem likely that improvements in the range of gunnery had rendered these forts obsolete as soon as they were completed.

One of the first of these new forts, and by far the largest, was **Fort Horsted**. The Fort was built in 1870 on land near where the present A228 joins the A229, adjacent to the former Mid-Kent College complex, and some 3 miles from Chatham dockyard. Named after the iconic Jutish warrior chief, Horsa (see Chapter 3), Fort Horsted was built using convict labour from the newly opened prison at Borstal, supervised by specialist officers from the Royal Engineers. The central tunnel and casemates were constructed of brick covered with several feet of solid concrete, and the whole surrounded by a 30-foot-deep ditch. The shape of the fort is a six-sided arrowhead, with the point facing southwards, and was designed for a garrison of some 400 men. Its armament was listed as eight 8-inch howitzers, four 6.5-inch howitzers, twelve 20-pounder RBLs (rifled breech-loaders), thirteen 64-pounder RMLs and twelve 32-pounder smooth bore breech-loading guns.

Once the fort was completed in 1889, it was the central garrison and store for the construction of Fort Luton and Fort Bridgewood. During the First and Second World Wars, the fort was used for the manufacture and storage of ammunition, and during the Second World War it also housed an anti-aircraft battery using 3.7-inch and Bofors guns.

The fort was demilitarized in the early 1960s and sold off, after which it had a number of commercial, industrial and local government occupiers. An application to demolish the fort to make way for housing was rejected, the fort being deemed an ancient monument of great local interest. In 1976, the fort was owned by a tyre remoulding firm when an enormous fire broke out, after which the fort rapidly deteriorated until English Heritage and the Environment Agency agreed to a proposal to develop the site into a number of small business units in 1997. As the proposal safeguarded the historic nature of the fort, the normal stringent rules were relaxed and work was allowed to go ahead. The site was cleared of the accumulated rubbish, and the Fort Horsted Business Centre opened six units in April 2007.

Fort Darland was built at the same time as Fort Horsted and on similar lines. It was intended to have a garrison of around seventy men and be armed with six 9-pounder guns. Completed in 1900, it was already obsolete and surplus to defensive requirements by 1910, and was used as an Army Technical School until 1914 when the 1st Battalion of the Middlesex Regiment was stationed there. During the First World War, Lance Corporal Walter Beard of the Royal Engineers was awarded the Albert Medal (the precursor of the George Medal) following an incident with a grenade. Between the two wars, the fort resumed its role as a training school until around 1940 when it was taken into use as a military detention centre or 'glasshouse'. It was during this time that the noble fort gained an ignominious reputation when two warrant officers of the Military Provost Staff Corps were charged with causing the death of one of the prisoners.

In 1943, an unlikely and recalcitrant soldier by the name of Rifleman William Clayton, nearly forty years of age, who suffered from chest troubles and was severely deaf, had been sentenced, not for the first time, to a period of detention. This was in fact his fourth period of detention and he was understandably regarded by the staff as a malingerer, a useless layabout who was trying to work his ticket. As such, the staff were prepared to give him a hard time and when he failed to keep up with the rest of the doubling inmates on the parade ground, Clayton was handed over to the regimental sergeant major and the quartermaster sergeant to be detained pending his appearance next day on a charge. When the breathless Clayton failed to keep up with these two warrant officers while being marched to the confinement cells, he was repeatedly slapped, punched and shaken. Nearly unconscious, the rifleman was eventually put in a wheelbarrow and trundled to the punishment block, where his condition began to worry his escort, who resorted to further violent methods to try to revive him, but he was certified dead before they had even got him into a cell. Rifleman Clayton's death was recorded as tuberculosis, aggravated by the violence of the two warrant officers, who were both charged with manslaughter and sentenced to imprisonment and reduced to the ranks. The incident caused a public uproar and the prime minister, Winston Churchill, ordered a full judicial enquiry that resulted in a much more humane, albeit strict, regime in all military prisons.

At the end of the war, the fort was relinquished by the War Office and was demolished in the 1960s to make way for a housing estate. Only some earthworks and encasement remain of this once proud but unutilized 'Palmerstone's Folly'.

There was a five- or six-year gap between the commencement of the construction of Fort Horsted and Fort Darland and that of the next two forts, Fort Borstal and Fort Luton.

It was not until 1875 that a start was made on the construction of **Fort Borstal**, the closest of the new forts to the River Medway and just a few yards from where the M2 Motorway now crosses the river. Commencement of the works was delayed pending the completion of the nearby convict prison, from whence the labour would be provided. It was not one of the forts recommended by the 1860 commission, but it was subsequently decided that another stronghold was needed on the high ground overlooking the river. Following the tradition of the time, Fort Borstal was an unequal pentagon in shape, with a longer loop-holed wall to the rear where the main entrance was situated and accommodation provided in casemates. There was a caponier at the gorge and counterscarp galleries at the centre and at each end of the front face. There were five expense magazines with the main magazines in the north-west portion of the fort. A dry ditch completely surrounds the fort.

It was completed in 1883, by which time the threat was over, and the fort was not armed until the Second World War. During and after the First World War, the fort was used to house troops, and as a TA centre whereby the fort's first aggressive role was assumed in 1940, when a battery of four 4.5-inch anti-aircraft guns were installed there. These were electronically fired simultaneously, resulting in an enormous bang and leading to an erroneous local belief that the fort was housing a 'Big Bertha' gun. It is claimed that these guns shot down six enemy aircraft in just twenty minutes during the Battle of Britain. In 1961, the fort, which is in a good state of preservation, became part of the nearby Borstal Institution, and was used as a pigsty and store. The fort was sold off in 2000 for £170,000, with a view to converting it into living accommodation, but this attracted strong local opposition as it is a scheduled ancient monument.

Fort Luton was built around the same time and on similar lines to Fort Borstal, although rather smaller in scale. It was not completed until 1892 and was never armed. During the Second World War, it was the anti-aircraft control centre for the Medway area. It was later taken over by the Kent County Council Education Department and finally sold off to a developer.

The last and most southerly of the forts to be built in the Medway Towns was **Fort Bridgewood**. Sited near what is now the M2 motorway and HMP Cookham Wood, work started in 1879 and took thirteen years to complete. It never saw any real action, although it sustained significant damage to the counterscarp in 1907 during a series of siege exercises carried out on several of the Medway forts. Unusually, the surrounding ditch was revetted with chalk blocks and flint. During the Second World War, it was the headquarters of the local Home Guard, ARP and Observer Corps, and in 1953, in the Cold War period, it was designated the Regional Seat of Government, but was disposed of in the 1960s and has since been demolished and built over in 1975.

Finally, **Grange Redoubt** and **Woodland Redoubt** were a pair of experimental infantry redoubts that were built close to where the present Grange Roundabout (B2004) now stands. Designed to be erected quickly and at low cost, they consisted of a palisade at the bottom of a ditch which could be raked by small arms fire from a firing step on a sloping glacis. Bombproof casemates were provided behind the firing step. Little, if anything, remains of these fortifications.

The Thames

The need to defend the access to London via the Thames river is obvious, but in earlier years the need was even more acute because of the importance of the installations along the mouth of the river: Woolwich Arsenal, Woolwich Dockyard, the Deptford stores and dockyard, the Purfleet powder magazines, and of course, the great congregation of shipping in the port of London itself. Due to its eminent strategic position, in 1539/40 two artillery blockhouses were built at **Gravesend** where the river narrows to around 800 metres. These were designed to provide crossfire in partnership with another blockhouse on the Essex side at Tilbury. Two further blockhouses were built some 5 kilometres downstream at Higham (Kent) and East Tilbury (Essex).

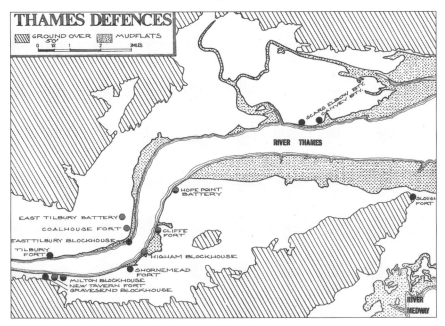

The nineteenth century Thames defences.

At the time of the Spanish Armada, the blockhouses at Gravesend and Tilbury were joined by a boom defence, consisting of hulks and other boats linked together by chains and anchored to the riverbed. A similar system was employed in 1667, when the Dutch brazenly sailed up the Medway and the lower reaches of the Thames.

After the excitement of the Dutch raid, although Tilbury Fort was substantially enlarged and improved, the Gravesend defences were left to decay for a century until, in 1780, a substantial new battery, the **New Tavern Fort**, was built further to the east of the old blockhouse, and a new line of gun emplacements was positioned along the riverbank between the two. In 1830, the old Gravesend blockhouse was demilitarized, full reliance being placed on the New Tavern Fort. This has a zig-zag earthen rampart bristling with fifteen heavy guns and fronted by a defensive ditch, the garrison being accommodated in a converted former inn, The New Tavern, which was itself a conversion of the medieval Chantry House.

A number of gun emplacements were also built in the 1790s on the Shorne Marshes to the east of Gravesend, to provide support for the New Tavern Fort. In the 1850s, one of these gun emplacements was converted to provide an additional, pentagonal fort. It was well placed, but there were considerable problems with the foundations. The intention to install thirteen 32-pounder guns on the roof had to be abandoned, and in the 1870s, eleven rifled muzzle-loading (RML) guns of 11-inch calibre and three 9-inch RMLs were mounted in an annexed up-river battery. The fort was deemed incapable of withstanding an attack in 1904, and the guns were removed – although two 5.5-inch guns were installed temporarily during the Second World War. It lies on a military firing range and has now been largely demolished by the Royal Engineers on exercises.

Despite these difficulties, during the nineteenth century the defences were principally provided by the New Tavern Fort and the **Shornemead battery** on the Kent side of the river, together with the large batteries on the Essex side at Tilbury Fort and Coalhouse Point.

Further down the river from Shornemead lies the well-preserved remains of **Cliffe Fort**, which was the only entirely new fort built in this area in the latter half of the nineteenth century. Lying directly opposite the Coalhouse Fort, about 1 kilometre across the river in Essex, Cliffe Fort suffered the same constructional problems as that at Shornemead, and here too it proved impracticable to mount the guns on the roof. Its main claim to fame was as a Brennan torpedo station towards the end of the century. The Brennan torpedo was invented by the Irish-American Louis Brennan and became the 'state-of-the-art' coastal defence weapon between 1887 and 1903. The torpedo had two propellers, turned by wires that were attached to winding

Cliffe Fort.

machines on the shore station and which played out after the torpedo was fired. By varying the speed at which the wires were extracted, the torpedo could be steered by the operator on shore. The only extant example of this device is in the Royal Engineers' Museum in Chatham. Although never fired in anger, the Cliffe Brennan Torpedo did succeed in sinking a ship when a practice torpedo struck and sank a small ketch.

The derelict fort is now owned by a private aggregate works and is not open to the public, although it is possible to walk around the outside. The launching rails used to guide the torpedo from the fort into the river can still be seen.

Further out into the Thames Estuary, a new fort was built between 1860 and 1868 at Allhallows-on-Sea on the northern edge of the Hoo Peninsular. Semi-circular in shape and known as the **Slough Fort**, it had casemates for seven 7-inch RMLs and provision for further guns on the roof. There was accommodation for three officers, an NCO and seventy men. Enthusiasm seems to have waned as time passed and more peaceful times were anticipated, so the fort appears never to have been fully finished. The iron shields for the guns were never fitted, although, as late as 1895, two wing batteries were added for barrel-loading guns on hydro-pneumatic disappearing carriages.

Slough Fort would seem to have been one of the first of the 'Royal Commission' forts to have been abandoned, and records show it to have been sold off in 1929. It is now used as a riding school.

Semaphore stations

From the very earliest time, the problem of how to pass messages and warnings over possibly long distances, especially in the event of an attack, has taxed the brains of military tacticians. Even as late as the Second World War, church bells were to be used in the event of an invasion and sirens to announce the impending arrival of enemy aircraft, even though wireless telegraphy and radio telephony were commonly available.

The most common of the early solutions was some form of beacon or signal fire, arranged ideally in a chain so that a message could be passed over great distances if need be. All visual signals have the disadvantage of requiring reasonable conditions of visibility, and the early burning beacons could be extinguished by heavy rain, but on the whole they proved reasonably successful in warning, for example, of the approach of the Spanish Armada in 1588. But beacons could only warn of a given situation, such as an attack or invasion; they were either alight or not. It was a question of yes or no, on or off, and nothing more sophisticated was possible until the end of the eighteenth century, when the French invented the idea of using levered semaphore signals to convey a range of simple messages. A drawing of such a device was found on a French prisoner of war in 1794, and the concept was quickly adopted and adapted by the Royal Navy. A range of towers were constructed between Plymouth and Yarmouth, capable of spelling out simple messages by a combination of flags and balls, the object being 'to convey ... to the Commanding Officers at the ports to HM Ships on the coast such information as may be discovered of such of the enemy's ships as may be discovered for any of the said stations.'

But it was soon evident that something more sophisticated was called for, and in response to a call from the Admiralty, two clerical gentlemen, the Reverend John Gamble and the Reverend Lord George Murray, submitted alternative designs for a system of shutter telegraph (as opposed to a semaphore system).

It was Lord Murray's work that held the attention of the Admiralty. This consisted of six, 3-foot square shutters arranged in two columns. These shutters could be opened or closed like a Venetian blind by means of ropes, the various combinations spelling out the letters of the alphabet or numbers.

Fifteen of these signal towers were erected in 1795/6 between London and Deal, with a branch connecting Sheerness to Beacon Hill near Faversham. So far as Kent was concerned, the line ran via Swanscombe, Higham, Lower Halstow, Beacon Hill, Selling, Barham Downs and Betteshanger to the Deal Navy Yard. The branch line ran from Beacon Hill via Tonge and Queenborough to Sheerness.

This comparatively sophisticated system had its drawbacks: visibility was hampered by fog, mist or heavy rain, and these also caused the shutters to warp and stick. High wind could also be a problem, but despite these drawbacks it was a reasonably reliable and fast system. The news of the execution of Peter Parker, the ringleader of the Nore Mutiny, was passed from Sheerness to London in six minutes.

With the end of the Napoleonic threat, the order for the closure of the stations between London and Sheerness, Chatham and Deal was issued in 1814, but soon afterwards the need for a permanent, peacetime signalling system was recognized. By this time the semaphore system had been improved and two alternative proposals were put forward: one by Major (later General Sir) Charles Pasley (the founder of the Royal School of Military Engineering at Chatham) and the other, a somewhat similar scheme, was submitted by Rear Admiral Sir Home Riggs Popham. The compromise solution was for a single 30-foot post with two 8-foot-long arms at differing heights.

The route for these semaphores was largely the same as the previous system, with an additional one at Hartshill between Swanscombe and Higham. The original site for the Chatham machine was in Brompton, but, because smoke tended to obscure it from the dockyard, it was later re-sited on the Great Lines. The use of such visual means of communication was not regarded by the Admiralty as a necessity following the definitive defeat of Napoleon, but part of the system remained operative for a time, mainly used by the customs and excise service. It was eventually supplanted in the middle of the nineteenth century by the introduction of Samuel Finley Breese Morse's invention of the electric telegraph and the Morse code.

The Volunteer Army

Throughout the latter part of the eighteenth century, Britain was very much preoccupied with her present and former possessions overseas. A large number of troops were engaged in keeping the peace in India and other colonial dependencies, while the recent revolutions in France and in America were causing considerable concern. With the army stretched to its limit, the defence of the realm rested largely in the hands of the county militias – a rag-tag bunch of poorly trained and ill-equipped part-time soldiers, selected by ballot to serve for five years. As unwilling conscripts, these militiamen were noted for their lack of discipline and lackadaisical attitude towards their responsibilities and duties. So concerned were the authorities that, in 1794, the Volunteer Act was passed, calling upon *gentlemen of weight or property* to form volunteer units to defend the kingdom. These could be infantry, cavalry or artillery companies.

The élite cavalry units, the *Gentleman* or *Yeoman Cavalry*, were largely composed of rural gentry commanding self-financing middle-class volunteers, wearing Light Dragoon-style uniforms and armed with pistols and curved, light sabres. Troops were formed in Elham and Lydd, which combined with others to form the East Kent Yeomanry.

The volunteer infantry and artillery units wore uniforms similar to those of the regular regiments, and like the Home Guard in 1940, they were at first armed with whatever weapon they could lay their hands on, be it pitch-fork, spade, sword or musket. Units were formed throughout Kent, including troops in Folkestone, Hythe, Lydd and New Romney, which later joined together to form the Cinque Ports Volunteers.

In 1799 a huge parade of the county's volunteers was held in Mote Park, Maidstone, attended by 6,000 yeomanry and volunteers. King George IV and the Royal Family, together with William Pitt, the prime minister, and other members of the government, attended this prestigious event, while 20,000 citizens enjoyed a picnic and watched the spectacle.

Apart from the mounted yeomanry, the volunteers were briefly stood down after the Peace of Amiens in March 1802, but were reformed when relations deteriorated in May 1803 and a new wave of volunteerism swept the country. This was encouraged by the government, which threatened a compulsory *levée en masse* if sufficient volunteers were not forthcoming, resulting in men volunteering to become soldiers to avoid being conscripted!

Such was the fear of a French invasion that, by 1804, there were nearly 400,000 men under arms in Britain, but once the immediate threat declined so did the governmental support for the volunteer movement, and funding dried up. By 1815, all the volunteer infantry units had been disbanded, although much of the cavalry continued and formed the basis of today's Territorial Army. In May 1837, 600 volunteers from the East and West Kent Regiments of Yeomanry Cavalry took part in a review in Mote Park, Maidstone, to celebrate the accession of Queen Victoria.

The somewhat fragile relations that had existed between France and England during the Crimean War deteriorated once more in 1858, when an Italian named Felice Orsini made an assassination attempt on the life of Napoleon III. It was known that Orsini had hatched his plan and made his bombs whilst in England, and the French suspected that the British government was somehow implicated, resulting in the concept of a volunteer force being raised anew. Earl Sydney, the Lord Lieutenant of Kent, together with some other county lieutenants, was authorized to form a rifle volunteer corps and an artillery volunteer corps, under the still valid Volunteer Act of 1804. The force would only be called out 'in case of actual invasion' or certain similar situations, when members would receive normal army pay and allowances. They were to provide their own weapons and equipment and meet their own costs. (Although volunteers had to pay for their personal firearms, these were supplied through the War Office to ensure standardization of gauge.)

A large number of enthusiastic civilians joined these units in a fever of patriotism and fear of invasion. Butts were erected in many towns where the volunteers could practice musketry under the eye of regular army instructors, and regular drill parades were held. But the danger was soon past and official support for the volunteers waned once more. A few units continued under their own steam but were subjected to a great deal of ridicule from the other citizens. Marching behind their band through the streets to the drill ground, the town urchins would follow them, calling out various unkind remarks. According to Earl Brownlow, a former Secretary of State for War, writing in the *North American Review* in 1900:

> Once the battalion had reached the drill ground and deployed into line, the gamins formed line opposite them, waiting, like the French line at Fontenoy, for the English to fire first. Then, as the rattle of the locks proclaimed the volley which terminated the exercise, they fell down with shrieks and groans and writhed in simulated agony of death on the battlefield, while the onlookers shouted with pleasure at the performance.

Volunteers saw service in the Second Boer War, and in 1907 the Volunteer Force and the Yeomanry merged to form the Territorial Army. Throughout its lifetime (1861–1907) the Volunteer Force had an effective strength of around 250,000 and would no doubt have played a significant role in repelling any invasion attempt.

Chapter 8

First World War (1900–1920)

The period covering the last quarter of the nineteenth century and the first decade or so of the twentieth was not lacking in British military ventures: troops were involved in battles and winning gallantry medals in Abyssinia, Afghanistan, the Andaman Isles, Assam, Baluchistan, Basutoland, Bhutan, Burma, Canada, China, Egypt, the Gambia, Ghana, Malaya, Manipur, Matabeleland, New Zealand, the North-west frontier, Persia, Peshawar, Rhodesia, South Africa, the Sudan, Tibet and Zululand. Was it perhaps the blood spilt by these men that justified colouring the British Empire on contemporary maps in red?

But these were all battles fought far away across the seas and generally had little effect on the daily routine of the 'man on the Clapham omnibus'. As we have seen, for centuries Britain in general and Kent in particular had been worried about some foreigner or other landing on our shores, but this possibility was far from the minds of the people as the new century dawned. Things were beginning to change, however, as the war clouds gathered over Europe. As early as 1905, the tension between Great Britain and Germany had become so serious that Major General Reginald Hart, VC, the former commandant of the School of Military Engineering at Chatham, was given the task of overhauling the Thames and Medway defences which will be covered below.

The origins of the First World War (or the 'Great War' as it was known at the time and up until the commencement of the Second World War) are, as is the case with most conflicts, very complex. The assassination of Archduke Ferdinand in Sarajevo on 28 June 1914 was simply the flashpoint for various grievances, imperial ambitions and other festering problems throughout Europe. So far as Britain was concerned, it was the violation by Germany of Belgium's neutrality that brought her into the escalating conflict, and on 3 August 1914 Great Britain declared war on Germany. Less than three weeks later, the British Expeditionary Force was in action at Mons, where they halted an enemy more than twice their size.

Other battles followed, and by November 1914 the two sides were entrenched along what was to become known as the Western Front, stretching nearly 500 miles from Dunkirk on the Channel coast to the Vosges Mountains. Very little change took place along this line for the next four years, despite some determined assaults by both sides. The trenches were deeply dug, and barbed wire, snipers and machine guns discouraged any movement. Constant shelling coupled with heavy rain turned the countryside into a quagmire; in places the mud was deep enough for a man to drown in it.

Any ambitions the Kaiser might have had to invade England were stifled by this virtual stalemate. Yet despite this, there was always the possibility of the Germans launching an invasion or a significant raid in order to relieve the pressure on the Western Front (especially in 1915), and so precautions were naturally taken to oppose any such action. In fact, despite the pressing need for more troops in France, the British General Staff insisted on allocating four divisions of Territorial Army infantry and one of cavalry to the defence of the east coast.

Nevertheless, the public fear of invasion never reached the levels experienced in the Napoleonic era or, later, in the Second World War. What was new was the use of aircraft to take the war to the homeland of the enemy.

As in the previous chapter, the anti-seaborne landing precautions taken were centred largely on the Dover and Medway areas; indeed, considerable use was made of the forts and fortifications built or improved during the Napoleonic threat, but the time of the great Norman and Tudor castles and Napoleonic forts was long past. Henceforth, the anti-invasion measures would concentrate on 'pill boxes' (named after the small, circular containers in which pharmacists used to supply pills and tablets), coastal artillery batteries, and certainly in the First World War, a series of trench-based field fortifications and earthworks, emulating those in use on the Western Front.

Dover was immediately designated a prohibited area into which no one was allowed without a permit, and a chain of field fortifications was constructed. These field redoubts were initially provided with a bombproof cover, but experience on the battlefields led to these being removed and the defences limited to trench systems. In addition, a number of field-gun emplacements were provided. In all, according to a map held in the National Archives (Public Record Office), there were some thirty field redoubts, trench systems and gun emplacements in the Dover area, of which little or nothing remains. Very few permanent defences were constructed during this period, apart from a number of concrete pill boxes, like the one at Fort Burgoyne (within the military barracks), which appears to be the only one still standing.

The artillery at Fort Burgoyne was removed in 1906 and replaced by Vickers machine guns, three in the fort itself and three in the wing redoubts, making it a defensible barracks and a base for mobile guns, rather than a permanent defence. During the First World War, further brick gun emplacements were constructed at the fort.

At Archcliffe Fort, some small, quick-firing guns were installed to prevent the enemy taking shelter under the cliff face. With no regular army garrison available, the fort was manned by a company of the 1st Volunteer Battalion of the Buffs, who provided two NCOs and nine privates each day. Above the fort, St Martin's Battery on the Western Heights was used in the First World War (and in the Second), as it commands unrivalled views of the harbour and the town. It was reached from the Grand Shaft stairway by way of the St Martin's steps. When German submarines attempted to enter Dover harbour in December 1914, they were met with a determined barrage from all the guns able to be used.

To the north of the county, a series of defences were constructed, known as the **Chatham Land Front**, divided into three main areas: The Isle of Grain; the Isle of Sheppey and along the ridge of the North Downs from Detling to Iwade; and following the main Maidstone to Sheppey road (A249). These defences included concrete pill boxes and barbed wire entanglements (much used on the Western Front), coastal artillery batteries and – a completely new innovation – anti-aircraft guns.

On the Isle of Grain, the defences closely resembled a section of the front line in France, being composed of a series of interconnected trenches, interspersed with pill boxes, machine gun nests and redoubts. The stretch of land between these earthworks and the sea was a mass of barbed wire. A battery was constructed at Whitehall Farm, intended to give crossfire across the Thames Estuary in conjunction with the already existing Grain Fort. The new battery's armament consisted of two 6-inch BLGs (breech-loading guns), while that of the fort was upgraded with two 4.7-inch quick-firing guns to protect the new Medway Boom, stretching across the Medway Estuary from the fort to the Garrison Point Fort, which would impede enemy submarines.

Across the estuary, on the Isle of Sheppey, similar entrenchments were made from Garrison Point at Sheerness in the northwest, as far as Shellness at the southeastern tip of the island – a distance of about 12 miles. Along its length there were fourteen redoubts and sixteen concrete pill boxes armed with Vickers or Lewis machine guns. Due to the nearby airfield, an entrenchment virtually enclosed the village of Eastchurch, to be manned by Royal Flying Corps men in the event of a landing. A further RFC defensive system, including machine guns in pill boxes, covered the Leysdown airfield.

At Fletcher's Battery (built in 1900, just north of the present Eastchurch caravan sites complex), a large, concrete underground redoubt was constructed and the existing battery augmented by two 9.2-inch BLGs. The Coastguard Station at Shellness was also converted into a machine gun nest, and the Shellness Battery's two 6-inch BLGs would thwart any attempted landing northwards up the coast towards Leysdown. At this point the island's defence lines joined up with the beginning of the Chatham Land Front via a pontoon bridge over the River Swale at South Marshes, near Kingsferry, and the main road bridge between the island and the mainland.

Sheerness itself was already well covered by coastal artillery on Garrison Point and elsewhere around the town, and other emergency batteries were constructed along the coastline at places such as Scrapsgate, Merryman's Hill, Pump Hill and Warden Point, using 6-inch BLGs or converted 18-pounder field guns.

On the mainland, a series of trenches and earthworks ran from Iwade to Keycol Hill, and other advanced works were sited at Key Street (A2), Chestnut Street (A249) and Oad Street, near Borden. From Keycol Hill, southwards along the line of the A249 to the top of Detling Hill, the defences closely resembled Flanders Field, with interconnecting trenches interspersed with strong points and redoubts at Keycol Hill (A2), Wormdale Farm (Newington), Danaway, Beauxaires Farm (1 mile north of Detling airfield), Stockbury Church Wood, Thrognal Farm near Hartlip and on Detling Hill, the pivot of the whole line. These were in addition to the pill boxes and earthworks set up to protect Detling airfield itself.

The pill boxes provided along this stretch of the line were of three types: those at Detling airfield were rectangular concrete ones with embrasures to facilitate the use of machine guns; those in Beauxaires Wood consisted of five elliptical concrete pill boxes housing Vickers .303 machine guns with restricted vertical field of fire; between Stockbury and Keycol there were widely spaced, partly buried square boxes made of brick and concrete and designed for rifle use.

In the Chatham Dockyard area, a large number of very small, virtually one-man, ten-sided pill boxes were built around the dockyard and the Naval hospital. These pill boxes, which were of a design unique to Naval establishments, were sealed by a concrete door and had three or four embrasures through which small arms could be fired. Completely surrounding the main Naval magazine at Chattenden, there was a complex system of six redoubts, linked by a series of trenches and combined with various obstacles.

Measures to protect the **Thames** approach to London followed the historical pattern, with the forts, such as the New Tavern Fort at Gravesend, being upgraded and equipped with new and more powerful breech-loading guns, co-ordinated by a system of range-finding and fire-control. In fact, these were never called upon to repel a maritime assault, and instead attempted to cope with raids by Zeppelin air-ships and bomber aircraft.

Air raids

The early pioneers of heavier-than-air flight were probably blissfully ignorant of the belligerent use to which their inventions would be put. Less than a decade after the Wright brothers' historic flight in 1903, the admirals and generals were eagerly examining how these innovative machines could be used in warfare. As an Italian staff officer presciently observed in 1909:

> The sky is about to become another battlefield no less important than the battlefields on land and sea ... In order to conquer the air, it is necessary to deprive the enemy of all means of flying, by striking at him in the air, at his bases of operation or at his production centres. We had better get accustomed to this idea and prepare ourselves.

> (Giulio Douhet, quoted in E Bowen, *Knights of the Air*)

Not all senior officers were convinced, however, and many generals were still picturing magnificent cavalry charges like those of yesteryear. In Germany, the importance of heavier-than-air machines was overshadowed by the success of the Zeppelin airships, and Britain too was slow in getting off the mark, relying initially on the more advanced French technology. But the outbreak of the war led to an unprecedented advance in technology in respect of aircraft design and the engines used to power them. The flimsy, kite-like machines of 1914 evolved rapidly as the war went on and became an essential weapon of modern warfare. Kent was in the forefront of the early aviation experiments and the development and production of military aircraft. The Short brothers, in particular, were closely involved in the making of balloons, seaplanes and land-based aircraft. Eustace Short devoted his time to balloons and airships in Battersea, while brother Horace continued their work at Eastchurch on the Isle of Sheppey (where the Royal Aero Club was based). Oswald's interest lay in seaplanes, and he set up a factory on the banks of the Medway at Rochester Esplanade that was to become the firm's predominant site for many years to come. By the time the First World War broke out, the firm of Short Brothers was one of the country's main aviation manufacturers, and the flying boats it produced in the inter-war years, such as the Short Empire, formed the basis for the highly successful Sunderland flying boat in the Second World War, while the all-new Short Stirling bomber was made in a new factory at Rochester airport.

In the early days of the war, unarmed aircraft were used mainly on the battlefields for reconnaissance purposes and as artillery spotting platforms, and there are tales of opposing pilots waving to each other or exchanging chivalrous salutes, but this obviously had to change. It was soon realized that aircraft would be much more effective if they were fitted with machine guns or could carry bombs. Some pilots took to carrying a rifle or a pistol to try to kill or disable an enemy opponent, and some two-seater aircraft had a Lewis gun installed for the observer to use, but this was merely a defensive approach to the problem: to become a true, single-seat fighter, what was needed was a means of firing to the front without destroying the aircraft's propeller. A few early aircraft, such as the FB.5 and the FE.2b, had their engine and propeller behind the pilot, facing backwards, but such a design, although ideal for mounting a forward-facing machine gun, was, by its very design, slower and less manoeuvrable than a conventional one. Experiments were made with guns mounted above the top wing of a biplane, but these were difficult to get at for reloading or in the event of a stoppage. Captain Lanoe Hawker of the RFC mounted a Lewis gun forward of his cockpit, fixed to fire slightly to the left of the propeller, which proved sufficiently successful to earn him a Victoria Cross in July 1915. The German Fokker E.1 *Eindecker* (monoplane) was the first to successfully use a machine gun synchronized to fire through the propeller arc and thus be a true fighter aircraft. However, it was not long before the RFC and RNAS machines were also fitted with synchronized machine guns and were able to attack other aircraft or observation balloons.

As the country went to war, Kent set up defensive airfields at Bekesbourne, Detling, and Throwley near Faversham. The Royal Naval Air Service had its main seaplane station on the Isle of Grain, with another station at Westgate. Airship stations were located at Capel-le-Ferne, near Dover, and Kingsnorth near Rochester. Ferry landing strips were provided at Lympne, Hawkinge and Swingate, near Dover. An airstrip at St Mildred's Bay proved unsatisfactory, since the flimsy aircraft parked on the cliff edge had a habit of being blown over the edge into the sea in a high wind! A solution was found by making another airstrip at Manston.

The pressing need for pilots and observers, because of their high mortality rate, led to the construction of a number of training airfields in Kent, including Wye, Swingate, Dymchurch, Penshurst, Lydd, New Romney and Joyce Green (Dartford).

So far as bombing was concerned, the early military aircraft had no bomb racks or release mechanism and the first bombs were small devices, dropped by hand by the pilot or observer. The first 'bombing raid' on England occurred in December 1914 when two German aircraft dropped two bombs in Dover harbour, followed by another on Christmas Eve, 1914, when a single aircraft dropped a bomb which landed near Dover Castle, causing little damage and minor injuries to one man.

In fact, the only way for an otherwise unarmed aircraft to destroy a Zeppelin was to drop bombs on it from above! It was such an action that won Sub-Lieutenant Rex Warneford RNAS a VC in June 1915 when his Hales bombs destroyed a Zeppelin that was trying to return to its base in Belgium from an abortive raid on England. It was not long before more sophisticated methods of carrying and dropping larger bombs were devised.

Again, although primarily used as a tactical weapon on the Western Front, the Germans soon realized that bombing raids on England would damage public morale and could possibly lead to a shortening of the war. The Germans also had the advantage of a number of Zeppelins or airships which, although cumbersome and slow, were well-armed, and could carry a considerable bomb load and could fly long distances. Together with the Gotha bomber, these represented a very real danger and raids were soon made on London and other strategic towns and cities. The county of Kent was not to be spared, especially where poor conditions of visibility rendered the primary target invisible and the bombers' lethal cargo was dropped on secondary targets or simply jettisoned.

Although the military use of aircraft reached its apogee in the Second World War, Kent was affected much earlier. The first bomb to be dropped on Great Britain fell on Dover on Christmas Eve, 1914, blowing a gardener out of a tree and merely injuring his pride. A piece of this bomb was presented to King George V when he paid a visit to the town shortly afterwards. A further raid on Kent was made on 16 April 1915, when a solitary Albatros BII dropped bombs on Sittingbourne and Faversham, causing some damage and killing a blackbird! Other attacks were later made, by both aircraft and Zeppelin airships, on Ramsgate, Sittingbourne, Gravesend, Dover, Margate and other places, causing damage and a number of casualties, including several children killed in Ramsgate. By 1916, such was the intensity of Zeppelin attacks that the RFC had to pull some of its squadrons from the front line in France to help defend the UK.

But the most disastrous of these incursions occurred on Friday 25 May 1917, when twenty-three Gotha G bombers (the first bomber aircraft to be used for strategic bombing) took off from their airfields in Belgium, heading for London via the Essex coast. On arrival over London, the raiders found, to their great disappointment, that the capital was under heavy cloud cover and they were unable to see their targets. Frustrated, they turned for home, and flying at an estimated 14,000 feet, found that the cloud cover disappeared as they flew southwards. Following the main railway line to the Channel ports, the bombers dropped high-explosives at various points along the way: Luddesdown, Linton, Marden, Pluckley, Smarden and Bethersden, causing little damage in these country parishes and killing just one sheep. Ashford offered a much more tempting target: the extensive and important railway works. Six bombs were dropped, but all missed the railway, although one girl was killed – the first fatality of the raid.

Having split into two wings, half the Gotha bombers dropped their load on Kingsnorth, Shadoxhurst and Mersham, while the other half attacked the Royal Military Canal and dropped several bombs on the Romney Marsh, before turning their attention to Lympne airfield. Little damage was caused and the planes droned on over Hythe, where two more fatal casualties were caused. Following the coast, the aircraft dropped further bombs on Sandgate, before heading inland a little to attack Shorncliffe military camp. Here matters took a more serious turn as the German bombs killed seventeen Canadian soldiers and one British 'Tommy'. Moving on to the nearby Folkestone suburb of Cheriton, bombs caused a further three fatalities. And now it was the turn of Folkestone itself – the climax of the raid.

Unlike during the Second World War, this country was ill-prepared for air attacks and no warning system had been set up. Communications were poor, relying on manually operated telephone switchboards and telegraph systems, and so no one in Folkestone was aware of the drama that had been unfolding over the county in the past hour or so.

A few distant explosions had been heard, but these were put down to the troops training at Shorncliffe Camp. These noises gradually came nearer until the Gothas were overhead and the true horror began. The first bombs fell in the West End of the town and around the Central Station, killing a total of four people. The second salvo killed another man. Eight bombs were dropped in the town centre, killing a further six.

In the early part of the twentieth century, the main shopping area of the town was in and around Tontine Street, and this being a Friday – pay day – the street was busy with shoppers and people simply strolling around the town, enjoying the warm early-summer evening. In those days it was normal for shops to be open well into the evening, and so, when the bombers arrived over the town at 6.22 pm, the scene was set for a catastrophe. Several of the shops had queues outside them, with war-weary housewives hoping to purchase some rare commodity such as the potatoes that were reported to be available at Stokes' large greengrocers shop.

Just two bombs fell in Tontine Street, one of which failed to explode (like many others during this raid). The other bomb, however, was a very different matter and took the lives of no less than sixty-one people. This bomb scored a direct hit on the greengrocers, the roof of which collapsed, killing forty-four customers and staff instantly, while a further seventeen later died in hospital. The victims were almost all women and children whose bodies were horribly mangled, some simply blown apart; severed limbs jostled with the carcases of horses among the rubble and debris, while the pathetic cries of mortally injured animals added to the horrific turmoil and uproar.

The German planes then moved on towards their prime target, Dover, but here a warm welcome awaited them. Six army gun batteries opened up on them, as did a number of naval vessels in the harbour, and three planes from the Royal Naval Air Service took off to do battle with the 'cultured Hun'. The raid on Dover was abandoned and the Gothas headed for home, harried all the way by British aircraft and shipping, a number of the raiders being destroyed or damaged on the way.

In all, ninety-six people, mainly civilians, were killed during this raid and nearly 200 seriously injured. Seventy-two of the fatalities occurred in Folkestone alone.

But soon Kent was in a better position to protect itself. Having been very much to the fore in the earliest experiments with heavier-than-air machines, especially at Eastchurch on the Isle of Sheppey, it was not surprising that there were some forty-five airfields available in Kent during the period from 1915 to 1918. From these, using tactics developed on the Western Front and equipped with modern weapons systems, fighter aircraft were ready to meet the incoming enemy and prevent him from reaching the capital. Some of these airfields, such as those at Joyce Green (Dartford), Detling, Throwley (Faversham), Bekesbourne (Canterbury) and Wye were built where they could provide patrols to cover the approaches to London. Others, simple fields, were designated Emergency Landing Grounds (ELGs) where our aircraft in difficulty could make an emergency landing, especially at night, when a flare path would be lit.

As soon as incoming raiders were reported, every available aircraft capable of flying took off, not only from Royal Flying Corps and Royal Naval Air Service bases but also from training establishments and works' air fields as well. Once in the air, they were in a position to give a good account of themselves and defend Kent and London from predatory Germans, but on the ground they were naturally sitting ducks. In the event of not all the aircraft being able to get airborne, reliance had to be placed on a number of anti-aircraft batteries that were sited on or around the county's airfields in view of their vulnerability.

But it was not only the airfields that were protected: anti-aircraft batteries sprang up everywhere, using adapted, and later dedicated, artillery weapons. Because of the novelty of air warfare, no anti-aircraft guns as such had been produced by the time war broke out in 1914, and so a range of other artillery pieces were adapted for this purpose. The whole area around the Chatham Dockyard was dotted with small, purpose-built anti-aircraft battery emplacements, using 1-pounder quick-firing guns and short-barrelled 3-inch guns. These were in addition to the 'ring of fire' represented by the Chatham Land Front batteries.

The Royal Navy bunkering depot on Grain was protected from air attack by the Port Victoria AA battery's 3-pounder quick-firing guns, although this installation was badly damaged in 1915 when the *Princess Irene*, a former Canadian Pacific liner that had been converted to a mine-layer, blew up while anchored just off Port Victoria Pier with the loss of 273 lives. Apart from the whole crew (bar one) and a number of dockyard workers, the explosion killed three civilians on shore, including a nine-year-old girl.

Observer Corps

The defence against air raids, whether directed at military and naval targets or against the civilian population on the 'shock and awe' principle, must always be reliant on an efficient means of advanced warning. Once the bombers arrive, it is too late to order the fighters into the air, and the anti-aircraft gunners are as likely to be enjoying a 'char and a wad' in the Salvation Army canteen as sitting alert at the controls of their guns. The government recommendations in 1915 were not a great help, suggesting that:

> If you see an aeroplane or airship, try and note these points. Run to the nearest telephone, call up anti-aircraft London and commence your message with these words: Aircraft Report. You then proceed to give your information in the following order . . .

There followed a long list of questions, to have answered which would have taken so long the raid would have been over before the report was complete. It was clear that a fast and reliable system of reporting the approach of enemy aircraft was urgently needed, and so Major General Edward B Ashmore, CB, CMG, MVO, a former RFC pilot, was appointed to devise an improved system of detection, communication and control. His solution took the form of the Metropolitan Observation Service (MOS), encompassing the London Air Defence Area and subsequently extended eastwards towards the Kent and Essex coasts. This comprised a national system of observers and some 200 observation posts to report the impending arrival of Zeppelins. Initially manned by army personnel, these were soon replaced by members of the Special Constabulary and the posts organized into areas with telephone contact with the anti-aircraft batteries or airfields with which they were associated. By 1917, bomber aircraft were superseding the huge and cumbersome Zeppelins, and although the MOS had some success, it did not become fully operational until the summer of 1918, and the last German raid on England took place in May of that year. However, the experience gained and the lessons learned were to prove invaluable in the formulation of arrangements for the future, and the MOS is generally accepted as the forerunner of the Royal Observer Corps, of which much more in the next chapter.

Sound Detection Systems

It was during the First World War that the first serious experiments were made into the detection of enemy aircraft by acoustic means. Some involved the use of a device that resembled a battery of hearing trumpets, while another more successful experiment used a system of 'fixed sound mirrors'.

First World War listening device.

The fixed sound mirror (which was defined as 'one in which the reflecting surface remains fixed in position, and the direction of the source of sound is found by means of a moveable arm carrying a sound collector') was operated by a listener who stood in front of it with a sound collector that had a trumpet-shaped end which acted as a microphone, and stethoscope earpieces through which the operator could hear the amplified engine noise. The sound collector was moved about the surface of the mirror until the aircraft sound was at its loudest, when a quite accurate bearing could be taken.

The first of these devices was in the form of a simple concave dish, 15 feet in diameter, carved into the hillside at the top of the cliff at Fan Bay, Dover. Originally faced with puddled chalk, this proved unsatisfactory, and the mirror was later relined with 6 inches of rendered concrete. Another, similar mirror was also sited at Joss Bay in Thanet.

As is so often the case, these mirrors were introduced too late in the war to be of much use, but the development of these, and other similar devices, continued during the inter-war years and will be examined in more detail in the next chapter.

Chapter 9

Second World War (1920–1945)

I have, myself, full confidence that ... we will prove ourselves once again able to defend our island home, to ride out the storm of war, and to outlive the menace of tyranny, if necessary for years, if necessary alone. At any rate, that is what we are going to try to do.

(Winston Churchill to the House of Commons, 4 June 1940)

Following the euphoria that marked the end of the 'Great War' of 1914–18, the populace looked forward to a promised period of 'peace in our time'. The 'war to end all wars' had been fought and won – albeit at an enormous cost in terms of lives and money. But, despite all these slogans and joyful expectations, there were some who were not prepared to lower the country's defences below an acceptable and prudent level. Quietly and with a minimum of publicity, the groundwork for the defence of the realm in the event of another war was laid.

Apart from the Air Raid Precautions (of which more later), experience over the centuries had shown that the usual precautions against a sea-borne invasion of Britain by some foreign power should always be maintained, at least at a minimum level. Political developments in Europe in the 1930s clearly demonstrated the value of this, as Adolf Hitler progressed from Chancellor in 1933 to outright dictator the following year. Germany began unlawfully to remilitarize and the Nazi forces started sabre-rattling. Between 1934 and 1936, the assassinations of the Austrian Chancellor and Alexander of Yugoslavia, followed by the Spanish Civil War, underlined the precarious political situation in Europe.

As early as 1934, Dr Ewald Banse, seen by some as the *éminence grise* of German military doctrine, published a book in which, although the main thrust of his plan for the conquest of England ('that proud and seemingly invincible nation ...') involved landings on the east coast, he also suggested that:

To get an army across the Channel to the Kent coast should prove a relatively simple business, particularly if the attacker is in possession of the French ports of Dunkirk, Calais and Boulogne, from which he can clear the Channel of English ships with artillery.

Although the (as yet) militarily unprepared Germany strongly repudiated this hypothesis, it was no doubt firmly lodged in the minds of certain National Socialists.

In 1938, the Nazis organized the *Anschluss* of Austria, followed by the annexation of Bohemia and Moravia, and an anti-Polish press campaign was started, correctly seen by many as the prelude to an invasion. It was time for Britain to get ready to go on a war footing, and in 1939, Kent was not only a fortress against incursions into the county, as was the case in the very early years, but was a veritable and significant bulwark in the defence of the capital and thus of the country as a whole.

With the defeat of France and the ultimate retreat from Dunkirk, Winston Churchill summed up the situation in his famous speech in which he asserted that 'we shall fight them on the beaches, we shall fight on the landing grounds, we shall fight in the fields and in the streets, we shall fight in the hills: we shall never surrender.' As he added a fortnight later, 'If the British Empire and its Commonwealth last for a thousand years, men will still say, "This was their finest hour."' The question was: how were we going to thwart or resist this threatened invasion?

Fallschirmtruppe

In July 1940, Hitler issued his Directive No. 16, setting in motion the preparations for a landing in Britain, stating that 'as England, in spite of the hopelessness of her military position, has so far shown herself unwilling to come to any compromise, I have decided to begin to prepare for, and if necessary to carry out, an invasion of England.' This directive set four pre-conditions for the invasion to take place; the first and foremost of these was for the RAF to be 'beaten down in its morale and in fact, that it can no longer display any appreciable aggressive force in opposition to the German crossing.' And so, in Churchill's words, the Battle of France was over: the Battle of Britain was beginning.

However, it is interesting to see that, even at this stage of the war, Hitler was only just 'beginning to prepare for' an invasion of England. Had he begun his preparations earlier, while Britain was still largely unprepared for war, he may have had greater success.

If Hitler was slow to foresee the possibilities of invasion, there is no doubt that the British were slow in recognizing the form this might take. Despite the lessons of history and Dr Banse's comparatively recent hypothesis, there was a strong feeling that any invasion would take the form of a large-scale airborne attack. Although the Red Army was the first to form and train airborne troops, and caused a considerable stir in 1935 when they demonstrated a parachute drop at battalion strength, the Germans' use of airborne troops (*Fallschirmtruppe*) at widely different locations during the battles for France and the Low Countries in May 1940 seemed to come as a surprise to the Allies and had an almost hypnotic effect on the military thinking of the time. Britain had no such troops and it was directly resulting from this experience that Churchill immediately called for the formation of what was to become the Parachute Regiment. But it would be around two more years before this regiment became an effective and experienced fighting force.

Even when every Channel port north of the Somme was in Nazi hands, thus meeting Balse's criterion for a sea-borne invasion, the British were still obsessed with the idea of a mass airborne invasion, and Churchill wrote to Roosevelt on 15 May 1940, 'We expect to be attacked here ourselves, both from the air [bombing] and by parachute and airborne troops, in the near future and are getting ready for them.'

In fact, the German potential for an airborne attack was still very small. The number of trained parachutists was probably no more than 6,000–7,000 and the very limited number of gliders only carried eight men each. The number of operational Junkers 52 transport aircraft was probably a few hundred and there was even a serious shortage of parachutes. In any event, a solely airborne invasion would have been seriously hampered by the lack of transport, armoured vehicles and artillery if it had no support from a beachhead.

Although the handful of Nazi airborne troops had enjoyed considerable success in the Low Countries, they had nevertheless suffered heavy casualties, and their commanders realized that an attack on Britain after Dunkirk, when the country was prepared and geared up to oppose it, was an entirely different proposition from a sneaky drop on a Sunday morning on what was technically still a neutral country.

Operation Sea Lion

Accepting that an invasion could only succeed if large numbers of troops could be quickly landed on the shores of England, the most obvious landing place would be in Kent or Sussex. This supposition was later borne out by the discovery of the German plans for 'Operation Sea Lion' (*Unternehmen Seelöwe*) that showed that the Germans intended to land in 1940 on a wide front from Thanet to Portsmouth, but with emphasis on the more accessible shores of Kent and Sussex. For example, two divisions of the German 16th Army were to land between New Romney and Sandgate, where there was a

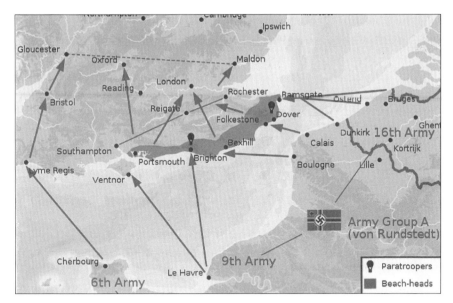

Operation Sealion.

gap in the cliffs, while the 7th Parachute Division would simultaneously land in the Elham Valley and Lyminge area, between the RAF airfields at Lympne and Hawkinge. And so Kent found itself once more in the front line and had to present an impregnable fortress.

The Battle of Britain

When the Roman Legions went into battle they would form phalanxes with shield-bearers on all sides and other legionnaires holding shields over their heads so that the phalanx resembled an armadillo, impervious to the slings and arrows of the enemy. Southern Britain was a bit like that armadillo in 1940. The coastal gun batteries and the precautions against a seaborne landing (including the warships of the Royal Navy) formed a tight shield around our coastline, while the Royal Air Force provided the overhead shield. Both types of defence depended on the other, and as Hitler knew, should the RAF fail to control the skies of England, the nation would be wide open to an airborne landing against which the coastal defences would be helpless.

To destroy the overhead cover, August 1940 saw the Luftwaffe commence a series of concentrated air attacks on British aircraft, both on the ground and in the air. The Kentish airfields at Hawkinge, Manston, Detling, West Malling, Biggin Hill and elsewhere were subjected to concentrated and repeated bombing raids with the two-fold aim of rendering the airfield so badly damaged that friendly aircraft would be unable to land or take off, whilst also destroying as many aircraft on the ground as possible. The story of the Battle of Britain is too well known to be retold here, and it is sufficient to say that, with the combined efforts of the anti-aircraft guns and the British fighter aircraft, Hitler failed to achieve his first pre-condition for the invasion, and Operation Sea Lion was put on hold.

It was now that the training and organization of the Civil Defence service was to prove its worth, as concentrated and large-scale bombing raids on the towns and cities of Britain began. Of course, the main target was London, but virtually every bomber heading for the capital had to pass over Kent and run the gauntlet of the Kentish anti-aircraft and fighter plane defences. Some German planes limped back to their bases before reaching the capital but took the opportunity to unload their destructive cargo over Kent. Other bombers were specifically sent to attack targets in the county, and a couple of brief but very heavy raids left Canterbury in ruins. The Ashford railway works were targeted and places like Dover and Folkestone suffered both tip-and-run raids and cross-Channel shelling, making these two towns among the most frequently raided towns in Britain.

Were the Blitz and these air raids the prelude to the anticipated invasion, or were they simply an attempt to destroy the morale of the British and cause them to capitulate without an invasion being necessary? Certainly, with the ignominious fate of France and the Low Countries still very fresh in British minds, this was no time to drop our defences and simply bemoan our lot. As the posters exhorted us, we should 'Keep Calm and Carry On'.

Coastal Defences

Although many people in high places held an early, but erroneous, conviction that any invasion would come solely or mainly from the air, by parachutists or other airborne troops, others fortunately recognized that the main body of troops and the necessary logistical support would have to come by sea. Therefore, the primary target had to be the ships and landing craft that would bring them across the English Channel or along the Thames Estuary. In order to combat this, the traditional and ancient coastal strongpoints had to be restored, renovated and rearmed with modern weapons.

Almost one thousand years after it was first built, the great castle at Dover was once more pressed into action. Apart from providing perhaps the most critical of all the various control rooms in the castle's tunnels in 1940 (see later), the ancient gun emplacements were strengthened and made capable of use by the latest artillery guns, as indeed were those of various other castles and forts. Many of the Napoleonic defences were brought back into use for either coastal guns or anti-aircraft weapons. For example, shortly before the

Second World War, two twin 6-pounder guns were installed on the roof of Garrison Point Fort at Sheerness and one 6-pounder at the front. These weapons remained there until 1956.

At Fort Burgoyne, Dover, the artillery that was removed in 1906 and replaced by Vickers machine guns returned in the form of two batteries of 25-pounder field guns for which concrete emplacements were provided. Fort Burgoyne remains virtually unchanged today, but is out of bounds to the public, being within the confines of Connaught Barracks and therefore subject to tight security.

In nearby Folkestone, four 6-inch naval guns of First World War vintage were installed on the East Cliff, together with a number of Bofors anti-aircraft guns and a 6-pounder anti-tank gun, augmented by five spigot mortars. On the other side of the town, on the famous Leas cliff-top promenade, four 5.5-inch naval guns, recently removed from HMS *Hood*, were ready to repel the enemy while further Bofors guns protected the skies.

Further along the coast, an observation post was constructed on top of the east tower of Lympne Castle (now roofed over), which gave a fine, un-interrupted view across the Romney Marsh to the sea. The remains of Stutfall Castle, the defences erected by the Romans nearly two millennia ago, are clearly visible from the top of the tower.

Another reuse of an older defensive system involved the use of off-shore forts. A four-storey observation tower was built on the nineteenth-century base of the Grain Tower between Sheerness and the Isle of Grain, with an accommodation block for the crews of new 6-pounder anti-E-boat guns. This post remained armed and ready for action until 1956 when the Coastal Artillery Unit was disbanded. Meanwhile, the nineteenth-century Shornemead Fort near Gravesend was brought back into use as barracks for a nearby battery of two 5.5-inch guns. A number of the Napoleonic Martello Towers were used as observation posts or for anti-aircraft weapon emplacements.

We have already seen how the Grain Tower was erected in the 1860s at the entrance to the River Medway, followed by Hoo and Darnet forts built further upstream in 1871: now a whole range of new forts would be built to replace or supplement these ancient edifices. Unlike their predecessors, which were constructed in situ on an island, sandbank or spit of land, these 'Maunsell' forts, as they were known (after their designer, Guy Maunsell), were built on shore at Gravesend and then towed out to their chosen sites, where they were secured to the seabed by flooding the concrete pontoon base.

Four naval forts were constructed, together with three army ones, and were all sited off the Kent and Essex coasts. The naval forts each consisted of a single, large and compact unit and were intended for an anti-shipping

Tongue Sands Fort.

role. Only one of these really concerns Kent – the Tongue Sands Fort that was sited off Margate. This, like the other naval forts, was intended to prevent the Luftwaffe from laying mines in the estuary and to sink any E-boats trying to get up the Thames or attack coastal targets. It is claimed that the Tongue Sands Fort was successful in disabling and capturing a U-boat that was trying to torpedo it.

In common with the other naval forts, the Tongue Sands Fort consisted of a pair of hollow cylindrical concrete towers, each having an external diameter of 24 feet and reaching 60 feet in height, mounted on a reinforced concrete pontoon. A platform or deck was placed across the two towers, on each end of which a 3.75-inch gun was mounted directly over the top of each tower. In the centre of the deck, steel-walled compartments provided some accommodation and a galley, on top of which two 40mm Bofors light anti-aircraft guns were mounted. The hollow interior of the towers provided the main storage and accommodation space, the latter being brightly decorated and provided with central heating and forced-air ventilation.

The completed fort, including the pontoon on which it was built, was towed out to sea and sunk in the shallow waters of the estuary, only the tops of the two towers and the gun platform remaining visible above the waves. It is interesting to note that the successful building of these forts demonstrated the practicability of constructing the Mulberry harbour for D-Day. The Tongue Sands Fort collapsed in a storm in 1996.

The three army forts were quite different from the naval ones. Being essentially intended to house anti-aircraft batteries, each army fort consisted of seven separate towers, linked by walkways, and had the dual task of giving early radar warning of any enemy aircraft formations approaching London up the estuary and helping to destroy them as they arrived. They provided a more accurate radar service than that supplied by most land-based stations. These forts, known (from west to east) as the Nore (off Sheerness), Red Sands (about six miles off Minster, Sheppey) and Shivering Sands (off Herne Bay), were all well within sight of the north Kent coast.

In each case, of the seven separate towers that comprised an army fort, five were gun platforms, surrounding a central control and radar tower, with a slightly detached searchlight tower close by. Four of the towers were equipped with a 3.7-inch quick-firing gun, while a fifth held two Bofors 40mm anti-aircraft guns.

The construction of the army forts was totally different to that of the naval forts. Each tower consisted of a two-storeyed octagonal 'house' on four hollow legs, made from reinforced concrete, 3 feet in diameter and 65 feet long, securely attached to a submerged base structure. The gun tower and searchlight 'houses' provided accommodation and storage for the total establishment of 120 NCOs and men, the officers messing in the central control tower. In the course of the war, the forts shot down twenty-two aircraft and about thirty flying bombs between them. Afterwards, the forts

Shivering Sands Fort.

were decommissioned and the last military maintenance teams were with-drawn in the winter of 1958/9, following which they were put to a number of other uses.

In 1953, a ship collided with the Nore fort, destroying two of its towers. Much of the weaponry and equipment was lost, and four civilian workers lost their lives in this incident. The ruined fort was finally dismantled in 1959/60.

A similar fate befell one of the Shivering Sands towers, which was lost in 1963 when a ship collided with it. The following year the Port of London Authority used the isolated searchlight tower to set up a weather and tide monitoring station, and in 1990 the top of the tower was removed to provide a helicopter landing pad for use when maintaining the equipment.

Red Sands was one of several forts that were taken over by pirate radio operators. For a time it operated as Radio Invicta, the co-owner of which, Tom Pepper, an engineer and one of the disc jockeys, were all drowned when their launch, delivering supplies to the fort, capsized. Apart from adverse sea conditions, static electricity and lightning strikes were among the other perils facing the occupants of the fort. Other radio stations operating from here included Radio King and Radio 390.

In 1964, Screaming Lord Sutch set up a pirate radio station on one of the forts that was extended to include the other four towers which remained connected at that time, and broadcast as 'Radio City'. One of the towers was lost when another ship ran into it in bad weather, killing four people.

All these Thames Estuary forts are now in a dilapidated condition and generally deemed to be dangerous. Nevertheless, members of certain bodies still visit them to examine, record and photograph these relics of seventy-odd years ago.

The Boche Buster

One early innovation was the provision of an 18-inch Mark 1 howitzer on the Elham Valley railway line that ran between Folkestone and Canterbury. Mounted on an adapted First World War carriage, the complete gun and mounting weighed 243 tons, the gun itself coming in at 81 tons. Each shell weighed 1.25 tons and stood over 6 feet in height. As a result, a number of adaptations had to be made to the railway line to accommodate this huge weapon which quickly became known as the 'Boche Buster'. The largest gun ever seen at the time, it was secreted in a tunnel between Bridge and Bishopsbourne when not in use.

Installed in early 1941, it was intended that the Boche Buster would cover the coastline between Dungeness and St Margaret's Bay. Unlike the German big guns installed in Northern France, the Boche Buster was not capable of lobbing a shell across to the other side of the Channel and was never intended to do so; its role was purely an anti-invasion one.

The initial firing of this enormous piece took place in February 1941, as a result of which every window in the nearby village of Barham was broken. It was decided that the locals would be informed of any future tests so that they could make sure their windows were open. In fact, since Operation Sea Lion never took place, the gun was never fired in anger, although some of the test firings had unexpected consequences. On one occasion, a shell exploded prematurely over the Royal Marine Barracks at Deal. The following day a large piece of metal, weighing about 14 pounds, arrived back at the Battery Headquarters with an attached note from the Royal Marines commanding officer that read 'Is this one of yours?' The battery commander's comments have been censored!

In November 1943, the Boche Buster was relocated to Elham station and eventually ended up on the Shoeburyness ranges in Essex before finally being broken up in the early 1960s. If it had not been called upon to play an active part in the war, its role as a publicity and morale-boosting propaganda tool must not be underestimated. It was often seen on the cinema newsreels (described as 'somewhere in England') and was visited by numerous VIPs such as Winston Churchill, and Mrs Eleanor Roosevelt, who inspected it in 1942.

A couple of other heavy railway guns, albeit not quite as large as the 'Boche Buster' being of 9.2-inch calibre, were positioned in Hythe and near Folkestone Junction Station.

Of course, the use of big guns mounted on railway lines was not new. In the First World War, the Germans had *Big Bertha*, named after Bertha Krupps of the great armaments family, as well as a number of railway-mounted naval guns such as the *Langer Max*. The value of such big guns was clearly demonstrated when *Big Bertha* destroyed the Belgian medieval forts or citadels at Liège, Namur and Antwerp. But nothing had been as big as the Boche Buster.

The Inner Line of Defence

All the foregoing measures were essentially aimed at keeping the enemy from attacking or landing on our shores, but if, as was highly likely, a significant number of the enemy managed to effect a landing, then they had to be stopped on the beaches, or at least delayed long enough for them to be destroyed by our land forces before they could establish a substantial beachhead or prosecute the war towards the interior.

To this end, there was not a Kentish beach that did not have a barrier of mines, barbed wire, anti-tank ditches, 'dragons' teeth' or some other major or minor obstacle to the enemy's progress. In Folkestone, for example, the whole of the beach and harbour area was out of bounds to the public and a wide gap was cut in the approach to the Victorian pier. The grounds of the great Royal Pavilion Hotel which faced the inner harbour (now demolished and replaced by the anodyne Burstin Hotel) were laid with anti-personnel mines. A workman who inadvertently wandered into the hotel's grounds in 1942 set one off and was badly injured. A courageous policeman, Constable Cyril Williams of the Folkestone Borough Police, hearing the explosion, made his way to the area, and despite the danger from other mines, went to the injured man, and with the assistance of another workman they brought him to safety. The two men were awarded the George Medal for their bravery.

Dragons' Teeth was the name given to pyramidal concrete blocks, usually 3 or 4 feet tall, that were placed in a way to prevent tanks and mechanized infantry from progressing in a certain direction, and to channel them into 'killing fields' where anti-tank guns awaited them. They were often used in conjunction with, or in place of, anti-tank ditches and the spaces between them filled with barbed wire or anti-personnel mines. Something similar was often used to cause a bottleneck on certain main roads – for example on the bridges over the River Medway at Maidstone and Rochester – the idea being that the remaining narrow gap could be rapidly filled with motor vehicles and/or other large obstructions to at least slow down the enemy's mechanized progress.

Another formidable defence weapon, installed at various points around the county and often in conjunction with a road block or pinch point of some sort, was the flame fougasse. A simple, cheap, but very effective weapon, this consisted of an oil drum filled with petrol and tar that could be detonated at a distance with the use of a self-igniting phosphorous grenade. The idea was that the tar would stick to the tank or other vehicle while the petrol would burn and thus 'cook' it. A much larger version of this concept was installed on Shakespeare Beach, Dover, where three large fuel tanks and a pump house were buried at the south end of the South Lines on the Western Heights. Released and ignited, this huge incendiary device would have swamped the beach, utterly destroying any enemy forces there.

On the hills behind Folkestone, where the Romans and the Normans had set up their forts, a white line of excavated chalk scarred the verdant pasture where a line of anti-tank ditches had been dug. Only now, some seventy years later, have the hills really regained their normal appearance, although the knowledgeable eye can still discern the line of the ditches.

Sugarloaf Hill, Folkestone, showing the 'tank trap' ditch cut into the hillside chalk in 1940.

On the beaches and further inland, a great rash of concrete pillboxes appeared – too many to enumerate here. Most were simple, unpretentious edifices, but some were thinly disguised as cafés, bus shelters, ice cream parlours, bungalows, chalets and other everyday buildings. Examples included a two-storey pillbox near the 'Valiant Sailor' public house at Capel-le-Ferne that was given the appearance of a garage, complete with dummy petrol pump. On the Leas at Folkestone there was the imitation café *J'ai de la Joie*, while at the foot of the Road of Remembrance, in the same town, there was a false toll house. In Margate, an ordinary hexagonal pillbox was given a false roof to make it appear to be a cigarette kiosk, complete with advertisements for 'Craven A' cigarettes. A few pillboxes sited in open fields near Cheriton were disguised as hay ricks by the use of straw-covered hessian. On some airfields, retractable pillboxes were installed, designed to sink into the ground while friendly aircraft were landing.

The basic round pillboxes used in the previous war, many of which still remained, were ideal for deflecting enemy fire but were difficult to build quickly, and so the new brick or concrete edifices were either square, rectangular or hexagonal in form. Using largely unskilled, unemployed labour, there were numerous hiccups in the construction of these defences. In one case in Dover, when the shuttering was removed, it was found that the loopholes were facing the wrong way, so new apertures had to be laboriously chipped out of the solid walls. Winston Churchill, visiting Folkestone, was invited to lay a brick at one box under construction. 'I hope he's got a Union

Card,' said one of the watching workers. Whereupon Winston produced with a flourish the honorary membership card he had been given when he was building the famous wall at Chartwell.

After the war, many of the 1940s pillboxes were demolished and farmers were paid a bounty to remove any on their land. In fact, many took the bounty and then 'forgot' to demolish the boxes, which were, in any case, very strong and difficult to destroy. A few cliff-top defences succumbed to erosion, while others became tool sheds, hen houses or pig pens. To judge from the litter to be found inside them, more than a few pillboxes have been used by courting couples for purposes that have nothing whatsoever to do with defence!

Great lumbering barrage balloons arose over major towns and military installations, their trailing cable designed to hamper any aerial support to a landing.

Evacuation

Something the army had discovered during its all too-brief stay in France was the detrimental effect fleeing refugees had on military movements. The roads were crowded with walkers, cyclists, motorcyclists, horse-drawn carts, cars, vans, lorries and every possible means of escape from the approaching German army. These were joined by a number of French and Belgian soldiers who had deserted in order to be with their families when the enemy arrived, rather than leaving them to their own devices.

Now that Britain stood alone, it was time to adopt a naval term, 'to clear the decks for action.' To this end, to avoid a similar refugee situation arising in this country, and also for simple humanitarian reasons, the government decided at an early stage that children of school age (or, in some cases, younger), together with their mothers should they so wish, were to be encouraged to leave vulnerable areas. The evacuation of schoolchildren from London to places like Kent in September 1939 was obviously ill thought out. To move them from a primary target to what was very likely to be a highly significant secondary target reeks of a panic decision. In the event, the so-called 'Phoney War' that followed Dunkirk lulled many into a false sense of security, and the evacuees from London and other big cities began to dribble back to their homes. In May 1940, those London evacuees who remained in Kent were relocated to Wales.

It was not until June 1940 that it was decided to remove the local children from Kent and send them (mainly) to Wales, exchanging the green fields and lush pastures of the Garden of England for the slag heaps of Merthyr Tydfil. The towns of Kent became ghost towns, but there were now far fewer vulnerable women and children for the defenders to worry about. As for those non-combatants who remained, they were firmly told that in the event of an invasion they were to stay put. The Chief Constable of the Maidstone Borough Police, Henry Vann, issued an instruction to his men to the effect that:

> Unless an ordered evacuation is effected some time before an invasion is imminent, and this is very unlikely, there will be no evacuation of the civil population. It is of paramount importance that when a crisis arises the public must remain where they are and any attempt at panic evacuation must be stopped, if necessary by force, regrettable though this course might be.

As for the police themselves, it was made clear to them that they were not part of the Armed Forces and therefore, in the event of the effective occupation of the area by the enemy, they should not use or carry arms in the occupied area. This instruction did not apply in the event of a landing by an isolated body that did not form part of an invasion force (i.e. a 'Commando' raid), in which case they were not debarred from resisting and if possible, destroying the enemy.

Although the police were instructed not to offer any resistance, since they would be required to maintain calm and order under the occupying force (as happened in the Channel Islands), no such restriction was placed on the Home Guard, as we shall see later.

Air Raid Precautions

The experience of the First World War had made it clear that air supremacy would be vital in any future war and that the civilian population of Great Britain would be in great peril from air raids – more frequent, more far-reaching and much heavier than it had just experienced. In the words of Giulio Douhet, 'the bomber will always get through.' (*Command of the Air*, 1921).

Acknowledging the verity of this maxim, the British government in 1924 created the Air Raid Precautions (ARP) organization, even though at that time there was no direct threat from any likely enemy. We were now friends with our traditional enemies, the French, and Germany was still struggling to recover from its recent comprehensive defeat. Adolf Hitler and Nazism would not really be felt for another decade. The ARP Committee estimated that, in the event of a war, London could expect 9,000 casualties in the first two days and then 17,500 every ensuing week. It added that it considered these figures to be on the conservative side. Widespread panic and chaos was anticipated and it would probably be necessary to declare martial law, at least in the capital. Over the years, as the situation in Europe deteriorated and the likelihood of war increased, the casualty rates were regularly adjusted upwards until, by 1938, the Air Ministry anticipated 65,000 casualties each week. It is claimed that the government ordered a million coffins to be made ready once the war was declared.

The Air Raids Commandant, Major General H Pritchard, RE, was more sanguine, however, and considered that this state of affairs could be avoided if the morale of the people could be upheld through appropriate training and organization, coupled with the provision of suitable air raid shelters. His scheme included the provision of Regional Seats of Government to maintain stability in the event of Parliament being rendered incapable of performing its proper governmental role. General Pritchard's more reasoned approach was supported by the biologist J B S Haldane, who published a book entitled *ARP (Air Raid Precautions)* aimed at 'the ordinary citizen, the sort of man and woman who is going to be killed if Britain is raided again from the air', written as a counter to the 'propaganda' that was being disseminated in the majority of works on the subject.

In 1937, the government decided to create an Air Raid Wardens Service, and over the ensuing year, recruited 200,000 part-time volunteer wardens. The increasing belligerence of Hitler in 1938 led to the mobilization of these ARP wardens who were given the role of assisting in the digging of trenches and the requisition of cellars and basements to be used as air raid shelters. Later, they were involved in the issue of Anderson garden shelters and Morrison indoor table shelters. Wardens were responsible for the issue of civilian gas masks of various types, ranging from the normal adult patterns, through the 'Mickey Mouse' fancy version for young children, to the all-enclosing device to be used for babies. They were not always welcomed and generally disliked, but accepted as a necessary evil. Waving his newly issued gas mask, one elderly gentleman plaintively asked the warden, 'How am I supposed to eat my dinner with this thing on?' In July 1939, the government issued a circular requiring 'all windows, skylights, glazed doors and other openings that would show a light, will have to be screened in wartime with dark blinds or brown paper on the glass so that no light is visible from outside.' Once war was declared, the wardens had a vital role in the maintenance of these blackout regulations.

Before long there were nearly 1,500,000 of these unpaid volunteers who carried out their duties in addition to their normal occupation, wearing a suit of overalls and an armlet, together with a black steel helmet with a white 'W' on it (chief wardens had a white helmet with black lettering).

Although the ARP wardens merged with the heavy and light rescue teams, first-aiders and others to come under the new Civil Defence Service in 1941, the ARP name remained in use on signs and in everyday use until the ARP was disbanded in 1946. However, the wardens did get the dark blue battle-dress issued to all members of the Civil Defence. In fact, virtually the whole of the Second World War defences of the county, once the initial invasion scare of 1940/41 was over, were concentrated on Air Raid Precautions (ARP) and various forms of anti-aircraft measures.

ARP Report and Control Centres

Most towns or other centres of population set up a Report and Control Centre to which all reports of enemy action were reported, and from where rescue and other local ARP operations were directed. The work of these centres was controlled from the main control room in Maidstone. In Folkestone, the report and control centre was set up in the early days of the war in the old, dark and gloomy Victorian police station beneath the town hall. In the (frequent) event of enemy action, the centre was manned by the chief constable of the Folkestone Borough Police, Alfred Beesley, or his deputy, Chief Inspector R Butcher (awarded the BEM in 1943 for his wartime work), together with representatives of the rescue and fire services. There was a controller (Captain Keary, ex Indian Army), a plotter and an adjacent telephone section, manned by six telephone operators and a couple of runners. The telephonists received messages from the ARP and police on the ground as to what had occurred and what services were required at the scene, which they recorded on triplicate message pads, sending a copy to the controller by runner for his attention. The plotter had a large scale map of the town on which all the incidents were indicated by coloured pins. This map, which showed every house, shop and even garden sheds, covered the whole of one wall.

The Report and Control Centre was responsible for causing the air raid sirens to be sounded – which they did in Folkestone on nearly 3,000 occasions. As there were only just over 100 actual air raids, it is understandable that the population (now reduced from a pre-war 50,000 to a wartime 15,000) soon became blasé and paid little or no attention to the sirens. And so a second alert with an intermittent note was sounded, known as the 'cuckoo' or 'warbling Minnie', whenever there were 'raiders overhead', which occurred 1,235 times.

As early as August 1940, the long range guns at Cap Gris-Nez began shelling the Kent coastal towns, 218 shells falling on Folkestone alone. Of course, it was not possible to anticipate when or where these shells would fall, and so any warning could only be sounded once the first shell had fallen. To advise the public that this explosion was the first of a salvo of shells, from

November 1942 the sirens were sounded twice at an interval of one minute. The 'all-clear' signal was also sounded twice.

And then, in 1944 came the 'doodlebugs'! Little warning was needed as these flying bombs made a very audible and distinctive sound, and people soon learned that they only needed to take shelter when they heard the engine stop. Although London was the main target, 1,422 of these devices exploded in Kent, either because this was where their fuel ran out or they were brought down by anti-aircraft gunfire or shot down by fighter aircraft over the county. An enormous number were destroyed over the English Channel before they had time to reach land.

The staff of the Report Centre worked twelve-hour shifts, but for half of this time they were only 'on call', during which time they could carry on a fairly normal life. They could go for a walk, to the cinema or to a dance, but they had to report back as soon as there was an alert, which in the case of the cinemas was indicated by a warning light that came up beside the screen. No announcements were made so as not to alarm the public.

To provide a measure of control over these centres and the various civil defence services, as well as to provide a continuation of administration in the event of central government being disrupted, a system of Regional Commissions, each under a Regional Commissioner, was set up. So far as Kent was concerned, the county came within No. 12 (South Eastern Region), which had its headquarters in Tunbridge Wells at Bredbury, Mount Ephraim.

In all, 29,272 HE bombs fell on Kent, together with around 728,000 incendiary bombs and 1,422 flying bombs. These resulted in the deaths of 1,608 Kent inhabitants, with around 8,000 suffering injuries.

Watching and listening

Although the expectation of an airborne invasion of Great Britain was misplaced, the anticipation of bombing raids was not. The important thing was to be ready for the bombers (and possible paratroop-carrying transports) when they arrived and to give them a warm welcome. It was now that the experiments carried out in the inter-war period proved invaluable.

As mentioned in the previous chapter, it was during the First World War that the first serious experiments were made into the detection of enemy aircraft by acoustic means, and by 1940 considerable strides had been made in this technology.

The first of these devices, a simple concave dish carved into the hillside at Fan Bay, Dover, was replaced by a 20ft-diameter concrete slab 'mirror', and similar devices were erected at Abbot's Cliff (west of Dover), Joss Gap (Thanet), Warden Point (Isle of Sheppey) and at Lade (sometimes referred to as Greatstone or Denge). The operator would stand on a plinth in front of

The three acoustic mirrors at Lade.

the mirror, holding a handle to which the sound collector was attached. A curved arm from the handle moved over a handrail marked off in degrees that ran around the plinth, thus giving the bearing of the approaching aircraft.

Later on, the mirrors at West Hythe and Lade were replaced by 30ft-diameter hemispherical dishes. Lade also had the only wall or strip mirror in Britain. This took the form of a curved concrete wall, 200 feet long and 26 feet high.

These rather simple devices were surprisingly accurate and could detect an aircraft around 10 miles away. The Lade wall mirror had an even greater range of around 25 miles with an impressive accuracy. Reception was, however, subject to interference from extraneous noises caused by the wind, waves and even the jingling of a horse-drawn milk cart!

But technology never stands still and by the time the Second World War began, these audio devices had already been overtaken by the new radar system. They were used briefly during the war when there were fears that some means of jamming the radar signals had been found, but their life was to be short. Today, the mirrors and wall still may be seen at Lade, West Hythe, Abbot's Cliff and Fan Bay – striking monuments to a brief contribution to Kent's defences.

Radar was the result of many years' experiments by various scientists and in many countries. In 1934, in response to fears and rumours that the Germans were developing a death ray, the government asked Sir Robert

Watson-Watt to assess the possibilities of using the known radio technology to develop such a weapon. His response after much research was that it was not possible to produce a death ray but the technology could be used as a defence against enemy aircraft.

Watson-Watt was then entrusted with the job of producing such an object-detection system, using radio waves to determine the range, altitude, direction and speed of objects by bouncing radio waves off the target. In order to conceal the range-finding capabilities of this new system, it was given the name Range and Direction Finding so that it could use the same acronym RDF as was commonly used to describe a *Radio* direction finding system. It was not until 1940 that the US Navy coined the acronym RADAR for this **RA**dio **D**etection **A**nd **R**anging system that has been used ever since.

Despite all the work being done on similar systems elsewhere, Great Britain was the first country to fully exploit it as a defence against aerial attack by setting up a nationwide ring of coastal early warning radar stations, known as the Chain Home stations. The earliest of these were all in the south-east, three of which were in Kent – Swingate, Dunkirk and Newchurch. These all used radio tower masts and were rushed into production just before and during the early days of the Second World War. The system was rather primitive and prone to bugs and glitches, but Watson-Watt, being a pragmatist, maintained that, in order to be battle-ready in time, it was better to go for a 'third-best' solution if a 'second-best' one would not be ready in time, and 'best' never available at all.

This 'third-best' system proved itself in the Battle of Britain when it was able to detect and give adequate warning of approaching Luftwaffe formations, and of course the military applications were rapidly expanded during the war. The Chain Home system was limited in that the towers were fixed and faced the sea, from whence an attack would come. So once the enemy had penetrated beyond the towers, he was lost to sight, and it was to cover this situation that the (Royal) Observer Corps was formed.

Once the Germans managed to determine what these towers were used for, they became targets. However, the open-work steel masts proved to be impervious to blast and nothing short of a direct hit would put them out of action, and so they were eventually left alone. Nevertheless, on one occasion, a number of the south-eastern stations, including Dover (Swingate), were temporarily put out of action by a direct hit on the power grid. This incident aside, the enemy concentrated on trying to jam the radio signals.

The Chain Home system was dismantled after the war, but some of the masts remain standing and are used for other purposes. The Swingate masts, rising proudly above the White Cliffs of Dover, are a familiar sight to travellers using the Cross-Channel ferries to this day. The two 111-metre-high towers here are the only radar stations from the Battle of Britain still in use today, although slightly modified and supporting FM transmitting and mobile phone antennas. A third tower was dismantled in March 2010, while the fourth was removed soon after the war.

The Swingate Chain Home radar tower.

Royal Observer Corps

In the early 1920s, Major General 'Splash' Ashmore was appointed the officer commanding the London Defence Area, a system for alerting London of an impending air raid in times of war. Although intended solely for the London area, the system proved so satisfactory that it was extended to the whole country. In 1922, the overall responsibility for air defence was transferred from the army to the newly created Air Ministry, and Kent was selected for the trial of a new system of listening posts. With the agreement of the Chief Constable of Kent, Major H E Chapman, a group of nine posts and a temporary operations room were set up in the Weald in 1924. These were manned by Special Constables and were sited at:

B1	Sutton Valence	C1	Goudhurst	D1	Bethersden
B2	Marden	C2	Cranbrook	D2	Ham Street
B3	Biddenden	C3	Hawkhurst	D3	Tenterden

The temporary operations room was installed in a small room over a shop in Cranbrook High Street.

On 12 August 1924, a Sopwith 'Snipe' fighter aircraft of the RAF took off from Kenley in Surrey and flew over the area to land at Hawkinge. Each of the listening posts duly recorded its passing and reported it to the operations room where the aircraft's movements were plotted. Three further experiments were carried out, all of which proved highly successful, and General Ashmore was able to report that such a system could work in war and in peace.

The aim was to now extend the system nationwide, starting with Kent and Sussex. A permanent operations room was set up in Maidstone, and the number of listening posts in Kent was increased to twenty-seven. Further exercises in 1925 proved an unqualified success, and the Observer Corps officially came into existence on 29 October that year, its members taking over from the Special Constabulary.

By 1926, the scheme had been extended to Hampshire and Essex, but after this, although the established groups continued to perform well, there was a distinct lack of enthusiasm from the government until the onset of the Second World War caused it to be extended across the whole country. The observers continued to be Special Constables (with a sergeant in charge of each post) until 1929, when control passed from the county constabularies to the Air Ministry, although chief constables maintained responsibility for recruiting and personnel matters.

On 24 August 1939, all members of the Observer Corps were issued with 'Mobilisation Notices' by chief constables, and from 3 September 1939 the observation posts and control centres were continuously manned until

12 May 1945. Observers were provided with a simple mechanical device known as a 'Micklethwaite Height Adjuster', by means of which they were able to determine the height and distance of any incoming aircraft.

During the war, the number of posts was revised and some were set up on places like the Martello Tower No. 3 on the East Cliff at Folkestone and Martello Tower No. 24 in Dymchurch, giving these old fortresses a new purpose and a new lease of life. The latter post was the first in Britain to report a flying bomb in 1944.

During the Battle of Britain, the Observer Corps formed the cornerstone of Air Marshal Hugh Dowding's air defence system, prompting him to write that it:

> constituted the whole means of tracking enemy raids once they had crossed the coastline. Their work throughout was quite invaluable. Without it the air raid warning systems could not have been operated and inland interceptions would rarely have been made.

In recognition of the vital role the corps played at this time, it was granted the prefix 'Royal' in 1941. Also around this time the personnel were issued with an RAF-style uniform, but, due to a shortage of Air Force blue berets, they were issued with the black Tank Corps berets which they wore ever since. The ROC was stood down on 12 May 1945, but was reactivated very shortly afterwards in light of the Cold War, and this part of the ROC's history is covered in the next chapter.

Listening posts

By 1940, wireless telegraphy (Morse) and radio telephony (voice) had come a long way since the end of the First World War, and much use was made of them in the later conflict. Apart from its obvious use on the battlefield and on aircraft and ships, on the Home Front a number of listening posts were set up to eavesdrop on the enemy's radio traffic.

In 1939, the War Office requisitioned Beaumanor Hall in Leicestershire, and it became a secret listening station where encrypted enemy Morse code signals were intercepted and sent to the famous Station X at Bletchley Park by motorbike everyday for decoding. Beaumanor Park was to be the home of the War Office 'Y' Group for the duration of the war.

In 1943, a special section was set up called the Frequency Measuring Section whose job was to monitor and measure the frequencies used by the enemy. The use of a radiogoniometer enabled the geographical locations of the transmitters to be pin-pointed and plotted at Beaumanor. There were six High Frequency Direction Finding locations scattered across England and Scotland, some of these being paired stations. There was only one station in Kent and this consisted of a pair of huts, less than a mile apart, near Maidstone. Each hut was in the middle of a field, one (known as Bill One) in Sutton Valence and the other (Bill Two) in Chart Sutton.

These huts were about 10 or 12 feet square, and each contained an operator's desk and chair, a radio receiver and the radiogoniometer and a small switchboard. There was also a direct telephone link to Beaumanor. Although ATS girls had been trained in direction finding, they were not used on these stations because of their primitive and isolated nature. Instead, young civilian men, mainly 17- to 19-year olds, manned them. They had all received previous training in wireless intercept work and were given further training in direction finding (D/F) work at Beaumanor before being posted to one or another posts. The initial training was carried out at Fort Clarence, Rochester, where they learned Morse code up to a 25/30 words per minute standard.

Each of the two Kentish huts was manned by a team of three young men who between them provided twenty-four hour cover, working eight-hour shifts; there were no days off and it was not unusual, when there was a quick changeover of shifts, for an operator to spend the intervening eight hours in the adjoining bicycle shed, rather than have to cycle perhaps 10 miles to his 'digs' and then cycle all the way back for his next tour of duty.

One day, the operator at Bill One was visited by two army officers who were very interested in what he was doing. In view of the highly confidential nature of the work, the operator was very cagey and revealed little about his task. Some time afterwards, the receivers at both Bill One and Bill Two were being swamped by an extremely loud signal that was obviously being broadcast from very close by. The operators reported the matter and a specialist team from the Royal Corps of Signals arrived and traced the location of the interfering transmitter which was being used by the two bogus army officers, who were in fact enemy agents. They were duly dealt with. In 1944, the operator in Bill Two was blown out of his hut by a flying bomb, but he escaped injury.

The accuracy and value of these simple listening posts was demonstrated in late 1944 when both Bill One and Bill Two reported signals from a particular German army group that was transmitting from a location in the Ardennes, which was known to be under Allied control. They were asked to recheck this information and they insisted it was correct. In fact, it transpired that this was the first news the British had concerning the German breakout, the American withdrawal and the beginning of the Battle of the Bulge.

Another branch of the Y Group was the listening posts that were not concerned with direction finding but instead listened in to conversations between various enemy naval vessels, and between such vessels and their bases. Manned by WRNS, these listening posts were scattered around the south and east coasts, including one on the cliff top between Dover and Folkestone. Their role was to search the airwaves, using VHF receivers to pick up transmissions from enemy ships (usually minesweepers or E-boats), get a bearing on the signal, and then write down what they heard, verbatim and in longhand, speedily but legibly, using triplicate message pads with carbon interleaves. Constantly twiddling the frequency knob, the operators endeavoured to catch both the question and the answer and get it down on the pad. On at least one occasion, a listening Wren was able to report a rubber dinghy had been sighted by a German vessel in the North Sea, and this early notification enabled the British air-sea rescue launch to reach the downed British flyers before the Germans.

Command and Control

It is all very well having listening posts, observer posts and other eyes and ears observing and listening to the enemy's movements, but this information has to be assessed, processed and acted upon. As a result, a number of control centres of varying types sprang up in Kent and elsewhere.

Perhaps the best known of these is the underground complex beneath Dover Castle. The six Napoleonic tunnels under the castle known as 'casemate' have been referred to in previous chapters, and it was in these that an important part of England's defence was planned and controlled.

During the inter-war years, the casemate level was again enlarged, and around 1938, plans were drawn up to use the most easterly of the tunnels as the naval headquarters, including a wireless office and communications centre. The adjacent tunnels were used as the operations rooms for the anti-aircraft and the coastal artillery detachments, the latter moving there from nearby Fort Burgoyne after Dunkirk. The remaining portions were converted to storage and sleeping accommodation for the staff of the various operations rooms.

It was in the naval headquarters in this complex that Operation Dynamo – the evacuation from Dunkirk in 1940 – was planned and co-ordinated, under the direction of Rear Admiral Bertram Ramsay, the Flag Officer commanding Dover. Again, the story of Dunkirk and the 'little ships' is too well known to need repeating here.

In 1943 the naval headquarters was designated a Combined Operations headquarters, and early the following year a decision was made to extend the tunnel system. The Royal Engineers and Pioneer Corps dug a further complex in the soft chalk above the casemate level, which became known as the annexe level. It was originally intended to be used as an emergency dressing station, kitchens and mess rooms, and the dressing station was subsequently upgraded to a full hospital with two operating theatres, although part of this was later used as additional sleeping quarters, since, at times of intense activity, the exhausted staff had been known to sleep on the floor of the tunnels, too tired to walk to their dormitory.

The Combined Operations centre was fed with a constant and almost indigestible diet of intelligence from coastal observation posts, RAF reconnaissance flights, allied warships, radar stations and various other sources, arriving in the form of telex, wireless telegraphy (Morse), Aldis lamp, telephone, teleprinter, radio telephony and every other conceivable type of communication.

A further tunnel complex, code named 'Bastion' was begun in 1941, but was abandoned and sealed off following severe subsidence. Instead, in later 1942, work was begun on the 'Dumpy' system (said to be an acronym for Deep Underground Military Position Yellow) on a level beneath the casemates. On completion, this was fitted out with everything needed to make it into a fully equipped combined operations headquarters.

The Enemy Within

We have seen how, in the past, whenever danger threatened, the defenders and the populace would retreat inside their fort or castle and prepare to repel any assailants who, given the strength of the fortress, would in most cases settle down for a long siege. It does not require a great leap of imagination to picture the whole of the British Isles as the nation's fortress in 1940, with our defenders manning the walls (or, in this case, the coastline) and the enemy just outside, waiting to starve the occupants out.

Britain could never be entirely self-sufficient in food or in raw materials or energy, but with careful conservation it should have been possible then to last out for quite a long time. We produced a reasonable crop of cereals and other foodstuffs and this was supplemented by the government's 'Dig for Victory' programme. Every bit of arable land was being conscripted to produce more food, and people's lawns and public open spaces were being dug up to assist in this. The dairy and livestock reserves were also augmented by rabbit hutches and chicken coops in gardens, and pig clubs wherever practicable. What food we had was carefully rationed to prevent waste and hoarding. We still had numerous working coalmines and a flourishing manufacturing industry.

But this was still not enough. Britain continued to rely on imports of wheat and raw materials from, in particular, America and Canada, and the Germans did their best to deny us these essential supplies by U-boat wolf packs attacking the convoys as they made their perilous way across the

Atlantic. The question was, would enough get through to prevent the people of Great Britain starving, or indeed prevent them from continuing to have the means to prosecute the war?

With hindsight we know that the answer to this question was, in the event, 'Yes, but only just!' However, these were very real worries at the time and they were fed by the fear of an 'enemy within'. Ever since the Spanish Civil War, when General Mola claimed to have four columns of troops outside the town of Madrid and a 'fifth column' of spies and saboteurs within, there had been fears that a similar situation might exist in beleaguered Britain. Were there people in Britain whose under-cover intention was to thwart the nation's war effort by means of sabotage, espionage or subversion? Experience proved that these did exist, although the threat was not as great as many anticipated.

It was known that enemy agents had been operating in Kent prior to the declaration of war; a German lawyer, Dr Albert Tester, had been living with his family in a house near the North Foreland lighthouse and was known to be a good friend of William Joyce – 'Lord Haw-Haw' – but there were no grounds for his arrest until war broke out, when orders were immediately given for him to be arrested. But he had not waited and was found to have fled back to Germany.

Thanet appears to have been popular with German agents since another couple arrived in Thanet before the war. Dr Hermann Goertz and a young girl, Marianne Emig travelled around the country in the guise of tourists, taking many photos and making a lot of sketches, which coincidentally always seemed to include an airfield or military installation, such as Manston. They returned to Germany, and in their absence, Special Branch searched their belongings and the incriminating pictures were discovered. A warrant was issued for their arrest, should they return to England. Surprisingly, Goertz did return and was arrested at Harwich. Charged with offences against the Official Secrets Act, he was sentenced to four years' imprisonment, which he served in Maidstone Prison. He was released just before the war and returned to Germany.

In a crude effort to remove any possible enemy agents, immediately after the declaration of war, aliens of German, Austrian and Italian extraction were rounded up and interned, mostly on the Isle of Man. It was ironic that a great many of these were in fact refugees from their native lands, including many persecuted Jews. Others, known to be sympathetic to the National Socialist cause, such as Sir Oswald Mosley and his wife, the former Diana Mitford, were also interned under the infamous Regulation 18b.

This knee-jerk reaction to a perceived threat failed to unmask many true spies or saboteurs. One spy, in the pay of the Germans for some years, was a British Army warrant officer who was arrested by a Kent constable in Bilsington.

A number of enemy agents were indeed sent to the United Kingdom in September 1940, all of whom, so far as is known, were apprehended by the British authorities. The quality of these early infiltrators was poor, as typified by the two pairs of agents who crossed the Channel from Le Touquet in a fishing boat in the early hours of 2 September 1940. The first couple landed near Hythe with a wireless and a codebook. They were detected and arrested by 5.30 am the same day by army sentries. They were both Dutchmen who spoke little English and were completely untrained.

The second couple consisted of a German, Jose Rudolf Waldberg, who spoke fluent French but no English, and a man of doubtful origins who claimed to be Dutch, Carl Heinrich Meier, who was the only one of the four who had a good command of English. This second pair landed at Dungeness where Meier, being thirsty, attempted to buy cider at the Rising Sun public house, well before opening hours. Being suspicious of someone so obviously unaware of English licensing laws, the barmaid suggested he have a look round the village church until opening time while the landlord phoned Lydd police station to voice his fears. Before the police could attend (on their bicycles), an army corporal and another man brought Meier to the police station, where he claimed to be a Dutchman who had just arrived as a refugee. Meier was held in custody at the police station with the other two suspected agents.

The next day a search was made for the fourth man, Waldberg, who was picked up on the beach. Nearby, the searchers found a wireless transmitter, and it was clear that Waldberg had already been in contact with the enemy, although he had no intelligence of any value to impart.

It appeared that the four agents had been sent to circulate among the local people and pick up anything they overheard that might be of use, although, given their poor command of English, it is not clear how they might have achieved this. In addition, details of any military installations were to be sent back to their spymaster in occupied France. The four were tried at the Old Bailey for espionage and three were hanged, the fourth being acquitted on the grounds that he had acted under duress and the threat of reprisals against his family.

That the authorities were concerned about the infiltration of the population by enemy agents is apparent by the poster campaign that warned people that 'Careless talk costs lives' and to 'Be like Dad – keep Mum'. Such a campaign joined the many others, such as those that exhorted the population to 'Dig for Victory' and warned them that 'Coughs and sneezes spread diseases.'

Occupation

So far we have considered the precautions made to prevent the invasion of Great Britain by the Nazis in the Second World War, but what if the unthinkable had happened and an invasion force had succeeded in landing and occupying at least part of the country? Considering the invasion was likely to have occurred on the shores of Kent, the county would assuredly have been among the first to be occupied.

Churchill had already expressed his determination that we should resist any invasion force 'on the beaches … on the landing grounds, … in the fields, in the streets, … and in the hills,' declaring that 'we shall never surrender.' But how was this to be achieved? Evidently, if the armed forces failed to stem the enemy's advance, then the only recourse would be through guerrilla warfare, sabotage and covert action. How successful this would have been, knowing as we now do that the Germans were not adverse to taking extreme action against innocent hostages, must remain questionable. Nevertheless, the need to think the unthinkable was appreciated and some plans and preparations were made in the dark days of 1940.

On 14 May 1940, Anthony Eden called for volunteers to report to their nearest police station to become what he termed 'Local Defence Volunteers'. The fact that the police received no prior warning of this caused some confusion and a degree of alarm, but they set about taking down names and addresses until such time as they received instructions for what to do with them. The only qualification was that volunteers should be between the ages of 17 and 65 and 'capable of free movement.'

In July 1940, the LDVs became the Home Guard. The fact that the press initially dubbed these volunteers 'Parashots' is a further indication that, at this stage of the war, thoughts were still concentrated on a threat from the skies. There was an obsession with parachuting nuns and paratroops in various disguises, but the Home Guard also did good work in defending sensitive installations, and although it is unlikely they could have overcome even a minor commando raid, they would have been in a position to report any landings and possibly hinder the raiders from reaching their objective.

In the event that the enemy succeeded in establishing a beachhead and advancing inland, it was proposed that some selected Home Guards should literally go underground. Colonel McVean Gubbins of Military Intelligence was put in charge of a department at the Foreign Office, known as Section D, tasked with investigating possible subversion and sabotage operations. This led to the formation of guerrilla units, known as Auxiliary Units, under the command of Captain Peter Fleming of the Grenadier Guards (the brother of Ian Fleming, author of the 'James Bond' books). Captain Fleming selected as his headquarters a house called The Garth in Bilting, on the edge of Challock Forest between Ashford and Canterbury.

Towards the end of 1940, on Fleming's instructions, the Royal Engineers made a number of subterranean chambers in remote areas such as woods, where their construction would not attract too much attention, and then carefully camouflaged them to prevent detection. The plan was that the selected Auxiliary Unit personnel would 'go to ground' once the enemy were about to occupy the area and then stealthily appear to make attacks on the enemy's installations from their hidey-hole behind their lines. The men chosen for this task were civilians (usually members of the Home Guard) who had an intimate knowledge of the area – poachers being very welcome! Each six-man unit had its own bunker and they acted independently from each other for security reasons, but the formation was known at government level as the 201 Battalion, Home Guard.

A police constable, prowling through Ruckinge Woods on the Romney Marsh looking for poachers, came across what appeared to be a truncated tree that had been made to pivot, giving access to a chamber underneath. He reported his find to his superiors at Ashford and was told to forget what he had seen and not repeat it to anyone.

However, it is known that one of these bunkers was sited in the middle of a coppice overlooking Drellingore, near Hawkinge on the road to Alkham. The entrance to this was concealed by a hinged tree stump (like the one in Ruckinge Woods) and led to a 3-foot wide concrete shaft descending some 8 feet underground. The shaft led in turn to a fairly large chamber about 16 feet square with a corrugated iron roof, covered over with earth and undergrowth. The bunker was furnished with two 3-tier bunks, a table and chairs and a water tank. An Elsan closet met the sanitary needs and a three-week stock of Army K rations provided nourishment.

Each man had a personal issue of weapons, including a revolver, a commando knife and a brass knuckleduster that he kept with him at all times. Other weapons and equipment were held in the bunker, including: rifles, a 'Tommy gun' (Thompson submachine gun), bayonets, grenades, phosphorous bombs, explosives and detonators. They met twice a week at the bunker and attended Sunday training sessions either at The Garth or at Wye Agricultural College where they learned the art of silent killing.

The primary targets for the units were supply dumps and lines of communication, but they would have also destroyed targets such as the great railway viaduct at Folkestone and certain important buildings to deny them to the enemy. Secrecy was of prime importance, as the members of the unit were not covered by the Geneva Convention and would have been shot out of hand if discovered by the enemy. A young girl walking her dog who bumped into one of the men as he emerged from the coppice at Drellingore was not convinced by his explanation as to what he was doing and was suspicious of him. After the matter was reported to the officer in charge of the unit, it was agreed that in the event of an invasion she would have to be shot to prevent her giving the game away!

Chapter 10

The Cold War (1945–1990)

The euphoria that greeted the end of the Second World War was very soon replaced by the fear of yet another, even more terrible war. The dropping of the atom bombs on Hiroshima and Nagasaki gave the world a horrific insight into what global warfare could be like in the second half of the twentieth century. Weapons now existed that could obliterate whole towns in an instant, and very soon it would be possible to deliver these apocalyptic warheads by rocket, giving the target no warning whatsoever.

Relations between Soviet Russia and the Western allies – the United States, Great Britain and France – were icy, with the Russians appearing to become more belligerent by the day. How long would it be before this precarious diplomatic situation escalated into all-out war, using weapons of terrifying destructive power?

The only hope was that, should the two sides come to blows, the mutually feared result of nuclear warfare might discourage the use of these early weapons of mass destruction. The precautions taken therefore were twofold; on the one hand, protection against the possibility of the worst-case scenario – all-out nuclear war led by the two super-powers, the United States and the USSR – whilst, on the other hand, alternative defences needed to be maintained against any aggressive action on the part of the Communist bloc using conventional forces and conventional weapons.

So far as Great Britain was concerned, this meant that the end of the Second World War did not mean the end of conscription for National Service, whereby every able-bodied young man was called up to serve in one or other of the armed forces (or go down the coal mines as a 'Bevin Boy') for a period of eighteen months.

There was thus a significant (although miniscule in comparison with the might of the Red Army) British army, navy and air force, trained and 'showing the flag' in Germany, along the borders with the Russian-occupied

East Germany. On both sides, much of the time was spent strutting up and down and looking formidable in the sight of the opposition.

The belligerence of the Soviets was first demonstrated with the Berlin Blockade and the consequent airlift, but the opening of the war in 1950, between communist North Korea and the non communist South, was the first real conflict which could have formed the catalyst for World War Three – possibly a nuclear war. Fortunately, although communist China came to the aid of North Korea against the American-supported South, Russia remained aloof, and a fragile truce was arrived at and has managed to hold for the past sixty years.

No sooner had the Korean War ended in 1953 than another flashpoint occurred with the beginning of the long-drawn-out and inconclusive Vietnam War, and while this was still going on, the Cuban missile crisis occurred in 1962. People were once more thinking the unthinkable. Fortunately common sense prevailed and disaster was averted. Nevertheless, the Communist threat was perceived as a real one for nearly half a century, lasting until the collapse of the Soviet Union.

But although Korea and Cuba were both far away on the other side of the world and did not directly affect the population of Great Britain, the fear of an all-out nuclear war was never far off. Normal, traditional means of repelling invaders would be applied in the event of a traditional war, but in the event of a nuclear war we were not talking about an invasion as such, but more about annihilation. Could anyone survive a nuclear war? No one could say for sure as it was an unknown quantity; all one could do was to make an inspired guess and take whatever precautions seemed appropriate. It would not be a question of repelling invaders, but a matter of simply surviving.

To survive, one had to avoid both the initial shock and blast effect, followed by the effects of radiation. Anyone in the open within a wide radius from ground zero would have no chance at all, so, in the 1950s in particular, the government embarked upon a comprehensive programme of information about what to do in the event of a nuclear attack. It was estimated that there would be a four-minute gap between the launch of a nuclear rocket and its arrival in Britain; four minutes between life and certain death. The satirists had a great time joking about what one could do in four minutes ('These days a man can run a mile in four minutes . . .'), but the feeling of the general public was one of fatalism – 'if it comes there's nothing we can do about it,' or misplaced optimism – 'Hitler couldn't crush us and neither will Stalin.'

The view of the authorities was perhaps somewhere in between the two, but it was generally agreed that something had to be done to cope with this new threat. The plan was threefold:

- Provide an adequate warning system.
- Organize suitable shelters and provide information for the population during a nuclear attack and in the initial aftermath thereof.
- Restructuring and reorganization of government and control of survivors in the aftermath.

Warning systems

Radar stations, such as that at Ash, were converted to a Cold War use, and it was felt that the now advanced radar systems could detect approaching enemy aircraft or the firing of rockets with a nuclear warhead much better than human eyes and ears. This information would be fed into the United Kingdom Warning and Monitoring Organisation (UKWMO), which was formed in 1957 under Home Office and police control. Its purpose was to provide both military and civilian authorities in the United Kingdom with essential information in the few minutes prior to, during and after a nuclear attack.

Government publications stated that 'full advice to the public about the warning system, and about measures to protect themselves, would be published and broadcast in good time. A wartime broadcast service would be brought into operation to transmit non-stop public information.'

The most consistent plan was to use the wartime air-raid sirens to give warning of an immediate nuclear or conventional attack. If and how these would differ was not generally known.

Shelters and information for the population during a nuclear attack and in the initial aftermath

The Royal Observer Corps, which had been stood down in 1945, was soon reformed and initially continued its wartime role as plane spotters. However, the greater speeds and altitudes attained by jet aircraft, together with the improved means of detection by radar, meant that, by the mid-1950s, the RAF no longer had need of these human eyes. However, instead of being stood down once again, in June 1955 the ROC was given a new task, not as part of a warning system but as a post-nuclear attack monitoring scheme.

The first major exercise involving a simulated nuclear attack was held in 1956, after which the government decided that future United Kingdom defence policy should be based on the need for a nuclear deterrent, coupled with the risk of a nuclear attack on this country. This effectively signalled the definitive end of the ROC's aircraft recognition and reporting role. In future, it would be required post-attack to gather data regarding the size and location of any atomic weapons detonated in the United Kingdom or which might affect it. Instrumentation would monitor fallout as and where it occurred, the actual location and strength being mapped by the ROC. By this means, and in conjunction with the Meteorological Office, accurate forecasts could be disseminated of the predicted distribution and strength of the fallout.

This new role meant that the ROC centres (later known as controls) and the monitoring posts had to be adapted to give protection against both blast and radiation. The centres also had to be furnished with the necessary means of survival for up to three weeks, since it could be impossible to emerge while there was still a danger from radioactive fallout. Between 1958 and 1968, more than 1,500 subterranean monitoring posts were built, spaced about eight miles apart and organized in clusters of three to five posts. Each post was built of waterproofed concrete, 25 feet deep and covered with a thick soil layer. Inside these somewhat spartan constructions there were all necessary ventilation, sanitary and electrical provisions, and the necessary instrumentation, such as bomb power indicators (BPI) and ground zero indicators (GZI).

The Group control centres, such as those at Maidstone and Gravesend (Category A, built 1954), provided living and operational accommodation for up to 100 persons, including, police, civil defence corps, army, observers and UKWMO warning teams, with full life support systems and decontamination facilities.

For the most part, members of the ROC continued to be part-time volunteers under a serving RAF air commodore, with just a few full-time ROC personnel, mainly in the more senior and training positions. The main ROC field force was stood down in September 1991, and the corps, together with the UKWMO, was officially disestablished the same year. The majority of the redundant posts were sold off, mainly to former ROC members who have turned them into museums or holiday accommodation. The larger control buildings have been disposed of to private purchasers and used for a variety of purposes. That of 1 Group at Maidstone is used by a firm of solicitors for their archive storage, while the one at Woodlands Park, Gravesend, has been re-equipped and is open to the public on certain days as a Cold War Heritage Centre.

By 1981, the risk of war was considered so slight that it was felt that it would be uneconomic and impracticable to meet demands for public nuclear shelters. Information about self-help shelters was promised from time to time if the situation deteriorated, although the HMSO published a number of booklets under such titles as 'Nuclear Weapons', 'Protect & Survive' and 'Domestic Nuclear Shelters'.

Restructuring and reorganization of government, and control of survivors in the aftermath

Although there were serious questions as to whether any of the population would survive a nuclear war, it seemed probable that a number, possibly only a small one, would remain largely or totally unaffected. These would perhaps be those living in remote, isolated corners of the realm or perhaps on one or more of the Scottish islands. Equally, if the attack was directed at the main industrial and governmental centres, London, Birmingham, Manchester, Liverpool, Edinburgh, etc., there could be many survivors in the areas distant from these towns.

Whatever the answer to this question might be, it was clear that survivors would need some assistance. Some people living in buildings destroyed by the blast might well escape the effects of radiation if they were upwind, but could be trapped in the debris and still need rescuing and access to first aid, food, water and accommodation. There was therefore an element of World War Two thinking behind the initial planning for a nuclear attack. The Civil Defence Corps, disbanded in the heady days of post-war England, was reformed in 1948 to take control in the aftermath of a nuclear explosion. Each county, such as Kent, constituted a Corps Authority and established its own Division of the Corps. Each Division had a Headquarters Section, covering Intelligence and Operations, Signals, and Scientific and Reconnaissance sub-sections, and also included the familiar wartime sections such as Wardens, Rescue, Welfare, Ambulance and First Aid. The Civil Defence Corps was finally stood down in 1968.

The aftermath of a nuclear attack would obviously call for the renewed provision of public utilities as soon as possible, together with such interim measures as might be possible in the shorter term. Survivors would soon be looking for advice and guidance on a wide range of matters, such as: emergency accommodation, missing persons, lost and damaged property, emergency repairs, and so on. It was to this end that plans were drawn up for the continuation of local government, if necessary supplanting central government in the event that the latter was put out of action for any reason.

The country was organized into a number of regions, each with its own designated regional commissioner and government, working from a pre-prepared, bomb-proof and secure command centre, known as the Regional Seat of Government.

Regional Seats of Government

Anticipating serious disruption of central administration and government in the event of an invasion or nuclear attack, plans were drawn up for the country to be divided up into a number of regions that could operate autonomously under a Regional Commissioner. The Regional Seats of Government (RSG) were known by a variety of names over the years as the strategies of the government developed.

In 1953, the construction of a series of two-storey, bomb-proof War Rooms was begun, designed to house around forty essential workers. The network of eleven regions was completed in the mid 1960s, the War Room for the South East (Region 11) being at Hawkenbury, Tunbridge Wells.

However, so fast moving was the contemporary arms race that no sooner were the War Rooms completed than they were obsolescent. They were designed for a long, drawn-out conflict, whereas the planners now anticipated a short, sharp bombardment of major cities for which the new War Rooms were too small and too close to important centres of population. And so as early as 1956, the Home Office produced a specification for a greatly extended system of large bunkers, capable of accommodating up to 300 persons. Designed to withstand a near miss, these new bunkers would be able to operate under 'siege' conditions for several months, but, in the event, financial considerations meant this plan had to be scaled back. Consequently, none of the proposed new centres were built and the existing War Rooms were simply updated and improved. The regional structure was overhauled and Kent now came under Region 6 (Southern), the RSG being located in a Second World War aircraft components factory in Henley-on-Thames.

All these preparations were conducted under conditions of top secrecy, but a 'mole' tipped off a small group of activists who called themselves the 'Spies for Peace'. These broke into the RSG at Henley-on-Thames in 1963 and produced a pamphlet entitled 'Danger! Official Secret', which brought the scheme into the open, suggesting that the government was spending a lot of money on creating safe havens for itself and a few officials, while the general public would be abandoned and sacrificed if a nuclear attack were to occur.

In the face of a public outcry, the existing plans were abandoned and the whole system of emergency government was overhauled. It was felt that a more flexible system of protected Sub-Regional Controls (SRCs) was required to reactivate a link between central and local government. Regional Seats of Government would no longer be buried in deep bunkers, but would be set up as soon as possible after the attack, under pre-arranged plans and at whatever location was the most suitable in the given circumstances. Some existing bunkers and disused military installations were pressed into service for the SRCs, but once more the full plans were never implemented.

By 1968, when the threat was deemed so remote that the Civil Defence Corps was disbanded, many of the old eleven Regional Seats of Government had been relocated and downgraded to SRCs, Region 6 (Southern) now being served by three SRCs: one in a protected basement built under the offices of the Civil Service Commission in Basingstoke (later moved to Crowborough, Sussex), one at Stoughton Barracks, Guildford, and the third in the 'Dumpy' tunnels under Dover Castle that had been used as the Combined Operations Naval Headquarters during the Second World War.

By the 1970s, the threat had diminished considerably and the network was placed on a Care and Maintenance basis only, and had become totally unfit for purpose by the time the Cold War ended in 1990. The installations were sold off to anyone who wanted one, that at Crowborough being used by the Sussex Police for training, while the Tunbridge Wells War Room was completely demolished (taking three months rather than the anticipated two weeks). The 'Dumpy' levels at Dover have been declared unsafe and are therefore closed to the public, unlike the remainder of the tunnels.

Chapter 11

Conclusion – the Future

In these few pages we have followed the manner in which Kent – and thereby often Britain itself – was defended against its enemies for over two thousand years. We have seen how this was achieved by means of wooden forts, stone castles, great gun batteries, off-shore towers, mined beaches and finally deep underground bunkers. And yet, despite all the progress and military developments over these two millennia, Britain in the twentieth century was still preparing to withstand a siege – whether conducted by U-boats or by the use of nuclear weapons – in a manner reminiscent of medieval times.

Weapons and tactics may change, but, in the end, the principles of our defences change very little. The tactics adopted by the Roman phalanxes, using their shields around and above them, were replicated in the Battle of Britain, albeit on a much larger scale and using guns on our flanks and aircraft covering our heads.

No one knows what the future holds for us and for Kent. Will there be an apocalyptic nuclear war triggered by some silly border dispute or someone's imperial pretensions? What about a sneaky germ-based attack? Will we see an invasion from Outer Space? Sci-fi and futuristic writers favour all of these scenarios, but a common denominator in all their works seems to be the survival of a few humans who go on to recreate and repopulate the world. Let us hope this is the ultimate worst-case scenario, never to be experienced.

At the time of writing (and things can change frighteningly quickly!) there is no real discernable threat to our shores, other than isolated and possibly concentrated terrorist activity. The armed forces have been reduced to what are possibly the lowest levels ever, despite military operations in the Far and Middle East. This being so, Fortress Kent has relaxed and lowered its guard and is now an open fortress; but, like the medieval castles, it will undoubtedly close up and stand ready to repel anyone who has the temerity to trespass on the White Cliffs of Dover – or anywhere else in the Garden of England.

Kent has resisted invasion for nearly one thousand years and there are grounds for hoping that, whatever threat the county and country might face in the future, Kent will be true to its motto '*Invicta*' and remain unconquered. The true Guardian of England.

Glossary of terms used

Array:	To marshal, to muster, to equip, to accoutre (medieval).
Bastion:	A projecting mass of earth or masonry at the corner of a rampart that can be defended by flank fire from other parts of the fort.
Battering ram:	Usually the trunk of a large tree, this was repeatedly rammed against gates in order to break them down.
Battery:	A parapet thrown up to cover the gunners from enemy shot. Also a number of guns or mortars.
Blockhouse:	A military installation or fort, chiefly constructed of hewn timber and defended by musketry.
Bombproofed:	Provided with a brick vault, usually covered with earth, for protection against mortar fire.
Bulwark:	An outwork for defence.
Caponier/caponiére:	A covered passage across the ditch around a fortified place (from the Spanish for 'chicken coop').
Carronade:	A short cannon, originally made at Carron in Scotland.
Casemate:	A bombproof vault built into the ramparts with loop-holes through which guns may be fired.
Case-shot:	Numerous small metal balls, etc. packed into a canister that bursts when fired from a muzzle-loading gun and used as an anti-personnel weapon.
Catapult:	A generic term covering mangonels, trebuchets and other devices which used a counter-weight to throw projectiles against and over the walls of a

castle or city. These projectiles could include rocks or other heavy solids, burning objects intended to cause a fire within the fortress, or even dead animals or human corpses with intent to spread disease and pollute water supplies.

Corbel: Stone projecting from the face of a wall to support floor joists or an overhanging parapet such as a machicolation.

Counterscarp: The outer slope of a defensive ditch.

Drum tower: A circular tower sited along a wall. These were often backless so that they could not provide cover for an attacker who managed to gain entry to it.

Embrasure: An opening in a wall, through which a gun may be fired.

Enfilade fire: Fire along the length of a ditch or work.

Expense magazine: A small magazine for storing ammunition for immediate use.

Faussebray: A mound of earth forming a rampart.

Fencible: A militiaman or volunteer soldier enlisted in a crisis, especially to fight in a local or regional conflict. The word is a corruption of 'defencible'.

Feoffment: A conveyance, in feudal times, with livery of *seisin* (a concept based on the physical occupation of the land).

Gorge: A narrow passageway.

Glacis: The outer sloping bank serving as a parapet to a covered way or the declivity in front of a ditch.

Gun room: A casemate with embrasures overlooking a ditch, with guns to protect the ditch.

Man-at-arms: A medieval professional soldier, often from the lower levels of nobility, who possessed full armour and was usually used as heavy cavalry.

Mangonel: See 'catapult' above.

Machicolation: An overhanging parapet supported on corbels, usually at the top of a tower.

Mining: The digging of tunnels under the foundations of a wall with a view to causing them to collapse, often using fires to decompose the mortar or ignite timber components. Used with some success against Dover and Rochester castles.

Petard:	A small explosive device, introduced when gunpowder was first used, and used to blow down a wall or gateway. The word comes from the French word *péter* meaning 'to break wind'. These unreliable devices were liable to go off prematurely, killing the handler, hence the expression 'hoist by his own petard' meaning a plot that backfires.
Rampart:	An elevation or mound of earth around a fortified place.
Ravelin:	A detached work with two embankments raised before the counterscarp.
Redoubt:	A detached defensive fort or outwork.
Revet:	To face a wall with bricks, masonry, sand-bags, etc.
Siege tower:	A tall wooden scaffold tower on wheels which could be pushed up against the wall of a fortress to enable attackers to reach the top and so force an entrance, providing a degree of protection for the attacking troops. These were often used during the Crusades.
Seisin:	A feudal concept based on the physical occupation of the land.
Stockade:	Fence of posts set into the ground, often sharpened.
Terreplein:	The level surface of a work behind a rampart.
Trebuchet:	See under 'catapult' above. A weapon frequently used by the Romans.

Chronological table of monarchs

William I	1066–1087	Mary I	1553–1558
William II	1087–1100	Elizabeth I	1558–1603
Henry I	1100–1135	James I	1603–1625
Stephen	1135–1154	Charles I	1625–1649
Henry II	1154–1189	Interregnum	1649–1660
Richard I	1189–1199	Charles II	1660–1685
John	1199–1216	James II	1685–1688
Henry III	1216–1272	William III	1689–1702
Edward I	1272–1307	And Mary II	1689–1694
Edward II	1307–1327	Anne	1702–1714
Edward III	1327–1377	George I	1714–1727
Richard II	1377–1399	George II	1727–1760
Henry IV	1399–1413	George III	1760–1820
Henry V	1413–1422	George IV	1820–1830
Henry VI	1422–1461	William IV	1830–1837
Edward IV	1461–1483	Victoria	1837–1901
Edward V	1483	Edward VII	1901–1910
Richard III	1483–1485	George V	1910–1936
Henry VII	1485–1509	Edward VIII	1936
Henry VIII	1509–1547	George VI	1936–1952
Edward VI	1547–1553	Elizabeth II	1952–

Select Bibliography

Balse, Dr Ewald (1934) *Raum und Volk in Weltkrieg*, Brunswick: (unknown).

Bennett, D (1977) *A Handbook of Kent's Defences, from 1540 until 1945*, Kent Archaeological Society.

Blaxland, Gregory (1981) *South-East Britain – Eternal Battleground*, Rainham: Meresborough.

Bowen, Ezra (1980) *Knights of the Air*, New York: Time Life.

Brooke, Christopher (1968) *The Saxon & Norman Kings*, London: Collins (Fontana).

Brooks, Robin J (1983) *Aviation in Kent*, Rainham, Meresborough.

Fleming, Peter (1958) *Invasion 1940*, London: Hamish Hamilton.

Forde-Johnston (1979) *Great Medieval Castles of Britain*, London: Book Club Associates.

George, Michael & George, Martin (2004) *Coast of Conflict: The Story of the South Kent Coast*, Seaford: S B Publications.

Guy, John (1980) *Kent Castles*, Gillingham: Meresborough.

Hasted, Edward (1797–1801) *The History & Topographical Survey of the County of Kent, Vol. IV*, Canterbury: Bristow.

Hewitt, H J (1966) *The Organization of War under Edward III*, Barnsley: Pen & Sword Military.

Hough, Richard & Richards, Denis (1990) *The Battle of Britain: The Jubilee History*, London: Guild Publishing.

Hitchings, Henry (2008) *The Secret Life of Words*, London: John Murray.

Humphreys, Roy (1990) *Target Folkestone*, Rainham: Meresborough.

Hylton, Stuart (2004) *Kent & Sussex 1940*, Barnsley: Pen & Sword Military.

Hyndman, Oonah (1990) *Wartime Kent, 1939–40*, Rainham: Meresborough.

Ingleton, Roy (1994) *The Gentlemen at War: Policing Britain 1939–45*, Maidstone: Cranborne Publications.

Jenner, Michael (1991) *Journeys into Medieval England*, London: Penguin Books.

Jessup, F W (1995) *A History of Kent*, Chichester: Phillimore & Co.

Lambarde, William (1570) *Perambulation of Kent*, Bath: Adams & Dart.

Mortimer, Ian (2009) *The Time Traveller's Guide to Medieval England*, London: Vintage.

Nicholls, Joan (2000) *England Needs You*, Cheam: Joan Nicholls.

Norman, Vesey (2010) *The Medieval Soldier*, Barnsley: Pen & Sword Books.

Ogley, Bob (1994) *Kent at War*, Westerham: Froglets Publications.

Oxford Dictionary of National Biography, (The).

Quennell, Marjorie & C H B (1948) *A History of Everyday Things in England*, London: Batsford.

Sutcliffe, Sheila (1972) *Martello Towers*, Newton Abbot: David and Charles.

Trow, M J (2008) *War Crimes – Underworld Britain in the Second World War*, Barnsley: Pen & Sword.

Welby, Douglas E (1991) *The History of Archcliffe Fort, Dover, Kent*, Dover: Polar Bear Press.

Index